Uncle John's

Portable Press
An imprint of Printers Row Publishing Group
10350 Barnes Canyon Road, Suite 100, San Diego, CA 92121
www.portablepress.com

Written and researched by Paul Terry

Top 10 Of Everything was devised and created by Russell Ash

All notations of errors or omissions should be addressed to Portable Press, Editorial Department, at the above address. All other correspondence (author inquiries, permissions) concerning the content of this book should be addressed to Octopus Publishing Group Ltd, Carmelite House, 50 Victoria Embankment, London EC4Y 0DZ

www.octopusbooks.co.uk

PORTABLE PRESS
Publisher: Peter Norton
Associate Publisher: Ana Parker
Publishing / Editorial Team: April Farr, Vicki Jaeger, Lauren Taniguchi, Kathryn C. Dalby
Editorial Team: JoAnn Padgett, Melinda Allman

OCTOPUS
Publishing Director: Trevor Davies
Designed and packaged by: XAB design
Assistant Editor: Ellie Corbett
Junior Designer: Jack Storey
Giulia Hetherington: Picture Research Manager
Senior Production Manager: Peter Hunt

Library of Congress Cataloging-in-Publication Data available on request.

ISBN: 978-1-68412-574-6

Printed in China

22 21 20 19 18   1 2 3 4 5

Movie and TV data provided by IMDb (https://www.imdb.com).

Video game data provided by VGChartz (www.vgchartz.com).

BUZZANGLE MUSIC

Music data provided by BuzzAngle Music (www.buzzanglemusic.com).

Uncle John's

TOP 10
OF EVERYTHING
2019

SPORTS

SPACE

MOVIES

GAMES

MUSIC

PAUL TERRY

What does the word "epic" mean to you? What images does it conjure up in your mind? Confrontations between alien beings and Earth's mightiest heroes in *Avengers: Infinity War*, or Earth-bound Olympic battles between athletes from around the world? Or does "epic" make you think of the awesome power of Mother Nature, or, simply, the gigantic jaws of the Tyrannosaurus rex? Whatever is most epic to you, we have got you covered in the *Top 10 of Everything 2019.*

For movie fans, we cover genres from vampires to animated robot tales, to the films the Marvel Cinematic Universe's stars have made when they're not saving the world. If you love the animal kingdom, we have fantastic facts about everything from otters to butterflies, and from wolves to snakes...we love critters and creatures of all shapes, species, and sizes.

With more than 10,000 facts crammed into these pages, expect to be amazed by the tallest mountains in space, the fastest electric cars, the most successful LEGO video games, the most-watched music videos of all time, and tons more data.

Read from front to back—or dive randomly into zones that intrigue you the most— and enjoy finding something that is truly epic to *you*...

PAUL TERRY is a best-selling author, music artist, and producer. He has written/ edited official publications for Marvel Studios; Bad Robot TV shows *Alias*, *Lost* and *Fringe*; as well as for *Stars Wars*, LEGO, DreamWorks, *The Simpsons*, and *Futurama*.

He coauthored (with Tara Bennett) *Marvel Studios: The First Ten Years*, *The Official Making of Big Trouble in Little China*, the official *Lost Encyclopedia*, *Fringe: September's Notebook* (an Amazon Book of the Year 2013), and many more.

When he's not writing books, Paul writes music. His film scores include the award-winning feature documentary *Sidney & Friends* (which he also executive produced), *So Much Damage* (the docuseries on the history of Image Comics), and *Emily* (starring Felicity Jones and Christopher Eccleston). Under the moniker of Cellarscape, Paul's albums include *Exo Echo* and the award-nominated *The Act of Letting Go*.

www.paulterryprojects.com

CONTENTS

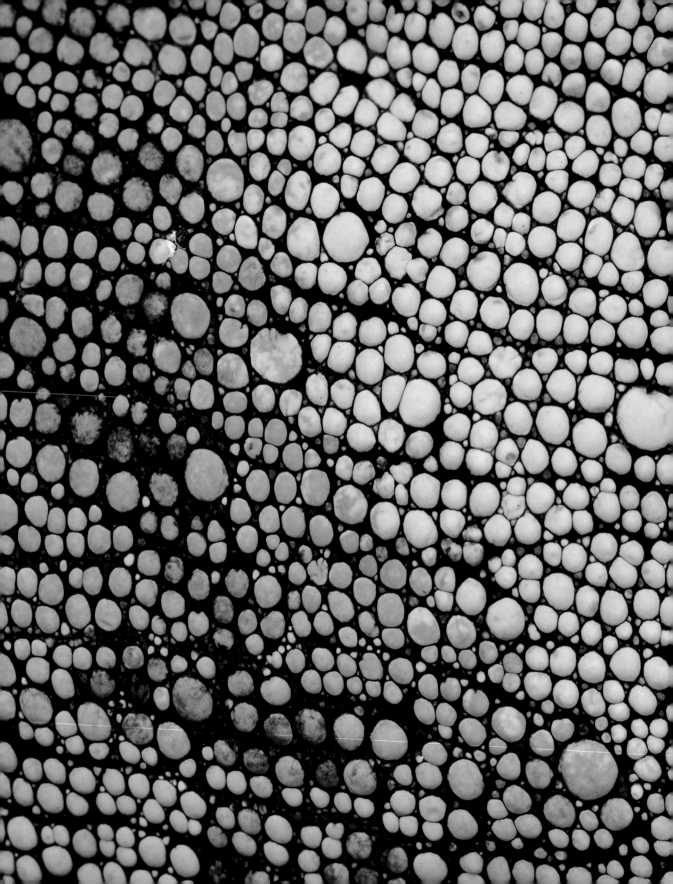

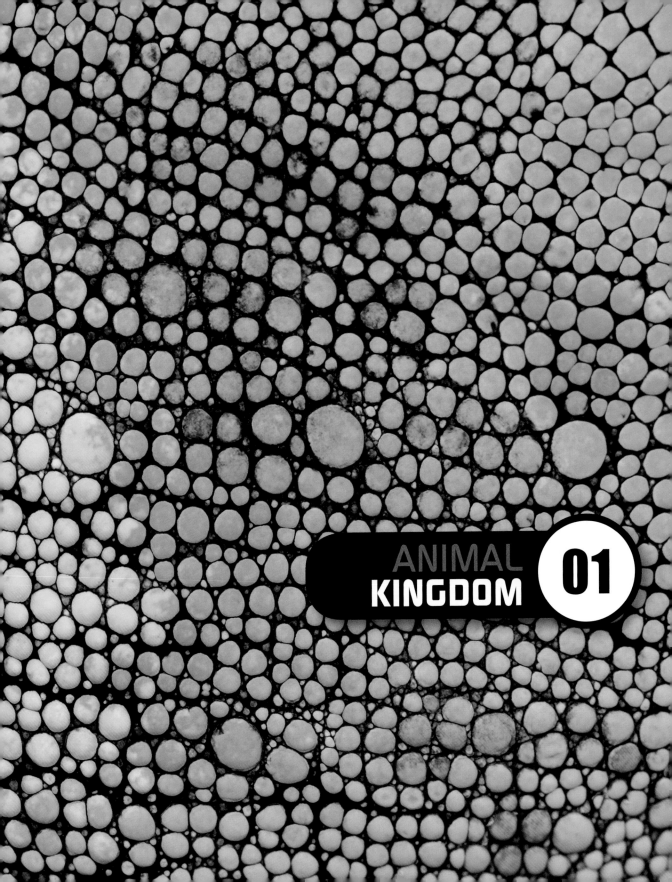

ANIMAL
KINGDOM 01

HUMANS VS. BEASTS

**USAIN BOLT
23.35 MPH
(37.58 KPH)**

**OMARA DURAND
19.62 MPH
(31.58 KPH)**

TOP 10

FASTEST ON LAND

In the wild, speed is the most important means of survival for predator and prey. If you don't have speed, then you have to be smart enough to outwit your predators...

	ANIMAL	SPEED (MPH)	(KPH)
1	CHEETAH	75	120.7
2	PRONGHORN	60.9	98
3	SPRINGBOK	60.3	97
4	OSTRICH	60	96.6
5	AMERICAN QUARTER HORSE	53.4	86
6	LION	49.7	80
7	AFRICAN WILD DOGS	44.7	72
=	ELK	44.7	72
9	EASTERN GREY KANGAROO	43.5	70
10	COYOTE	42.9	69

5 AMERICAN QUARTER HORSE

This breed of short, stocky horse is a result of native horses that stemmed from Spanish breeds crossing with the English breeds of settlers in Virginia. By the end of the 1600s they were being raced over a distance of a quarter of a mile, hence the name "quarter horse." The breed is enormously versatile and is used not only for pleasure riding, but for roping and barrel racing, and as a working cow horse. There are more than 3 million registered in the United States.

TOP 10

HEAVIEST **ON LAND**

Powerful, majestic, and beautiful–some of the most popular land animals in the world are also the biggest and heaviest...

	ANIMAL	WEIGHT (LB)	(KG)
1	AFRICAN BUSH ELEPHANT	12,000	5,400
2	ASIAN ELEPHANT	11,464	5,200
3	SOUTHERN ELEPHANT SEAL	11,000	5,000
4	COMMON HIPPOPOTAMUS	9,920.8	4,500
5	SOUTHERN WHITE RHINOCEROS	8,818.5	4,000
6	PACIFIC WALRUS	5,000	2,268
7	SALTWATER CROCODILE	4,409	2,000
8	ROTHSCHILD GIRAFFE	4,254.9	1,930
9	CHIANINA	3,924.2	1,780
10	SHIRE HORSE	3,306.9	1,500

4 ▸ COMMON HIPPOPOTAMUS

A hippopotamus will often spend 16 hours a day in the coolness of the river water, and can hold its breath for up to five minutes. When out of the water, it secretes a fluid that acts as a sunblock and moisturizer. Because the fluid is red, it gave rise to the myth that hippos sweat blood.

6 ▸ SMILODON

Despite being commonly known as the "saber-toothed tiger," the *Smilodon* isn't from the same Pantherinae family as tigers and lions, but a catlike group called Machairodontinae. There are three species of *Smilodon* recognized, with *Smilodon populator* being the largest, standing 4 ft (1.2 m) tall and 4 ft (1.2 m) long. It had a mouth that could open extremely wide (120 degrees, compared to a lion's 65 degrees).

TOP 10

BIGGEST **PREHISTORIC CARNIVOROUS MAMMALS**

Following the mass extinction of the cold-blooded reptilian dinosaurs, Earth was populated by an astonishing variety of warm-blooded mammals. These were the biggest meat eaters...

	CREATURE	WEIGHT (LB)	(KG)
1	ARCTOTHERIUM	3,855.9	1,749
2	ANDREWSARCHUS	2,204.6	1,000
3	SHORT-FACED BEAR	2,109.8	957
4	PSEUDOCYON	1,704.2	773
5	AMPHICYON	1,322.8	600
6	SMILODON	1,036.2	470
7	THYLACOSMILUS	264.6	120
8	PACHYCROCUTA	242.5	110
9	DIRE WOLF	174.2	79
10	EPICYON	150	68

TOP 10

LARGEST
PREHISTORIC HERBIVORES

Scientists believe that these "mega herbivores" acted as "ecosystem engineers," reducing tree cover, keeping watering holes and landscape clear, and distributing plant seeds...

	DINOSAUR	LENGTH (FT)	(M)
1	AMPHICOELIAS	196.8	60
2	ARGENTINOSAURUS	118.1	36
3	MAMENCHISAURUS	114.8	35
4	FUTALOGNKOSAURUS	111.5	34
=	SAUROPOSEIDON	111.5	34
6	DIPLODOCUS	108.3	33
7	XINJIANGTITAN	105	32
8	PUERTASAURUS	98.4	30
=	TURIASAURUS	98.4	30
10	DREADNOUGHTUS	85.3	26

3 MAMENCHISAURUS

Weighing the same as two adult African elephants, this enormous sauropod weighed around 12 tons. It had an incredibly long neck, the longest of any known dinosaur, measuring up to 36 ft (11 m) and consisting of 19 vertebrae (in comparison to a human or giraffe neck, which contains seven). Some scientists think it could have reared up on its hind legs to feed on high-up foliage.

LARGEST **PREHISTORIC BIPEDAL CARNIVORES**

Some dinosaurs—those with powerful back legs—stopped walking on all fours and rose up on their hind legs in an effort to run faster and for longer distances...

	DINOSAUR	LENGTH (FT)	(M)
1	SPINOSAURUS	59	18
2	CARCHARODONTOSAURUS	43.3	13.2
=	GIGANOTOSAURUS	43.3	13.2
4	CHILANTAISAURUS	42.7	13
5	TYRANNOSAURUS REX	40.4	12.3
6	TYRANNOTITAN	40	12.2
7	TORVOSAURUS	39.4	12
=	ALLOSAURUS	39.4	12
9	ACROCANTHOSAURUS	37.7	11.5
10	DELTADROMEUS	36.1	11

10 ▶ DELTADROMEUS

What marks *Deltadromeus* out from the rest of the dinosaurs on this list is its agility and speed. Its hind legs are long and slender, designed for fast running. This would have been advantageous in both hunting down its prey of ornithopod dinosaurs and avoiding predators such as numbers one and two on the list.

TOP 10

SMALLEST PREHISTORIC CARNIVORES

These little dinosaurs, probably about the size of a chicken, were bipedal and covered with feathers, solidifying the link between birds and dinosaurs...

	CREATURE	WEIGHT (LB)	(KG)
1	PARVICURSOR REMOTUS	0.31	0.14
2	EPIDEXIPTERYX HUI	0.35	0.16
3	COMPSOGNATHUS LONGIPES	0.57	0.26
4	CERATONYKUS OCULATUS	0.66	0.3
5	JURAVENATOR STARKI	0.75	0.34
6	LIGABUEINO ANDESI	0.77	0.35
7	MICRORAPTOR ZHAOIANUS	0.88	0.4
8	SINOSAUROPTERYX PRIMA	1.2	0.55
9	RAHONAVIS OSTROMI	1.3	0.58
10	MAHAKALA OMNOGOVAE	1.7	0.76

7 MICRORAPTOR ZHAOIANUS

Microraptors shared many features with our modern-day birds. They were small and fully feathered, but had four "wings," one on each limb. Scientists aren't sure whether the *Microraptor zhaoianus* could fly, but believe it could scale trees using its large claws, and glided among the forest canopy.

TOP 10

HEAVIEST **LIZARDS**

Most of the lizards listed below, including the Komodo dragon, are called monitor lizards possibly because of their occasional habit of standing on their back legs to "monitor" the presence of venomous predators...

	LIZARD	WEIGHT (LB)	(KG)
1	KOMODO DRAGON	366	166
2	ASIAN WATER MONITOR	110	49.9
3	CROCODILE MONITOR	44	20
=	PERENTIE	44	20
=	LACE GOANNA	44	20
6	ROCK MONITOR	37	16.8
7	NILE MONITOR	33	15
8	NORTHERN SIERRA MADRE FOREST MONITOR	22	10
9	GREEN IGUANA	18	8.2
10	BENGAL MONITOR	15.9	7.2

1 KOMODO DRAGON

Native to a few islands in Indonesia, the largest of all lizards grows to 10 ft (3 m) in length and can manage short bursts of 11 mph (18 kph). They are an ambush predator, "smelling" the air like a snake does with a large forked tongue, and they prey mainly upon pigs, deer, and cattle. They have large, curved, serrated teeth, and a venom that stops the prey's blood from clotting. Komodos can eat 80 percent of their own body weight in one sitting.

THE EXTINCT MEGALANIA **COULD HAVE WEIGHED MORE THAN 4,000 LB (1,814 KG)**

BIGGEST **RODENTS**

Much of the early exploration of North America was driven by the quest for beaver fur (used for clothing and hats) and meat...

	RODENT	WEIGHT (LB)	(KG)
1	CAPYBARA	201	91.2
2	NORTH AMERICAN BEAVER	110	49.9
3	LESSER CAPYBARA	100	45.4
4	EURASIAN BEAVER	88	39.9
5	CAPE PORCUPINE	66	29.9
6	CRESTED PORCUPINE	60	27.2
7	NORTH AMERICAN PORCUPINE	39.7	18
=	INDIAN CRESTED PORCUPINE	39.7	18
9	COYPU	37	16.8
10	PHILIPPINE PORCUPINE	11.9	5.4

2 NORTH AMERICAN BEAVER

The largest rodent in North America is this tree-felling, dam-building mammal that has an enormous impact on its environment. With its large incisors—colored orange from a protective coating—it will create dams that change river flow, purifying the water of silts and breaking down toxins. The dams prevent river erosion, and the clean ponds they create provide a fresh ecosystem for aquatic life and food for larger animals.

TOP 10

BIGGEST CANINES

Wolves feature heavily in this list of dental prowess: 42 sharp teeth and a powerful bite allow them to crush hard bone and leave very little of their prey uneaten...

	CANINE	WEIGHT (LB)	(KG)
1	EURASIAN WOLF	190	86.2
2	NORTHWESTERN WOLF	175	79.4
3	ARCTIC WOLF	155	70.3
4	GREAT PLAINS WOLF	150	68
5	TUNDRA WOLF	115	52.2
6	INDIAN WOLF	90	40.8
=	RED WOLF	90	40.8
8	STEPPE WOLF	88	39.9
9	MEXICAN WOLF	80	36.3
10	DINGO	77	34.9

EXTRA

	WEIGHT (LB)	(KG)
DEER WOLF	67	30.4
AFRICAN WILD DOG	66	29.9
ARABIAN WOLF	55	24.9

3 ARCTIC WOLF

A subspecies of the gray wolf, the smaller Arctic wolf is found in areas of North America (mainly Alaska) and Greenland, and hunts musk oxen and caribou. Its fur (which is unique among wolves for being mostly white all year round) has two layers, with the short, thick under layer being shed in the spring.

5 SNOW LEOPARD

With a long tail that provides balance, and a build that allows it to leap six times the length of its own body, the snow leopard is uniquely adapted for the mountainous regions of Central Asia. Incredibly elusive, they are known by some locals as "the ghost of the mountains." Numbers have decreased dramatically over the decades due to hunting for fur and conflict with livestock owners.

TOP 10 — BIGGEST **FELINES**

Domestic cats make great pets. Despite the enormous differences in size, those in our homes are very similar to the bigger versions that live in the wild...

	FELINE	WEIGHT (LB)	(KG)
1	SIBERIAN TIGER	1,025.2	465
2	LION	595.2	270
3	JAGUAR	308.6	140
4	COUGAR	264.5	120
5	SNOW LEOPARD	160.9	73
6	LEOPARD	141.1	64
7	CHEETAH	121.2	55
8	LYNX	77.2	35
9	CLOUDED LEOPARD	55.1	25
10	CARACAL	44.1	20

TOP 10

HEAVIEST WHALES

Whales' large mass helps them stay warm in cold seas and travel long distances, and provides a good deterrent against predators...

	WHALE	WEIGHT (LB)	(KG)
1	BLUE WHALE	418,877	189,999.4
2	BOWHEAD WHALE	219,999.3	99,790
3	NORTH ATLANTIC RIGHT WHALE	210,559.1	95,508
4	NORTH PACIFIC RIGHT WHALE	197,119.7	89,412
5	SOUTHERN RIGHT WHALE	190,400	86,364
6	FINBACK WHALE	165,760	75,187.5
7	SPERM WHALE	125,440	56,898.6
8	GRAY WHALE	88,184	39,999.6
9	HUMPBACK WHALE	88,050	39,938.8
10	SEI WHALE	62,720	28,449.3

7 SPERM WHALE

A sperm whale can dive to depths of up to 1.9 miles (3 km), although it typically dives down 1,312 ft (400 m) to feed on prey. An average adult will eat thousands of pounds of squid a day. The sperm whale has the largest brain of any creature ever to have lived on Earth, weighing about 17 lb (7.1 kg), compared to a human brain of 3 lb (1.4 kg).

TOP 10

LONGEST **WHALES**

The longest ever blue whale is reported to be one caught by whalers in Antarctica, a female that measured 110.17 ft (33.58 m), weighing in at 440,925 lb (203,765 kg)...

	WHALE	LENGTH (FT)	(M)
1	BLUE WHALE	110.17	33.58
2	FINBACK WHALE	89.5	27.3
3	SPERM WHALE	67	20.4
4	NORTH PACIFIC RIGHT WHALE	65	19.8
5	HUMPBACK WHALE	62	18.9
6	SOUTHERN RIGHT WHALE	59	18
=	BOWHEAD WHALE	59	18
8	SEI WHALE	56	17
9	GRAY WHALE	49	14.9
=	BRYDE'S WHALE	49	14.9

8 SEI WHALE

Sei whales are thought to be the fastest of all whales and dolphins, being able to reach speeds of 30 mph (48 kph). Their name (pronounced "say" or "sigh") is derived from the Norwegian word for pollack, as the creatures tended to appear at the same time as schools of the fish.

3 › MAKO SHARK

Named after the Maori word for "shark," the mako's anatomy is different from other sharks. It is more similar to that of its common quarry, the tuna, with a centralized muscle structure and main red swimming muscles closer to its spine. This limits lateral movement and focuses on propelling the fish forward at incredible speeds. Bursts of acceleration can hit 59 mph (95 kph), and its sustained speed is 22 mph (35 kph).

TOP 10

FASTEST IN THE SEA

Fish swim by moving their tails from side to side; the fastest, including sharks and tuna, are those that produce the most thrust and create the least drag...

	NAME	SPEED (MPH)	(KPH)
1	BLACK MARLIN	80	128.7
2	SAILFISH	68.3	110
3	MAKO SHARK	59	95
4	WAHOO	48.5	78
5	BLUEFIN TUNA	43.5	70
6	GREAT BLUE SHARK	42.9	69
7	ORCA WHALE	40.1	65
8	BONEFISH	39.8	64
=	SWORDFISH	39.8	64

WALRUS TUSKS CAN GROW TO A LENGTH OF 3 FT (0.9 M)

TOP 10

BIGGEST **SEALS, SEA LIONS, AND WALRUSES**

These three species of marine mammals, with front and rear flippers, are all members of the pinniped family, which means "fin-footed" in Latin...

	NAME	WEIGHT (LB)	(KG)
1	SOUTHERN ELEPHANT SEAL	11,000	4,989.5
2	NORTHERN ELEPHANT SEAL	8,000	3,628.8
3	PACIFIC WALRUS	4,151.3	1,883
4	STELLER SEA LION	2,500	1,134
5	ATLANTIC WALRUS	2,000	907.2
6	CALIFORNIA SEA LION	1,000	453.6
7	NEW ZEALAND SEA LION	992	450
8	GALÁPAGOS SEA LION	880	400
9	SOUTH AMERICAN SEA LION	772	350
10	AUSTRALIAN SEA LION	661.4	300

1 SOUTHERN ELEPHANT SEAL

The largest of all seals, male elephant seals can be up to 10 times the weight of an adult female. The males also have a large "trunk" (giving the species its name), which can be inflated to intimidate rivals during the mating season. While lumbering and bulky on land, they are accomplished swimmers and can dive up to 5,000 ft (1,500 m), staying submerged for up to two hours.

TOP 10

BIGGEST OTTERS

Otters utilize both water and land environments, so when their numbers decline, it indicates that something is wrong with the ecosystem...

	OTTER	WEIGHT (LB)	(KG)
1	SEA OTTER	119	54
2	AFRICAN CLAWLESS OTTER	80	36.2
3	GIANT OTTER	75	34
4	EURASIAN OTTER	37	16.8
5	NORTH AMERICAN RIVER OTTER	33	15
=	NEOTROPICAL RIVER OTTER	33	15
7	SMOOTH-COATED OTTER	24	10.9
8	SOUTHERN RIVER OTTER	22	10
9	SPOTTED-NECKED OTTER	14	6.4
10	HAIRY-NOSED OTTER	13	5.9

1 SEA OTTER

Sea otters are one of the few animals in the world that are able to use tools while they hunt. They keep their favorite stone tools, for cracking open shellfish, in specialized pouches under their arms. This evolutionary advancement allows them to consume 25 percent of their body weight in food every day. They also have a keen sense of social awareness and hold hands while they are floating in the sea, so as not to lose each other.

SIZE COMPARISON

MARINE OTTER
12.8 LB (5.8 KG)

ASIAN SMALL-CLAWED OTTER
11.9 LB (5.4 KG)

LARGEST **SQUID / OCTOPODES**

Although both are cephalopods with eight arms, these two species differ in a number of ways: by anatomy, by habitat, and, most importantly, by size, as you can see from the table below...

	NAME	TYPE	LENGTH (FT)	(M)
1	COLOSSAL SQUID	SQUID	45.9	14
2	GIANT SQUID	SQUID	42.7	13
3	BIGFIN SQUID	SQUID	26.2	8
4	GIANT PACIFIC OCTOPUS	OCTOPUS	20	6.1
5	ASPEROTEUTHIS ACANTHODERMA	SQUID	18	5.5
6	COCKATOO SQUID	GLASS SQUID	14.1	4.3
7	ROBUST CLUBHOOK SQUID	SQUID	13.2	4.02
8	SEVEN-ARM OCTOPUS	OCTOPUS	11	3.4
9	MEGALOCRANCHIA FISHERI	GLASS SQUID	8.9	2.7
10	DANA OCTOPUS SQUID	SQUID	7.5	2.3

4 ▶ GIANT PACIFIC OCTOPUS

This is the biggest octopus in the oceans, with the heaviest specimen recorded weighing in at 600 lb (272 kg), although adults usually reach 110 lb (50 kg). They survive mainly on a diet of clams and shrimps, but have been known to attack birds and even sharks. They are extremely intelligent, with the ability to learn quickly and solve problems.

6 ORINOCO CROCODILE

The Orinoco crocodile is the largest predator in the Americas and one of the rarest. It lives only in the Orinoco river and its tributaries in Venezuela and Colombia. In the second quarter of the 20th century the species was almost hunted out of existence for its skin, and its numbers have struggled to recover.

TOP 10

LONGEST **CROCODILES & ALLIGATORS**

Florida's Everglades is famous for many things, one of which is that it is the only environment on Earth where alligators and crocodiles coexist in harmony...

	NAME	LENGTH (FT)	(M)
1	GHARIAL	23	7
2	NILE CROCODILE	21.2	6.45
3	SALTWATER CROCODILE	20.7	6.32
4	AMERICAN ALLIGATOR	17.4	5.31
5	AMERICAN CROCODILE	17.1	5.2
6	ORINOCO CROCODILE	16.8	5.1
7	BLACK CAIMAN	16	4.9
8	MORELET'S CROCODILE	14.8	4.5
9	SLENDER-SNOUTED CROCODILE	13.8	4.2
10	FRESHWATER CROCODILE	13.1	4

TOP 10

BIGGEST **PREHISTORIC FISH**

Prehistoric fish represent the first vertebrates that thrived on planet Earth. They are identified only through fossil data and archaeological evidence...

	NAME	LENGTH (FT)	(M)
1	MEGALODON	52.5	16
2	DUNKLEOSTEUS	32.8	10
=	LEEDSICHTHYS	32.8	10
4	ONCHOPRISTIS	26.2	8
5	RHIZODUS	23	7
6	CRETOXYRHINA	20	6.1
7	ISURUS	19.7	6
=	XIPHACTINUS	19.7	6
9	MAWSONIA	13.1	4
=	ONYCHODUS	13.1	4

2 DUNKLEOSTEUS

Living between 360 and 380 million years ago, *Dunkleosteus* weighed nearly three tons. It didn't have teeth, but used two large bony plates, which could snap and crush prey. Scientists believe its bite force was double that of today's crocodiles. Sharks, and even other *Dunkleosteus*, have been found in fossil specimens' bellies.

TOP 10

BIGGEST
DOLPHINS & PORPOISES

These marine mammals belong to a suborder of the cetacean family. Along with some whale species, they have teeth and possess a single blowhole...

	NAME	WEIGHT (LB)	(KG)
1	ORCA WHALE	22,000	9,979
2	SHORT-FINNED PILOT WHALE	6,613.9	3,000
3	LONG-FINNED PILOT WHALE	5,070.6	2,300
4	FALSE KILLER WHALE	2,200	998
5	COMMON BOTTLENOSE DOLPHIN	1,433	650
6	MONK DOLPHIN	1,102	500
7	BURRUNAN DOLPHIN	992.1	450
8	MELON-HEADED WHALE	606.3	275
9	LONG-BEAKED COMMON DOLPHIN	518.1	235
10	CHINESE WHITE DOLPHIN	507.1	230

EXTRA

INDO-PACIFIC BOTTLENOSE DOLPHIN	502.7	228
ATLANTIC WHITE-SIDED DOLPHIN	496	225
DALL'S PORPOISE	485	220
SHORT-BEAKED COMMON DOLPHIN	440.9	200
PACIFIC WHITE-SIDED DOLPHIN	440.9	200

10 ► CHINESE WHITE DOLPHIN

Despite its name, the adult Chinese white dolphin is actually pink with gray spots. It is beloved of the people of Hong Kong, where it was first recorded by British explorer Peter Mundy in July 1637. As the human population of the area has grown over the decades, affecting the dolphins' environment, numbers have plummeted. An estimated 47 remain in Hong Kong waters.

TOP 10

BIGGEST **SHARKS**

Sharks are feared by most and some can be ferocious. Ironically, the two species at the top of this list are virtually harmless plankton eaters...

SHARK	LENGTH (FT)	(M)
1	WHALE SHARK	41.7	12.7
2	BASKING SHARK	40.4	12.3
3	GREAT WHITE SHARK	24.6	7.5
4	PACIFIC SLEEPER SHARK	24.3	7.4
5	GREENLAND SHARK	21	6.4
6	GOBLIN SHARK	20.24	6.17
7	GREAT HAMMERHEAD SHARK	20	6.1
8	TIGER SHARK	19.7	6
=	THRESHER SHARK	19.7	6
10	MEGAMOUTH SHARK	18.4	5.6

= 8 ► THRESHER SHARK

The thresher shark's tail is the key reason it makes this list. Its scythe-like caudal fin is elongated and constitutes a third of its total length. Using the fin to herd squid and schooling fish, the thresher shark also stuns its prey with a thrashing of its tail. In 2007 a specimen weighing 1,250 lb (510 kg) was caught by fishermen off the Cornish coast of the UK.

6 › WASP

There are 30,000 different species of wasp, most of which are solitary, non-stinging varieties. Wasps are vital to the ecosystem as they prey upon nearly every type of pest insect. They are so efficient that the agriculture industry now uses them to protect crops. The bigger species of wasps (the hornets – *Vespa crabro*) have the fastest wing beats, and can fly at 12.8 mph (30 kph).

TOP 10 — FASTEST INSECT WINGS

Insects use their wings for protection, as musical instruments, as camouflage, as signals to recognize one another, for attracting mates, and even as tools to fly...

	INSECT	BEATS PER SECOND (MAXIMUM)
1	MIDGE	1,046
2	GNAT	950
3	MOSQUITO	600
=	BUMBLEBEE	600
5	FRUIT FLY	300
6	WASP	247
7	HOUSEFLY	190
8	BLOWFLY	150
9	HOVERFLY	120
10	HORNET	100

TOP 10

LARGEST
PREHISTORIC FLIERS

Number one on this chart, *Hatzegopteryx*, is known from a single specimen discovered in Romania. Its wingspan indicates it was about the size of a Spitfire airplane...

	PTEROSAUR	WINGSPAN (FT)	(M)
1	HATZEGOPTERYX	34.4	10.5
=	QUETZALCOATLUS	34.4	10.5
3	ARAMBOURGIANIA	32.8	10
4	ORNITHOCHEIRUS	23	7
5	PTERANODON	21.3	6.5
6	COLOBORHYNCHUS	19.7	6
7	MOGANOPTERUS	15.4	4.7
8	ISTIODACTYLUS	14.1	4.3
9	TUPUXUARA	13.1	4
10	ZHENYUANOPTERUS	11.5	3.5

4   ORNITHOCHEIRUS

One of the earliest-discovered pterosaurs, *Ornithocheirus* is distinctive for its crested beak, which grabbed fish from the surface of the seas during the late Cretaceous period around 110 million years ago. It had fewer teeth than other pterosaurs, leading scientists to believe it survived on large fish. Its body was small but very muscular.

WINGED CREATURES

HEAVIEST BIRDS

Ostriches are too heavy to fly (see just how massive they are in the chart below), but they are built for speed and can run at over 40 mph (65 kph)...

	BIRD	WEIGHT (LB)	(KG)
1	OSTRICH	346	156.8
2	DOUBLE-WATTLED CASSOWARY	190	85
3	EMU	130	60
4	GOLD-NECK CASSOWARY	128	58
5	EMPEROR PENGUIN	100	45.4
6	GREATER RHEA	88	40
7	DARWIN'S RHEA	63	28.6
8	LITTLE CASSOWARY	57	26
9	KING PENGUIN	35	16
10	DALMATIAN PELICAN	33	15

5 EMPEROR PENGUIN

The emperor penguin (*Aptenodytes forsteri*) is the largest of all the penguins. It has adapted to survive the harshest winters on the planet, where temperatures can reach -58°F (-50°C) and winds can reach 124 mph (200 kph). They can swim to depths of 1,850 ft (564 m), which is nearly twice the height of the Shard in London, UK.. They are able to stay underwater for up to 28 minutes.

2 GOLDEN EAGLE

The golden eagle (*Aquila chrysaetos*) is a giant among birds of prey (the biggest in North America). Like the number one bird on the below list (the peregrine falcon), golden eagles drop from the skies to swoop on prey such as rabbits. It's mating ritual sees pairs take turns to drop and catch sticks and stones in midair.

DALMATIAN PELICAN

IS THE HEAVIEST BIRD THAT CAN FLY

TOP 10

FASTEST **IN THE AIR**

The impressive speeds on this chart, reached using muscle power and navigation skills alone, make the fastest bird the fastest living creature...

	BIRD	MAXIMUM KNOWN SPEED	
		(MPH)	(KPH)
1	PEREGRINE FALCON	241.7	389
2	GOLDEN EAGLE	198.8	320
3	GYRFALCON	129.9	209
4	SWIFT	106.3	171
5	WHITE-THROATED NEEDLETAIL	105	169
6	EURASIAN HOBBY	100	161
7	FRIGATEBIRD	95.1	153
8	SPUR-WINGED GOOSE	88.2	142
9	RED-BREASTED MERGANSER	80.8	130
10	GREY-HEADED ALBATROSS	78.9	127

TOP 10

BIGGEST
BEES, WASPS & HORNETS

Bees get a good press: they rarely sting, produce honey and beeswax, and pollinate plants. But wasps and hornets are useful too, as they help out by eating other insects...

	NAME	TYPE	SIZE (LENGTH) (IN)	(CM)
1	TARANTULA HAWK SPIDER WASP	WASP	2.5	6.4
2	EASTERN CICADA KILLER	WASP	2	5
=	WESTERN CICADA KILLER	WASP	2	5
4	GIANT SCOLIID	WASP	1.9	4.8
5	JAPANESE GIANT HORNET	HORNET	1.8	4.5
6	ASIAN GIANT HORNET	HORNET	1.6	4
=	BOMBUS DAHLBOMII	BEE	1.6	4
8	MEGACHILE PLUTO	BEE	1.5	3.9
9	EUROPEAN HORNET	HORNET	1.4	3.5
10	GREATER BANDED HORNET	HORNET	0.9	2.5

2 ▷ EASTERN CICADA KILLER

These large wasps are different from hornets or social wasps in that they use their stings to paralyze their prey. They wouldn't sting a human unless handled roughly. Males can't sting at all. A female wasp will stun a cicada and fly it back to its burrow for food for its larvae. As a cicada is usually twice the size of the wasp, the wasp will often haul its prey up a tree to gain sufficient height to propel itself into its nest chamber.

TOP 10

SMALLEST
PREHISTORIC FLIERS

We're all familiar with the birds and the bees, but prehistoric skies were filled with an array of fliers including ancient birds, bats, insects, and even reptiles...

	NAME	WINGSPAN	
		(IN)	(CM)
1	IBEROMESORNIS ROMERALI	7.9	20
2	NEMICOLOPTERUS CRYPTICUS	9.8	25
3	PALAEOCHIROPTERYX TUPAIODON	11.8	30
4	ANUROGNATHUS AMMONI	13.8	35
5	ICARONYCTERIS INDEX	14.6	37
6	PREONDACTYLUS BUFFARINII	17.7	45
7	PETEINOSAURUS ZAMBELLI	23.6	60
8	CONFUCIUSORNIS SP.	27.6	70
9	JEHOLOPTERUS NINCHENGENSIS	35.4	90
10	ARCHEOPTERYX SP.	39.4	100

3 PALAEOCHIROP-TERYX TUPAIODON

Adapted to prey upon low-flying insects in the forests of the Eocene period some 46 million years ago, this ancient bat is very similar to modern-day tropical species. It had a broad, primitive-looking snout and skull, but a wing structure very similar to today's flying mammals.

BIGGEST MOTHS

Scientists estimate there are more than 150,000 moth species worldwide; some in bright colors with dazzling patterns, and a myriad of shapes and sizes...

	MOTH	SIZE (WIDTH)	
		(IN)	(CM)
1	WHITE WITCH MOTH	12.2	31
2	ATLAS MOTH	10.3	26.2
3	MADAGASCAN MOON MOTH	8.9	22.6
4	CECROPIA MOTH	7	17.8
5	IMPERIAL MOTH	6.9	17.4
6	BLACK WITCH MOTH	6.7	17
7	EMPEROR GUM MOTH	5.9	15
=	POLYPHEMUS MOTH	5.9	15
9	OWL MOTH	5.5	14
10	LUNA MOTH	5	12.7

RAJAH BROOKE'S BIRDWING
6.7 IN (17 CM)

SINO-KOREAN OWL MOTH
4.7 IN (12 CM)

4 ▶ CECROPIA MOTH

This is the biggest moth in North America, *Hyalophora cecropia* (sometimes called the robin moth). Living in hardwood forests throughout the continent, this giant silk moth has a life span of only a few days. It has no mouth parts or digestive organs; its sole function is to mate. The males can detect female pheromones over a mile away.

LARGEST **BUTTERFLIES**

Similar to their bigger moth cousins in many ways, butterflies are generally brighter in color, fold their wings vertically, and have antennae with a long shaft and a bulb at the end...

	BUTTERFLY	SIZE (WIDTH)	
		(IN)	(CM)
1	QUEEN ALEXANDRA'S BIRDWING	11.8	30
2	GOLIATH BIRDWING	11	28
3	GIANT AFRICAN SWALLOWTAIL	9.8	25
4	RIPPON'S BIRDWING	7.9	20
=	WALLACE'S GOLDEN BIRDWING	7.9	20
6	PALAWAN BIRDWING	7.5	19
=	PRIAM'S BIRDWING	7.5	19
8	MAGELLAN BIRDWING	7.1	18
9	RAJAH BROOKE'S BIRDWING	6.7	17
10	CHIMAERA BIRDWING	6.3	16

3 — GIANT AFRICAN SWALLOWTAIL

Africa's largest butterfly can be found along the rivers and primary tropical rain forests in central and western Africa. They have no known natural predators as their bodies contain toxic chemicals called glycosides and they can spray a cloud of foul-smelling chemicals if disturbed. However, numbers are dwindling due to habitat destruction and poaching by insect collectors.

TOP 10

HEAVIEST
TORTOISES & TURTLES

Although they are both egg-laying reptiles with protective shells, turtles have webbed feet and live in or near water, while tortoises are almost exclusively land dwelling...

	NAME	WEIGHT (LB)	(KG)
1	LEATHERBACK SEA TURTLE	2,120	961.1
2	LOGGERHEAD TURTLE	1,202	545.2
3	GALÁPAGOS GIANT TORTOISE	919.3	417
4	GREEN SEA TURTLE	871	395.1
5	ALDABRA GIANT TORTOISE	793.7	360
6	YANGTZE GIANT SOFTSHELL TURTLE	550	249.5
7	HAWKSBILL TURTLE	280	127
8	INDIAN NARROW-HEADED SOFTSHELL TURTLE	260	117.9
9	ALLIGATOR SNAPPING TURTLE	236	107
10	AFRICAN SPURRED TORTOISE	231.5	105

5 ▷ ALDABRA GIANT TORTOISE

Giant tortoises exist in only two remote places in the world: the more famous is the Galápagos Islands in Ecuador and the other is the Aldabra Atoll in the Seychelles. These ancient giant creatures can live up to 120 years, and it's believed some individuals have seen their 250th birthday. They sleep an average of 18 hours a day.

THE LONGEST
BLUE WHALE
EVER RECORDED:
110.17 FT
(33.58 M)

TOP 10

BIGGEST CARNIVORES

Carnivores are animals whose diet consists of other animals; the list below naturally features predators at the very top of the food chain...

	TYPE	NAME	WEIGHT (LB)	(KG)
1	WHALE	BLUE WHALE	418,877	189,999.4
2	SHARK	WHALE SHARK	47,000	21,318
3	DOLPHIN	ORCA WHALE	22,000	9,979
4	SEAL	SOUTHERN ELEPHANT SEAL	11,000	4,989.5
5	CROCODILE	SALTWATER CROCODILE	4,409.2	2,000
6	WALRUS	PACIFIC WALRUS	4,151.3	1,883
7	BEAR	POLAR BEAR	2,209	1,002
8	STINGRAY	GIANT FRESHWATER STINGRAY	1,320	600
9	SQUID	COLOSSAL SQUID	1,091.3	495
10	BIG CAT	SIBERIAN TIGER	1,025.2	465

5 SALTWATER CROCODILE

The saltwater crocodile (*Crocodylus porosus*) is the world's largest reptile, reaching lengths of 20 ft (6 m). By reducing its heart rate to a mere 2–3 beats per minute, and with its hemoglobin dispensing oxygen to only the essential parts of the body, it can stay submerged for more than an hour.

FASTEST ANIMAL SPECIES

Swim, fly, run—could be the description of an animal triathlon; even the fastest athletes would be impressed by the speedy species listed below...

	TYPE	ANIMAL	FASTEST RECORDED SPEED (MPH)	(KPH)
1	RAPTOR	PEREGRINE FALCON	242	389
2	BAT	MEXICAN FREE-TAILED BAT	99.4	160
3	BONY FISH	BLACK MARLIN	80	128.7
4	BIG CAT	CHEETAH	75	120.7
5	ARTIODACTYL MAMMAL	PRONGHORN	61	98.2
6	SHARK	SHORTFIN MAKO SHARK	60	96.6
=	FLIGHTLESS BIRD	OSTRICH	60	96.6
8	HORSE	AMERICAN QUARTER HORSE	55	88.5
9	DOLPHIN	ORCA WHALE	40.1	65
10	REPTILE	CENTRAL BEARDED DRAGON	24.9	40

2 MEXICAN FREE-TAILED BAT

While birds of prey can achieve record speeds by diving on their prey in short bursts, these insect-hunting mammals can reach flying speeds of nearly 100 mph (160 kph). During World War II, the US Army hatched a plan to drop a bomb that contained hundreds of hibernating free-tailed bats with tiny incendiaries attached to them to start fires in Japanese homes and factories. Project X-ray, as it was called, was shelved because of the length of time it took to develop.

LONGEST **MIGRATIONS**

Species in all major animal groups migrate with the changing seasons, to find warmer weather, better food supplies, or a safe place to give birth to their young...

ANIMAL	DISTANCE (MI)	(KM)
1 ARCTIC TERN	59,650	96,000
2 SOOTY SHEARWATER	40,000	64,000
3 ELEPHANT SEAL	20,000	32,200
4 PECTORAL SANDPIPER	18,000	28,000
5 HUMPBACK WHALE	16,000	25,700
6 GRAY WHALE	14,000	22,500
7 LEATHERBACK TURTLE	12,000	19,300
8 PIED WHEATEAR	11,200	18,000
9 SHORT-TAILED SHEARWATER	10,600	17,000
10 BAR-TAILED GODWIT	7,200	11,500

1 ARCTIC TERN

In 2016, one bird was recorded flying 59,650 miles (96,000 km) from its breeding grounds off the west coast of Great Britain to Antarctica, taking in West Africa, the Cape of Good Hope, and the Indian Ocean en route. That's equal to circling Earth 2.4 times. During its lifetime, a typical tern can fly the equivalent of three trips to the moon and back.

TOP 10

BIGGEST SPIDERS

Arachnophobes, beware: research suggests that you are never more than 10 ft (3 m) away from a member of one of over 30,000 different species of spider...

	SPIDER	LEG SPAN (IN)	(CM)
1	HUNTSMAN	11.8	30
2	BRAZILIAN SALMON PINK	10.6	27
3	GOLIATH BIRDEATER	10	25.4
=	WOLF SPIDER	10	25.4
5	PURPLE BLOOM BIRD-EATING SPIDER	9	23
6	HERCULES BABOON	8	20.3
7	HYSTEROCRATES SPELLENBERGI	7	17.8
8	BRAZILIAN WANDERING SPIDER	5.9	15
=	CERBALUS ARAVENSIS	5.9	15
10	TEGENARIA PARIETINA	5.5	14

5 | ## PURPLE BLOOM BIRD-EATING SPIDER

Native to Colombia and Ecuador, these large-bodied tarantulas are among the most striking in the world. The male of the species has a purple hue all over its body. Although called "bird-eating," they mainly prey upon crickets, cockroaches, and mice.

TOP 10

BIGGEST **BLOODSUCKERS**

Bloodsuckers are parasites. They rarely kill their hosts because hosts will make more blood alive. Blood is full of iron and protein, essential for animals to live and grow...

	BLOODSUCKER	LENGTH (IN)	(CM)
1	SEA LAMPREY	35.5	90
2	GIANT AMAZON LEECH	18	45.7
3	CANDIRU	16	40
4	VAMPIRE BAT	7	18
5	VAMPIRE FINCH	4.7	12
6	MADRILENIAL BUTTERFLY	2.76	7
7	ASSASSIN BUG	1.6	4
8	FEMALE MOSQUITO	0.6	1.6
9	BEDBUG	0.2	0.5
10	FLEA	0.09	0.25

7 ASSASSIN BUG

The assassin bug lives up to its name by pouncing on unsuspecting insects and piercing them with its deadly proboscis. This carries a lethal saliva whose enzymes break down body tissue, allowing the bug to feed on its prey. In the United States, Triatominae (a subgroup of assassin bugs) are known as "kissing bugs," due to their habit of biting humans on the face.

8 HERCULES BEETLE

Native to the rain forests of Central and South America, the Hercules beetle is a species of rhinoceros beetle, with males having enormous horn-like pincers that make them the longest of all beetles. They feed on fresh and rotting fruit and are incredibly strong for their size, able to carry 850 times their own body weight.

TOP 10

BIGGEST
FLYING & GLIDING INSECTS

There is a "bushel" of stick insects in the list below. These species live in trees and bushes and the males are able to fly in search of females...

	INSECT	SIZE (LENGTH) (IN)	(MM)
1	CHAN'S MEGASTICK	22.3	567
2	BORNEO STICK INSECT	21.5	546
3	WHITE WITCH MOTH	12.2*	310*
=	QUEEN ALEXANDRA'S BIRDWING	12.2*	310*
5	GIANT AFRICAN STICK INSECT	11.6	295
6	ATLAS MOTH	10.3*	262*
7	MEGALOPREPUS CAERULATUS DAMSELFLY	7.5*	190*
8	HERCULES BEETLE	6.9	175
9	TITAN BEETLE	6.6	167
10	GIANT WATER BUG	4.75	120.7

*WINGSPAN, THE REST ARE LENGTHS.

TOP 10

LONGEST SNAKES

Fear of snakes is one of the most common phobias for humans. Looking at the list below, it seems we have good reason to be scared of them...

	SNAKE	LONGEST FOUND (FT)	(M)
1	RETICULATED PYTHON	49	14.94
2	GREEN ANACONDA	37	11.28
3	SCRUB PYTHON	26	7.92
4	AFRICAN ROCK PYTHON	20	6.1
5	KING COBRA	18.5	5.64
6	BOA CONSTRICTOR	13	3.96
7	BUSHMASTER	10	3.05
8	INDIAN PYTHON	9.8	2.99
9	DIAMONDBACK RATTLESNAKE	8.9	2.74
10	WESTERN RAT SNAKE	8	2.44

5 KING COBRA

The king cobra (*Ophiophagus hannah*) is the world's largest poisonous snake. Its neurotoxic venom is so powerful and copious that elephants are known to have died within three hours of a bite. That bite is delivered through short, half-inch (1 cm), powerful fangs.

FORCES OF **NATURE** 02

HIGHEST **WATERFALLS**

Visit the tallest building in the world, Dubai's Burj Khalifa, at 2,717 ft (828 m) high, to get a sense of how massive these waterfalls are...

	WATERFALL	LOCATION	HEIGHT (FT)	(M)
1	ANGEL FALLS	BOLÍVAR STATE (VENEZUELA)	3,212	979
2	TUGELA FALLS	KWAZULU-NATAL (SOUTH AFRICA)	3,110	948
3	CATARATAS LAS TRES HERMANAS	AYACUCHO (PERU)	3,000	914
4	OLO'UPENA FALLS	MOLOKAI, HAWAII (USA)	2,953	900
5	CATARATA YUMBILLA	AMAZONAS (PERU)	2,940	896
6	VINNUFOSSEN	MØRE OG ROMSDAL (NORWAY)	2,822	860
7	BALÅIFOSSEN	HORDALAND (NORWAY)	2,788	850
8	PU'UKA'OKU FALLS	HAWAII (USA)	2,756	840
=	JAMES BRUCE FALLS	BRITISH COLUMBIA (CANADA)	2,756	840
10	BROWNE FALLS	SOUTH ISLAND (NEW ZEALAND)	2,743	836

1 ▶ ANGEL FALLS

American aviator Jimmie Angel was the first person to fly over this waterfall, hence its name. It is located in Venezuela's Canaima National Park, which covers 12,000 square miles (30,000 square km). The park, a protected World Heritage Site, was established June 12, 1962.

9 CONGO-CHAMBESHI

This is the deepest river in the world, with the depth of some sections at 720 ft (220 m). The Congo is home to more than 1,000 species of animal, including hippopotami, lions, hyenas, crocodiles, okapi, and gorillas. There are more than 4,000 islands along the river.

TOP 10

LONGEST RIVERS

Diverse wildlife, including the colossal anaconda snake and the ancient, air-breathing fish, the arapaima, dwells along the Amazon river...

	RIVER	OUTFLOW	LENGTH (MI)	(KM)
1	AMAZON – UCAYALI – APURÍMAC	ATLANTIC OCEAN	4,345	6,992
2	NILE – KAGERA	MEDITERRANEAN	4,258	6,853
3	YANGTZE	EAST CHINA SEA	3,917	6,300
4	MISSISSIPPI – MISSOURI – JEFFERSON	GULF OF MEXICO	3,902	6,275
5	YENISEI – ANGARA – SELENGE	KARA SEA	3,445	5,539
6	HUANG HE	BOHAI SEA	3,395	5,464
7	OB – IRTYSH	GULF OF OB	3,364	5,410
8	PARANÁ – RÍO DE LA PLATA	RÍO DE LA PLATA	3,030	4,880
9	CONGO – CHAMBESHI	ATLANTIC OCEAN	2,922	4,700
10	AMUR – ARGUN	SEA OF OKHOTSK	2,763	4,444

WATER WORLD

▶ **LAKE SUPERIOR**

With an average depth of 480 ft (146 m), the deepest areas of Lake Superior reach 1,333 ft (406.3 m). There have been sightings of what has become known as Pressie, or the Lake Superior Dragon, for hundreds of years. Native Americans call it Mishipeshu, and pictograms of the creature can be seen on the shoreline.

BIGGEST LAKE IN THE WORLD

CASPIAN SEA, IRAN, RUSSIA, TURKMENISTAN, KAZAKHSTAN, AZERBAIJAN

CASPIAN SEA
143,000 MI²
371,000 KM²

LAKE SUPERIOR
31,700.1 MI²
82,103 KM²

TOP 10 — LARGEST LAKES IN THE USA

Although these are huge lakes, they are a long way away from the vastness of the largest lake in the world, the Caspian Sea, at 143,000 square miles (371,000 square km)...

	LAKE	LOCATION	AREA (SQUARE MI)	(SQUARE KM)
1	LAKE SUPERIOR	MICHIGAN – MINNESOTA – WISCONSIN – ONTARIO	31,700.1	82,103
2	LAKE HURON	MICHIGAN – ONTARIO	23,000.1	59,570
3	LAKE MICHIGAN	ILLINOIS – INDIANA – MICHIGAN – WISCONSIN	22,300.1	57,757
4	LAKE ERIE	MICHIGAN – NEW YORK – OHIO – ONTARIO – PENNSYLVANIA	9,910.1	25,667
5	LAKE ONTARIO	NEW YORK – ONTARIO	7,340.2	19,011
6	GREAT SALT LAKE	UTAH	2,117	5,483
7	LAKE OF THE WOODS	MANITOBA – MINNESOTA – ONTARIO	1,679.2	4,349
8	ILIAMNA LAKE	ALASKA	1,013.9	2,626
9	LAKE OAHE	NORTH DAKOTA – SOUTH DAKOTA	684.9	1,774
10	LAKE OKEECHOBEE	FLORIDA	662.2	1,715

TOP 10

LARGEST **OCEANS & SEAS**

Which ocean or sea is nearest where you live? Find out what kinds of marine life exist in that body of water, and which ones travel the greatest distances...

	NAME	TYPE	SIZE (SQUARE MI)	(SQUARE KM)
1	PACIFIC	OCEAN	64,196,000	166,266,876
2	ATLANTIC	OCEAN	33,400,000	86,505,602
3	INDIAN	OCEAN	28,400,000	73,555,662
4	SOUTHERN	OCEAN	20,327,000	52,646,688
5	ARCTIC	OCEAN	5,100,000	13,208,939
6	PHILIPPINE	SEA	2,000,000	5,179,976
7	CORAL	SEA	1,850,000	4,791,478
8	ARABIAN	SEA	1,491,000	3,861,672
9	SOUTH CHINA	SEA	1,148,000	2,973,306
10	CARIBBEAN	SEA	971,000	2,514,878

5 ARCTIC

The Arctic is home to polar bears, walruses, narwhal, and other species of whale including beluga and bowhead whales. Several species of seal also live in the Arctic. Scientific bodies such as the Intergovernmental Panel on Climate Change are working to educate the world on climate change and humankind's impact on our planet.

1 ▸ TROMELIN ISLAND

This island is a recognized IBA (Important Bird Area) as it provides a significant haven for nesting seabirds. The endangered green sea turtle also uses Tromelin Island as a place to lay its eggs.

GREENLAND: COASTLINE LENGTH = **27,394 MILES (44,086.4 KM)**, OVER **44,000 TIMES LONGER** THAN **TROMELIN ISLAND'S**

TOP 10

SMALLEST **ISLANDS / TERRITORIES**

Many of these islands / territories comprise multiple land masses. Find out which has more islands than any of the others...

	ISLAND / TERRITORY	CLAIMED OWNERSHIP BY	LENGTH OF COASTLINE (MI)	(KM)
1	TROMELIN ISLAND	MAURITIUS / FRANCE	0.39	1
=	KINGMAN REEF	USA	0.39	1
=	BAKER ISLAND	USA	0.39	1
4	HOWLAND ISLAND	USA	0.77	2
5	JOHNSTON ATOLL	USA	1.16	3
=	CORAL SEA ISLANDS	AUSTRALIA	1.16	3
7	JUAN DE NOVA ISLAND	FRANCE	1.54	4
8	JARVIS ISLAND	USA	1.93	5
=	SPRATLY ISLANDS	SEVERAL	1.93	5
=	GLORIOSO ISLANDS	FRANCE	1.93	5

1 VREDEFORT CRATER

This crater is located 74 miles (120 km) southwest of Johannesburg. Scientists estimate that the asteroid that struck Earth, to create the Vredefort Crater, may have been around 9 miles (14.5 km) wide. Calculations suggest the impact occurred around two billion years ago.

NEARLY **200 BURJ KHALIFAS,** WHICH IS 2,717 FT (828 M), LYING END TO END, WOULD FIT INTO THE **VREDEFORT CRATER**

TOP 10

LARGEST IMPACT CRATERS

These deep impressions on our planet's surface were caused by gigantic comets or meteorites smashing into Earth's surface many, many years ago...

	CRATER	LOCATION	DIAMETER (RIM TO RIM) (MI)	(KM)
1	VREDEFORT	SOUTH AFRICA	99.4	160
2	CHICXULUB	MEXICO	93.2	150
3	SUDBURY	CANADA	80.8	130
4	POPIGAI	RUSSIA	55.9	90
=	ACRAMAN	AUSTRALIA	55.9	90
6	MANICOUAGAN	CANADA	52.8	85
7	MOROKWENG	SOUTH AFRICA	43.5	70
8	KARA	RUSSIA	40.4	65
9	BEAVERHEAD	USA	37.3	60
10	TOOKOONOOKA	AUSTRALIA	34.2	55

SHORTEST **COASTLINES**

Compare the length of these coastlines with the chart on the opposite page to truly get an idea of just how small these ones are...

	COUNTRY	LENGTH OF COASTLINE	
		(MI)	(KM)
1	BOSNIA AND HERZEGOVINA	14.3	23
2	JORDAN	16.8	27
3	MACAU	22.4	36
4	SLOVENIA	25.5	41
5	TOGO	32.9	53
6	BELGIUM	47.2	76
7	BARBADOS	60.3	97
8	IRAQ	65.2	105
9	ARUBA	66.5	107
10	DOMINICA	94.4	152

INFO

Measuring the exact length of coastlines is problematic. Some methods involve "drawing" long straight lines along the coastline. Other methods use shorter-measurement lines that capture much more detail, resulting in a longer, but more accurate, overall distance.

3   MACAU

Located 37 miles (59.5 km) southwest of Hong Kong, Macau is also known in Chinese as Jinghai, which means "Mirror Sea." Its total area is 44.5 square miles (115.3 square km).

6 AUSTRALIA

The waters off the Australian coastline are home to the critically endangered speartooth shark and the grey nurse shark. Other vulnerable species in these waters include the great white shark and the whale shark.

TOP 10

LONGEST **COASTLINES**

Some countries are way more connected to the sea than you'd initially think, although there is a paradox of measuring coastlines (see the info box)...

	COUNTRY	LENGTH OF COASTLINE (MI)	(KM)
1	CANADA	164,988.34	265,523
2	USA	82,836.24	133,312
3	RUSSIA	68,543.46	110,310
4	INDONESIA	59,142.73	95,181
5	CHILE	48,816.78	78,563
6	AUSTRALIA	41,339.83	66,530
7	NORWAY	33,056.33	53,199
8	PHILIPPINES	21,064.48	33,900
9	BRAZIL	20,740.75	33,379
10	FINLAND	19,336.45	31,119

4 ▶ GANGKHAR PUENSUM

The name of Bhutan's highest mountain translates as "White Peak of the Three Spiritual Brothers." Out of respect for spiritual beliefs, the Bhutan government has banned mountaineering on Gangkhar Puensum. Everything from eerie lights to yeti sightings have been reported in the area.

TOP 10

COUNTRIES WITH
THE HIGHEST POINTS OF ELEVATION

The top of Mount Everest is a staggering 5.5 miles (8.8 km) high, which means that the air is a lot thinner than at sea level, making it much harder to breathe...

	PLACE	COUNTRY / COUNTRIES	HIGHEST POINT ABOVE SEA LEVEL (FT)	(M)
1	MOUNT EVEREST	CHINA, NEPAL	29,029	8,848
2	K2	PAKISTAN	28,251	8,611
3	KANGCHENJUNGA	INDIA	28,169	8,586
4	GANGKHAR PUENSUM	BHUTAN	24,836	7,570
5	ISMOIL SOMONI PEAK	TAJIKISTAN	24,590	7,495
6	NOSHAQ	AFGHANISTAN	24,580	7,492
7	JENGISH CHOKUSU	KYRGYZSTAN	24,406	7,439
8	KHAN TENGRI	KAZAKHSTAN	22,999	7,010
9	ACONCAGUA	ARGENTINA	22,835	6,960
10	OJOS DEL SALADO	CHILE	22,615	6,893

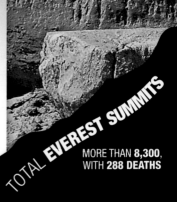

TOTAL **EVEREST SUMMITS**

MORE THAN **8,300**, WITH **288 DEATHS**

5 QATTARA DEPRESSION

This covers an area of 7,570 square miles (19,606.2 square km). It is home to the Qara Oasis, where more than 300 Berbers (indigenous people of North Africa) live. The golden jackal, cheetah, and gazelle also live in the Qattara Depression.

TOP 10

COUNTRIES WITH
THE LOWEST POINTS OF ELEVATION

To compare two well-known places on this chart: Badwater Basin in California's Death Valley is the lowest point in the USA, but the number one on this chart is more than five times lower...

	PLACE	COUNTRY / COUNTRIES	LOWEST POINT BELOW SEA LEVEL (FT)	(M)
1	DEAD SEA	ISRAEL, JORDAN, PALESTINE	-1,402	-428
2	SEA OF GALILEE	SYRIA	-702	-214
3	LAKE ASSAL	DJIBOUTI	-509	-155
4	AYDINGKOL	CHINA	-505	-154
5	QATTARA DEPRESSION	EGYPT	-436	-133
6	KARAGIYE DEPRESSION	KAZAKHSTAN	-433	-132
7	DANAKIL DEPRESSION	ETHIOPIA	-410	-125
8	LAGUNA DEL CARBÓN	ARGENTINA	-344	-105
9	BADWATER BASIN	USA	-279	-85
10	VPADINA AKCHANAYA	TURKMENISTAN	-266	-81

TOP 10

BIGGEST COUNTRIES

How many countries have you visited? With nearly 200 in total, there are 48 in Asia alone, with Europe consisting of 44...

	COUNTRY	SIZE (SQUARE MI)	(SQUARE KM)
1	RUSSIA	6,601,668	17,098,242
2	CANADA	3,855,100	9,984,670
3	CHINA	3,747,879	9,706,961
4	USA	3,705,407	9,629,091
5	BRAZIL	3,287,612	8,514,877
6	AUSTRALIA	2,969,907	7,692,024
7	INDIA	1,222,559	3,166,414
8	ARGENTINA	1,073,500	2,780,400
9	KAZAKHSTAN	1,052,100	2,724,900
10	ALGERIA	919,595	2,381,741

9 ▶ KAZAKHSTAN

This Central Asian country has a population of around 18 million across its 14 regions. It has more than 20 national parks and nature parks. Filmmaker Timur Bekmambetov, director of *Night Watch* (2004) and *Abraham Lincoln: Vampire Hunter* (2012), is from Kazakhstan.

TOP 10

SMALLEST COUNTRIES, SOVEREIGN STATES & ISLAND COUNTRIES / NATIONS

To be the best opposite version of the Biggest Countries chart, as the above title conveys, this now covers all key types of smaller nations...

	NAME	SIZE (SQUARE MI)	(SQUARE KM)
1	VATICAN CITY	0.17	0.44
2	MONACO	0.75	1.95
3	NAURU	8.1	21
4	TUVALU	10	26
5	SAN MARINO	23.6	61.2
6	LIECHTENSTEIN	61.8	160
7	MARSHALL ISLANDS	69.9	181
8	SAINT KITTS & NEVIS	100.8	261
9	MALDIVES	115.8	300
10	MALTA	122	316

3 ▶ NAURU

This island country has a population of around 13,000. Its capital, Yaren (formerly Moqua), in southern Nauru, was founded in 1968. Its currency is the Australian dollar. Nauru's nearest neighbor—and fellow island country—is Banaba Island.

3 ▶ SAHARA DESERT

The Great Desert covers almost a third of Africa. Its wildlife, adapted to its extremely hot climate, includes more than 100 different kinds of reptile, including skinks, cobras, and chameleons.

TOP 10

LARGEST **DESERTS**

The frozen deserts that occupy the top two positions in this chart cover more ground than the total sum of the rest of the deserts listed...

	DESERT	LOCATION	AREA (SQUARE MI)	(SQUARE KM)
1	ANTARCTIC POLAR DESERT	ANTARCTICA	5,500,000	14,244,935
2	ARCTIC POLAR DESERT	ARCTIC	5,400,000	13,985,936
3	SAHARA DESERT	NORTHERN AFRICA	3,500,000	9,064,959
4	ARABIAN DESERT	WESTERN ASIA	900,000	2,330,000
5	GOBI DESERT	ASIA	500,000	1,294,994
6	KALAHARI DESERT	SOUTHERN AFRICA	360,000	932,396
7	PATAGONIAN DESERT	ARGENTINA, CHILE	259,847	673,000
8	SYRIAN DESERT	SYRIA	200,773	520,000
9	GREAT BASIN DESERT	USA	190,000	492,098
10	GREAT VICTORIA DESERT	AUSTRALIA	163,862	424,400

5 KURIL-KAMCHATKA TRENCH

This deep realm is located in the northwest region of the Pacific. Expeditions have brought to light a vast amount of deep-sea pollution in the trench, including plastics, microplastics, and paint chips, which severely damage the underwater ecosystem.

TOP 10

DEEPEST **REALMS**

At 6.86 miles (11 km) deep, the distance from sea level to the Mariana Trench is equal to one ninth the distance between sea level and the Kármán line, the edge of space above Earth...

	NAME	LOCATION	DEEPEST POINT BELOW SEA LEVEL (FT)	(M)
1	MARIANA TRENCH	PACIFIC OCEAN	36,197.5	11,033
2	TONGA TRENCH	PACIFIC OCEAN	35,702.1	10,882
3	JAPAN TRENCH	PACIFIC OCEAN	34,593.2	10,544
4	PHILIPPINE TRENCH	PACIFIC OCEAN	34,580	10,540
5	KURIL-KAMCHATKA TRENCH	PACIFIC OCEAN	34,448.8	10,500
6	KERMADEC TRENCH	PACIFIC OCEAN	32,962.6	10,047
7	IZU-OGASAWARA TRENCH	PACIFIC OCEAN	32,086.6	9,780
8	PUERTO RICO TRENCH	ATLANTIC OCEAN	28,372.7	8,648
9	SOUTH SANDWICH TRENCH	ATLANTIC OCEAN	27,650.9	8,428
10	ATACAMA TRENCH	PACIFIC OCEAN	26,460	8,065

EXTRA

	LOCATION		
ROMANCHE TRENCH	ATLANTIC OCEAN	25,459.3	7,760
JAVA TRENCH	INDIAN OCEAN	25,344.5	7,725
EURASIAN BASIN	ARCTIC OCEAN	17,877.3	5,449

TOP 10

DEEPEST **CANYONS**

To illustrate just how deep the number one entry is, you would need 11 copies of New York City's One World Trade Center, end to end, to reach the bottom...

	CANYON	LOCATION	DEEPEST POINT (FT)	(M)
1	YARLUNG TSANGPO GRAND CANYON	TIBET	19,714.6	6,009
2	KALI GANDAKI GORGE	NEPAL	18,277.6	5,571
3	INDUS GORGE	PAKISTAN	17,060.4	5,200
4	COLCA CANYON	PERU	13,648.3	4,160
5	TIGER LEAPING GORGE	CHINA	12,434.4	3,790
6	COTAHUASI CANYON	PERU	11,597.8	3,535
7	URIQUE CANNON (ONE OF THE 6 COPPER CANYONS)	MEXICO	6,164.7	1,879
8	GRAND CANYON	USA	5,997.4	1,828
9	BLYDE RIVER CANYON	SOUTH AFRICA	4,537.4	1,383
10	TARA RIVER CANYON	MONTENEGRO	4,265.1	1,300

4 COLCA CANYON

Colca Canyon is a four-hour trip from Peru's former capital city, Arequipa. Visitors often hike to Cruz del Condor to get the best view of the entire canyon, and to see the Andean condor, a bird of prey with a 10.8 ft (3.3 m) wingspan. More than 100,000 people explore Colca Canyon annually.

2 MID-ATLANTIC RIDGE

This is a divergent tectonic plate boundary that lies at the very bottom of the Atlantic Ocean.
It was created by continental plates moving apart, forming a ridge.
On Iceland's Reykjanes coastline, the Mid-Atlantic Ridge rises above sea level.

TOP 10

LONGEST **MOUNTAIN RANGES**

Contrary to what you would expect this chart to contain, there are as many entries underneath the waves as above them, with the number one almost double the length of all the others combined...

	RANGE	MOUNTAIN TYPE	LOCATION	LENGTH (MI)	(KM)
1	MID-OCEANIC RIDGE	OCEANIC	GLOBAL	40,389	65,000
2	MID-ATLANTIC RIDGE	OCEANIC	ATLANTIC OCEAN	6,214	10,000
3	ANDES	LAND	SOUTH AMERICA	4,350	7,000
4	ROCKIES	LAND	NORTH AMERICA	2,983	4,800
5	TRANSANTARCTIC	LAND	ANTARCTICA	2,201	3,542
6	GREAT DIVING RANGE	LAND	AUSTRALIA	1,901	3,059
7	HIMALAYAS	LAND	ASIA	1,601	2,576
8	SOUTHEAST INDIAN RIDGE	OCEANIC	INDIAN OCEAN	1,429	2,300
9	SOUTHWEST INDIAN RIDGE	OCEANIC	RODRIGUEZ ISLAND TO PRINCE EDWARD ISLAND	1,200	1,931
10	PACIFIC-ANTARCTIC RIDGE	OCEANIC	SOUTH PACIFIC OCEAN	639	1,029

METEOROLOGY

3 MT. WAIALEALE, KAUAI, HAWAII

The name of this place means "Rippling Waters." The high rainfall means that places like the Alaka'i Wilderness Preserve, governed by the Hawaii Division of Forestry and Wildlife, are home to an abundance of rare plant life.

TOP 10

HIGHEST **RECORDED RAINFALL**

Climate change is seeing new records of all kinds of meteorological events occurring, and these 10 places are, to date, the wettest on record...

	LOCATION	COUNTRY	HIGHEST RAINFALL RECORDED (IN)	(MM)
1	CHERRAPUNJI, MEGHALAYA	INDIA	1,041.8	26,461
2	MAWSYNRAM, MEGHALAYA	INDIA	1,023.6	26,000
3	MT. WAIALEALE, KAUAI, HAWAII	USA	681.1	17,300
4	LÓPEZ DE MICAY, CAUCA DEPARTMENT	COLOMBIA	507.6	12,892
5	LLORÓ, CHOCÓ DEPARTMENT	COLOMBIA	500.7	12,717
6	TUTENDO	COLOMBIA	463.4	11,770
7	CROPP RIVER	NEW ZEALAND	453.4	11,516
8	SAN ANTONIO DE URECA, BIOKO ISLAND	EQUATORIAL GUINEA	411.4	10,450
9	DEBUNDSCHA	CAMEROON	405.5	10,299
10	BIG BOG, MAUI, HAWAII	USA	404.4	10,272

TOP 10

LEAST ANNUAL RAINFALL

Do you live in a part of the world that experiences high or low volumes of rain? See if your driest seasons get anywhere near as arid as these...

	LOCATION	COUNTRY	AVERAGE ANNUAL RAINFALL	
			(IN)	(MM)
1	MCMURDO DRY VALLEYS	ANTARCTICA	0	0
2	ARICA	CHILE	0.029	0.76
3	KUFRA	LIBYA	0.034	0.86
=	ASWAN	EGYPT	0.034	0.86
=	LUXOR	EGYPT	0.034	0.86
6	ICA	PERU	0.09	2.3
7	WADI HALFA	SUDAN	0.1	2.45
8	IQUIQUE	CHILE	0.2	5.1
9	PELICAN POINT	NAMIBIA	0.3	8.1
10	AOULEF	ALGERIA	0.48	12.2

1 MCMURDO DRY VALLEYS

Although located in the Antarctic, the McMurdo Dry Valleys are, as they sound, completely absent of snow. They are found in the region of Victoria Land, named after the United Kingdom's Queen Victoria in 1841.

TOP 10

CLOUDIEST CITIES
IN EUROPE

Some people in places with little sunshine suffer from SAD (seasonal affective disorder), a form of depression related to the change in the seasons...

	CITY	COUNTRY	HOURS OF SUNLIGHT PER YEAR
1	GLASGOW	SCOTLAND	1,203
2	REYKJAVÍK	ICELAND	1,268
3	BIRMINGHAM	ENGLAND	1,364
4	LONDON	ENGLAND	1,410
5	MANCHESTER	ENGLAND	1,416
6	DUBLIN	IRELAND	1,424
7	COLOGNE	GERMANY	1,504
8	VADUZ	LIECHTENSTEIN	1,517
9	BRUSSELS	BELGIUM	1,546
10	HAMBURG	GERMANY	1,557

EXTRA

CLOUDIEST CITIES **IN THE USA**

Continuing the cloud theme, here are the cities in the United States with the most annual cloud cover...

	CITY	STATE	NUMBER OF DAYS WITH CLOUD COVER PER YEAR
1	BUFFALO	NEW YORK	311
2	SEATTLE	WASHINGTON	308
3	PITTSBURGH	PENNSYLVANIA	306
4	ROCHESTER	NEW YORK	304
5	CLEVELAND	OHIO	299

2 ▶ REYKJAVÍK

This is the capital of Iceland, home to more than 120,000 people. Reykjavik spans 105 square miles (271.9 square km). One of the most popular tourist attractions is a trip to see the Northern Lights—colorful, dancing lights in the sky, generated in the upper atmosphere by electronically charged particles.

SUNNIEST LOCATIONS
IN THE WORLD

A year is made up of 8,760 hours, which emphasizes just how sunny these places are, five of which are in the United States...

	LOCATION	COUNTRY	HOURS OF SUNLIGHT PER YEAR
1	YUMA, ARIZONA	USA	4,015
2	PHOENIX, ARIZONA	USA	3,872
3	ASWAN	EGYPT	3,869
4	LAS VEGAS, NEVADA	USA	3,826
5	DONGOLA	SUDAN	3,814
6	TUCSON, ARIZONA	USA	3,808
7	FAYA-LARGEAU	CHAD	3,800
8	KHARGA	EGYPT	3,796
9	EL PASO, TEXAS	USA	3,763
10	TENNANT CREEK	AUSTRALIA	3,614

2 ▶ PHOENIX, ARIZONA

Phoenix is the capital of the state of Arizona, with a population of 1.6 million. This was the location of the famous Phoenix Lights incident of March 13, 1997, when thousands of eyewitnesses reported—and video-recorded—strange, unidentified lights and shapes in the sky, over a three-hour period.

HUMANKIND 03

TOP 10

FIRST STORIES PUBLISHED **IN THE JAMES BOND UNIVERSE**

Acclaimed author and James Bond creator, Ian Fleming (May 28, 1908–August 12, 1964), was also a naval intelligence officer...

	TITLE	FIRST PUBLISHED
1	CASINO ROYALE	APR 13, 1953
2	LIVE AND LET DIE	APR 5, 1954
3	MOONRAKER	APR 5, 1955
4	DIAMONDS ARE FOREVER	MAR 26, 1956
5	FROM RUSSIA, WITH LOVE	APR 8, 1957
6	DR. NO	MAR 31, 1958
7	GOLDFINGER	MAR 23, 1959
8	QUANTUM OF SOLACE	MAY 1, 1959
9	FROM A VIEW TO A KILL	SEP 21, 1959
10	THE HILDEBRAND RARITY	MAR 1, 1960

1 CASINO ROYALE

Casino Royale was first published by Jonathan Cape. It has been adapted into a film on two occasions. The 1967 film is a spoof of the story—and the spy genre—with David Niven as Bond. The 2006 movie was an action-adventure, and introduced Daniel Craig as James Bond for the first time.

PEOPLE WHO HAVE **PLAYED JAMES BOND**

SEAN CONNERY = 7
ROGER MOORE = 7
DANIEL CRAIG = 5
PIERCE BROSNAN = 4
TIMOTHY DALTON = 2
GEORGE LAZENBY = 1
DAVID NIVEN = 1

TOP 10

FIRST STORIES PUBLISHED
IN THE OUTLANDER UNIVERSE

Born in Scotsdale, Arizona, Diana Gabaldon, the creator of the *Outlander* books, is also a co-producer and consultant on the television series that adapts her epic historical fiction...

	TITLE	FIRST PUBLISHED
1	OUTLANDER	JUN 1, 1991
2	DRAGONFLY IN AMBER	JUL 1, 1992
3	VOYAGER	DEC 1, 1993
4	DRUMS OF AUTUMN	DEC 30, 1996
5	LORD JOHN AND THE HELLFIRE CLUB	NOV 12, 1998
6	THE FIERY CROSS	NOV 6, 2001
7	LORD JOHN AND THE PRIVATE MATTER	SEP 30, 2003
8	LORD JOHN AND THE SUCCUBUS	DEC 30, 2003
9	A BREATH OF SNOW AND ASHES	SEP 27, 2005
10	LORD JOHN AND THE BROTHERHOOD OF THE BLADE	AUG 28, 2007

DIANA GABALDON

Gabaldon is a *New York Times* bestselling author. Her *Outlander* universe of novels has been published in 24 languages and in 26 countries. She has won multiple awards for the book series, including a 1991 RITA Award and a 2006 Quill Award. On Starz' *Outlander* TV series, Gabaldon has a cameo role as Iona MacTavish in season one's fourth episode, "The Gathering."

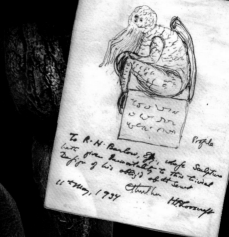

FIRST PUBLISHED TALES
BY H. P. LOVECRAFT

If you like creepy, mysterious tales that are full of highly original ideas, then look into the vast works of H. P. Lovecraft, beginning with the following...

	TITLE	FIRST PUBLISHED
1	A REMINISCENCE OF DR. SAMUEL JOHNSON	SEP 1917
2	BEYOND THE WALL OF SLEEP	OCT 1919
3	DAGON	NOV 1919
4	THE WHITE SHIP	NOV 1919
5	THE STATEMENT OF RANDOLPH CARTER	MAY 1920
6	THE DOOM THAT CAME TO SAMATH	JUN 1920
7	THE CATS OF ULTHAR	NOV 1920
8	NYARLATHOTEP	NOV 1920
9	POLARIS	DEC 1920
10	THE STREET	DEC 1920

H. P. LOVECRAFT

American master of the macabre, Howard Phillips Lovecraft (August 20, 1890–March 15, 1937) has influenced everything from table-top role-playing games like *Dungeons & Dragons*, through to modern creature features like *Cloverfield* (2008). His most famous tale, *The Call of Cthulhu*, was adapted into a multi-award-winning silent film in 2005.

TODD McFARLANE

The Canadian artist, writer, and creator of *Spawn* is working with Blumhouse Productions—the production company behind Jordan Peele's *Get Out* (2017)—on a dark, gritty new *Spawn* feature film. An Emmy Award–winning animated TV series based on *Spawn* ran from 1997–99, with three-time Emmy-winning actor Keith David voicing the title character.

TOP 10

DEBUT ISSUES IN TODD McFARLANE'S
SPAWN UNIVERSE

The monthly, ongoing *Spawn* comic book (created by Image Comics' co-founder Todd McFarlane) is the longest-running independent comic book in the USA...

IMAGE COMICS CELEBRATED THEIR **25TH ANNIVERSARY** IN 2017

	TITLE	DEBUT ISSUE / EDITION	PUBLICATION DATE
1	SPAWN	SPAWN #1 (OF 300+)*	MAY 1992
2	ANGELA	ANGELA #1 (OF 3)	DEC 1994
3	SPAWN: BLOOD FEUD	SPAWN: BLOOD FEUD #1 (OF 4)	JUN 1995
4	CURSE OF THE SPAWN	CURSE OF THE SPAWN #1 (OF 29)	SEP 1996
5	SPAWN THE IMPALER	SPAWN THE IMPALER #1 (OF 3)	OCT 1996
6	SPAWN: THE DARK AGES	SPAWN: THE DARK AGES #1 (OF 28)	MAR 1999
7	SPAWN: BLOOD AND SHADOWS	(ONE-SHOT / SPECIAL)	JUN 1999
8	SAM & TWITCH	SAM & TWITCH #1 (OF 26)	AUG 1999
9	SPAWN: BLOOD AND SALVATION	(ONE-SHOT / SPECIAL)	DEC 1999
10	HELLSPAWN	HELLSPAWN #1 (OF 16)	AUG 2000

*THE MONTHLY, ONGOING SERIES.

TOP 10

FIRST FEMALE NOBEL PRIZE
IN LITERATURE WINNERS

The 10 female recipients of this award span nearly a century on this Top 10, showing that there needs to be quite a rebalancing of male / female award-winners...

	NAME	COUNTRY	YEAR
1	SELMA LAGERLÖF	SWEDEN	1909
2	GRAZIA DELEDDA	ITALY	1926
3	SIGRID UNDSET	NORWAY	1928
4	PEARL S. BUCK	USA	1938
5	GABRIELA MISTRAL	CHILE	1945
6	NELLY SACHS	SWEDEN	1966
7	NADINE GORDIMER	SOUTH AFRICA	1991
8	TONI MORRISON	USA	1993
9	WISŁAWA SZYMBORSKA	POLAND	1996
10	ELFRIEDE JELINEK	AUSTRIA	2004

10 ▸ ELFRIEDE JELINEK

Austrian novelist, playwright, screenwriter, composer, and multimedia artist Elfriede Jelinek is no stranger to receiving awards for her work. Her other accolades include winning the coveted Mülheimer Dramatikerpreis, a theatrical award in Germany, four times.

ONLY AWARDED TO 14 WOMEN, FROM 113 TOTAL WINNERS.

WINNERS INCLUDE:

DORIS LESSING,
UK, 2007

HERTA MÜLLER,
GERMANY, 2009

ALICE MUNRO,
CANADA, 2013

SVETLANA ALEXIEVICH,
BELARUS, 2015

MOST RECENT NOBEL PRIZE
IN PHYSICS WINNERS

This Nobel Prize has been awarded since 1901, and has been given to more than 200 individuals, even though some winners can be teams...

	NAME	COUNTRY	YEAR
1	BARRY BARISH	USA	2017
=	KIP THORNE	USA	2017
=	RAINER WEISS	USA	2017
4	F. DUNCAN M. HALDANE	UK	2016
=	JOHN M. KOSTERLITZ	UK	2016
=	DAVID J. THOULESS	UK	2016
7	TAKAAKI KAJITA	JAPAN	2015
=	ARTHUR B. MCDONALD	CANADA	2015
9	SHUJI NAKAMURA	USA	2014
=	ISAMU AKASAKI / HIROSHI AMANO	JAPAN	2014

1 BARRY BARISH, KIP THORNE, RAINER WEISS

The LIGO (Laser Interferometer Gravitational-Wave Observatory) included more than 1,000 researchers from over 20 countries, all striving to observe the universe's gravitational waves. Scientists Barish, Thorne and Weiss received the Prize due to their LIGO work. The waves were finally observed on September 14, 2015.

TOP 10

MOST RECENT
NOBEL PEACE PRIZE WINNERS (INDIVIDUALS)

This is the most well-known of the five Nobel Prizes, created by Swedish philanthropist and businessman Alfred Nobel, and was first awarded in 1901...

	NAME	COUNTRY	YEAR
1	JUAN MANUEL SANTOS	COLOMBIA	2016
2	MALALA YOUSAFZAI	PAKISTAN	2014
=	KAILASH SATYARTHI	INDIA	2014
4	LEYMAH GBOWEE	LIBERIA	2011
=	ELLEN JOHNSON SIRLEAF	LIBERIA	2011
=	TAWAKKUL KARMAN	YEMEN	2011
7	LIU XIAOBO	CHINA	2010
8	BARACK OBAMA	USA	2009
9	MARTTI AHTISAARI	FINLAND	2008
10	AL GORE	USA	2007

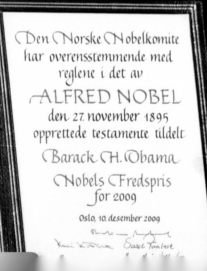

Den Norske Nobelkomite har overensstemmende med reglene i det av

ALFRED NOBEL

den 27. november 1895 opprettede testamente tildelt

Barack H. Obama

Nobels Fredspris for 2009

Oslo, 10. desember 2009

8 ▷ BARACK OBAMA

On March 2, 2017, the John F. Kennedy Presidential Library and Museum awarded the Nobel Peace Prize-winning President Obama the Profile in Courage Award "for his enduring commitment to democratic ideals and elevating the standard of political courage."

1 INTERNATIONAL CAMPAIGN TO ABOLISH NUCLEAR WEAPONS

The group is known as ICAN (as in, "I can"). It is a collection of non-governmental organizations across 100 countries working toward achieving a planet-wide agreement on banning all nuclear weapons.

TOP 10

MOST RECENT **NOBEL PEACE PRIZE WINNERS (ORGANIZATIONS)**

This Nobel Prize is given to groups of people who are striving to encourage international peace, and has been awarded to 27 different organizations between 1901 and 2017...

	ORGANIZATION	LOCATION	YEAR
1	INTERNATIONAL CAMPAIGN TO ABOLISH NUCLEAR WEAPONS	SWITZERLAND	2017
2	TUNISIAN NATIONAL DIALOGUE QUARTET	TUNISIA	2015
3	ORGANISATION FOR THE PROHIBITION OF CHEMICAL WEAPONS	(WORLDWIDE)	2013
4	EUROPEAN UNION	EUROPE	2012
5	INTERGOVERNMENTAL PANEL ON CLIMATE CHANGE	UNITED NATIONS	2007
6	GRAMEEN BANK	BANGLADESH	2006
7	INTERNATIONAL ATOMIC ENERGY AGENCY	UNITED NATIONS	2005
8	UNITED NATIONS	UNITED NATIONS	2001
9	MÉDECINS SANS FRONTIÈRES	SWITZERLAND	1999
10	INTERNATIONAL CAMPAIGN TO BAN LANDMINES	SWITZERLAND	1997

HUMAN DEVELOPMENT

CITIES WITH **THE MOST SUBWAY STATIONS**

How many subway stations do you have where you live? Find out, then compare it to these cities that feature in this infrastructure and development chart...

	CITY	COUNTRY	TOTAL SUBWAY STATIONS
1	NEW YORK CITY	USA	425
2	SHANGHAI	CHINA	337
3	SEOUL	SOUTH KOREA	307
4	PARIS	FRANCE	302
5	MADRID	SPAIN	301
6	BEIJING	CHINA	278
7	LONDON	UK	270
8	MOSCOW	RUSSIA	206
9	SHENZEN	CHINA	199
10	GUANGZHOU	CHINA	184

3 SEOUL

Appropriately, for such an advanced city, Seoul's full name is Seoul Special Metropolitan City. It is the capital city of South Korea. The Seoul Metropolitan Subway has a total of 21 lines. Its first line opened in 1974.

TOP 10

COUNTRIES WITH
THE MOST ROADS

Guess the total length of all the roadways in the area you live in, then compare that number to the millions of miles in this chart...

	COUNTRY	TOTAL LENGTH OF ALL ROADWAYS (MI)	(KM)
1	USA	4,177,072.8	6,722,347
2	INDIA	3,400,232.6	5,472,144
3	CHINA	2,918,145.5	4,696,300
4	BRAZIL	1,088,560.3	1,751,868
5	RUSSIA	867,434.2	1,396,000
6	JAPAN	754,966	1,215,000
7	CANADA	647,655.2	1,042,300
8	FRANCE	639,046.7	1,028,446
9	SOUTH AFRICA	588,447.2	947,014
10	AUSTRALIA	511,523.3	823,217

8 ▶ FRANCE

The *Autoroute* system of France is a network of more than 7,000 miles (11,265 km) of highways. Many of them are toll roads, meaning there is a fee for driving on them. With normal weather conditions, France recognizes an 80 mph (130 kph) speed limit on highways.

HUMAN **DEVELOPMENT**

COUNTRIES WITH
THE MOST AIRPORTS

There are more than 40,000 airports on our planet, with the most popular airlines carrying more than 100 million passengers each year...

	COUNTRY	TOTAL AIRPORTS
1	USA	19,536
2	BRAZIL	4,093
3	MEXICO	1,714
4	CANADA	1,467
5	RUSSIA	1,218
6	ARGENTINA	1,138
7	COLOMBIA	992
8	BOLIVIA	952
9	PARAGUAY	798
10	INDONESIA	683

3 MEXICO CITY
INTERNATIONAL AIRPORT

This is the busiest airport in Mexico. The site of the airport has a long history of aviation, dating back to 1910. A new airport called NAICM (Mexico City's New International Airport) is scheduled to open in 2020.

COUNTRIES WITH
THE MOST PORTS

For countries to successfully import and export cargo, ports and harbors are often the key, and they create employment for coastal regions...

	COUNTRY	TOTAL NUMBER OF PORTS
1	USA	552
2	UK	391
3	ITALY	311
4	JAPAN	292
5	FRANCE	268
6	CANADA	239
7	CHINA	172
8	DENMARK	159
9	INDONESIA	154
10	AUSTRALIA	106

RUSSIA	105
SPAIN	105
GREECE	103
GERMANY	98
NORWAY	83

4   TOKYO BAY PORT

This port is found in the southern Kanto region of Japan. The bridge and tunnel combination, the Tokyo Bay Aqua-Line, first opened in 1997. The bay is home to a natural, uninhabited island called *Sarushima* (which means "Monkey Island"), which is a popular tourist attraction.

OPULATIONS

CHRISTMAS ISLAND

...ddition to humans, this ...nd is home to two species ...at, the black-eared flying ...and the Christmas ...nd pipistrelle. Off the ...st, dugong and several ...cies of dolphins and ...ales inhabit the waters.

CHRISTMAS ISLAND'S
TOTAL AREA:
52 SQUARE MILES
(135 SQUARE KM)

CHRISTMAS ISLAND

LEAST POPULATED
COUNTRIES, ISLAND COUNTRIES & NATIONAL JURISDICTIONS

Compare the population numbers from the charts on both these pages to really get a sense of the wildly different land masses we call home...

NAME	POPULATION
PITCAIRN ISLANDS	57
COCOS (KEELING) ISLANDS	596
VATICAN CITY	1,000
TOKELAU	1,499
NIUE	1,624
CHRISTMAS ISLAND	2,205
NORFOLK ISLAND	2,302
FALKLAND ISLANDS	3,398
MONTSERRAT	4,900
SAINT HELENA, ASCENSION, AND TRISTAN DA CUNHA	5,633

5 PAKISTAN

In terms of the size of its land area, Pakistan is the 33rd largest country on Earth. Its capital is Islamabad, and its largest city is Karachi, home to Jinnah International Airport, the busiest airport in Pakistan.

TOP 10

MOST POPULATED COUNTRIES

With over 7 billion people on Earth, most of them can be found in these 10 countries. Plus, there is a bonus chart underneath showcasing 11–20...

	COUNTRY	POPULATION
1	CHINA	1,388,170,000
2	INDIA	1,325,460,000
3	USA	326,075,000
4	INDONESIA	262,173,000
5	PAKISTAN	209,970,000
6	BRAZIL	205,593,000
7	NIGERIA	185,990,000
8	BANGLADESH	163,680,000
9	RUSSIA	146,855,000
10	JAPAN	126,700,000

EXTRA

MEXICO	125,594,000
PHILIPPINES	105,367,000
ETHIOPIA	99,391,000
VIETNAM	96,655,000
EGYPT	94,667,000
IRAN	84,273,000
GERMANY	82,800,000
TURKEY	81,485,000
DEMOCRATIC REPUBLIC OF THE CONGO	77,267,000
FRANCE	66,991,000

POPULATIONS

MOST POPULATED
COUNTRIES IN ASIA

Asia is our planet's largest continent, and accounts for almost one third of the total land area, totaling a combination of more than 50 countries / dependent nations...

	COUNTRY	POPULATION
1	CHINA	1,388,170,000
2	INDIA	1,325,460,000
3	INDONESIA	262,173,000
4	PAKISTAN	209,970,000
5	BANGLADESH	163,680,000
6	RUSSIA	146,855,000
7	JAPAN	126,700,000
8	PHILIPPINES	105,367,000
9	VIETNAM	96,655,000
10	IRAN	84,273,000

2 INDIA

India is the seventh biggest country in the world. Although Mumbai is its largest city, New Delhi is its capital. India is home to tigers, lions, rhinos, and elephants. The Bengal tiger is its national animal, and the peacock is its national bird. The rare Ganges river dolphin is India's national aquatic animal.

TOP 10

MOST POPULATED
REGIONS OF AUSTRALIA

Some scientists estimate that Indigenous Australians date back more than 100,000 years ago, with artwork on natural formations dating back 30,000 years...

	REGION	POPULATION
1	NEW SOUTH WALES	7,704,300
2	VICTORIA	6,039,100
3	QUEENSLAND	4,827,000
4	WESTERN AUSTRALIA	2,613,700
5	SOUTH AUSTRALIA	1,706,500
6	TASMANIA	518,500
7	AUSTRALIAN CAPITAL TERRITORY	397,397
8	NORTHERN TERRITORY	244,000
9	NORFOLK ISLAND	2,302
10	CHRISTMAS ISLAND	2,205

1 NEW SOUTH WALES

The region is located on the east coast of Australia. Sydney is its capital city. New South Wales is home to Australia's tallest mountain, Mount Kosciuszko, which is 7,310 ft (2,228 m) high. There are 780 national parks and reserves in the state, including outback regions and waterfalls.

TOP 10

MOST POPULATED
COUNTRIES IN THE
EUROPEAN UNION

As of 2018, these are the 10 most populous countries that are officially part of the European Union, which comprises more than 500 million people...

	COUNTRY	POPULATION
1	GERMANY	82,800,000
2	FRANCE	66,991,000
3	UK	64,596,800
4	ITALY	60,788,845
5	SPAIN	46,449,565
6	POLAND	38,494,000
7	ROMANIA	19,822,000
8	NETHERLANDS	17,097,900
9	BELGIUM	11,370,968
10	GREECE	11,183,716

7 ROMANIA

Bucharest is the capital, and the largest city of Romania. It attracts filmmakers from all over the world to shoot there. Productions to date include *Cold Mountain* (2003), and the 2008 caper *The Brothers Bloom* by *Star Wars: The Last Jedi* director Rian Johnson.

THERE ARE 54 COUNTRIES IN AFRICA

7 KENYA

Kenya's capital, Nairobi, is the hub of the country's thriving music scene. The multi-award-winning Kenyan group, Sauti Sol, performed for President Barack Obama at Kenya's 2015 Global Entrepreneurship summit.

TOP 10

MOST POPULATED
COUNTRIES IN AFRICA

Africa is the second largest continent in the world, and of its many countries, these are the ones with the largest populations...

	COUNTRY	POPULATION
1	NIGERIA	185,990,000
2	ETHIOPIA	99,391,000
3	EGYPT	94,667,000
4	DEMOCRATIC REPUBLIC OF THE CONGO	77,267,000
5	SOUTH AFRICA	54,957,000
6	TANZANIA	51,046,000
7	KENYA	45,533,000
8	SUDAN	40,235,000
9	ALGERIA	39,670,000
10	UGANDA	37,102,000

TOP 10

MOST POPULATED STATES / TERRITORIES OF THE USA

More than half of the entire population of the USA is accounted for in the total population of the 10 states in this chart...

	STATE	POPULATION
1	CALIFORNIA	39,250,017
2	TEXAS	27,862,596
3	FLORIDA	20,612,439
4	NEW YORK	19,745,289
5	ILLINOIS	12,801,539
6	PENNSYLVANIA	12,784,227
7	OHIO	11,614,373
8	GEORGIA	10,310,371
9	NORTH CAROLINA	10,146,788
10	MICHIGAN	9,928,300

4 NEW YORK

New York is one of the founding states of the United States—part of the 13 colonies that declared independence from Britain in 1776. New York City is the most populated city in the USA, with more than 8.5 million residents spread across its five boroughs of the Bronx, Brooklyn, Manhattan, Queens, and Staten Island.

TOP 10

LEAST POPULATED
STATES / TERRITORIES
OF THE USA

Along with its 50 states, the United States also has 16 territories, some of which made it into the chart below...

	STATE	POPULATION
1	NORTHERN MARIANA ISLANDS	52,344
2	AMERICAN SAMOA	54,343
3	U.S. VIRGIN ISLANDS	103,574
4	GUAM	161,785
5	WYOMING	585,501
6	VERMONT	624,594
7	DISTRICT OF COLUMBIA	681,170
8	ALASKA	741,894
9	NORTH DAKOTA	757,952
10	SOUTH DAKOTA	865,454

8   ALASKA

Alaska became the 49th state of the USA on January 3, 1959. On August 21, 1959, Hawaii became the 50th. Alaska's state motto is "North to the Future." Its state sport is dog mushing, made famous in events such as the Iditarod Trail Sled Dog Race.

SPORTS **04**

TOP 10

MOST SUCCESSFUL **OLYMPIANS**

Comparing every medal winner from the 1896 Summer Olympics held in Athens, Greece, through to the 2018 Winter Olympics in Pyeongchang, South Korea, these are the greatest champions to date...

	OLYMPIAN	DISCIPLINE	COUNTRY	YEARS	GOLD	SILVER	BRONZE	TOTAL
1	MICHAEL PHELPS	SWIMMING	USA	2004–12	23	3	2	28
2	LARISA LATYNINA	GYMNASTICS	SOVIET UNION (NOW RUSSIA)	1956–64	9	5	4	18
3	MARIT BJØRGEN	CROSS-COUNTRY SKIING	NORWAY	2002–18	8	4	3	15
4	NIKOLAI ANDRIANOV	GYMNASTICS	SOVIET UNION (NOW RUSSIA)	1972–80	7	5	3	15
5	OLE EINAR BJØRNDALEN	BIATHLON	NORWAY	1998–2014	8	4	1	13
6	BORIS SHAKHLIN	GYMNASTICS	SOVIET UNION (NOW RUSSIA)	1956–64	7	4	2	13
7	EDOARDO MANGIAROTTI	FENCING	ITALY	1936–60	6	5	2	13
8	TAKASHI ONO	GYMNASTICS	JAPAN	1952–64	5	4	4	13
9	PAAVO NURMI	ATHLETICS	FINLAND	1920–28	9	3	0	12
10	BIRGIT FISCHER / BJØRN DÆHLIE	CANOEING / CROSS-COUNTRY SKIING	GERMANY / NORWAY	1980-2004 / 1992-98	8	4	0	12

10 ▸ BIRGIT FISCHER

German kayaker Birgit Fischer won gold medals at all six Summer Olympics that she competed in, and multiple medals in five of the Games. At the 1998 Seoul Olympics, Fischer had her best result of one silver and two gold medals. Between 1978 and 2005, at the ICF Canoe Sprint World Championships, she won a further 28 gold, 6 silver, and 4 bronze medals.

10 ▶ DANIEL DIAS

Swimming champion Daniel Dias was born on May 24, 1988, in Campinas, São Paulo, Brazil. His career medals of 65 gold, 13 silver, and 3 bronze include nine medals at the 2016 Summer Paralympic Games in Rio de Janeiro. Dias is 5.6 ft (1.71 m) tall.

TOP 10

MOST SUCCESSFUL **PARALYMPIANS**

Similarly, this chart shows the Paralympic athletes who have won the most medals in the history of the Paralympic Games, from the 1960 Summer Games up to 2018's Winter Paralympics in Pyeongchang, South Korea...

	PARALYMPIAN	DISCIPLINE(S)	COUNTRY	YEARS	GOLD	SILVER	BRONZE	TOTAL
1	TRISCHA ZORN	SWIMMING	USA	1980–2004	41	9	5	55
2	HEINZ FREI	ATHLETICS, CYCLING, CROSS-COUNTRY SKIING	SWITZERLAND	1984–2000	15	7	12	34
3	JONAS JACOBSSON	SHOOTING	SWEDEN	1980–2012	17	4	9	30
4	ZIPORA RUBIN-ROSENBAUM	ATHLETICS, SWIMMING, TABLE TENNIS, WHEELCHAIR BASKETBALL	ISRAEL	1964–92	15	8	7	30
5	RAGNHILD MYKLEBUST	BIATHLON, CROSS-COUNTRY SKIING, ICE SLEDGE RACING	NORWAY	1988–2002	22	3	2	27
6	ROBERTO MARSON	ATHLETICS, FENCING	ITALY	1964–76	16	7	3	26
7	BÉATRICE HESS	SWIMMING	FRANCE	1984–2004	20	5	0	25
8	SARAH STOREY	SWIMMING, CYCLING	UK	1992–2016	14	8	3	25
9	CLAUDIA HENGST	SWIMMING	GERMANY	1988–2004	13	4	8	25
10	DANIEL DIAS	SWIMMING	BRAZIL	2008–16	14	7	3	24

TOP 10

MOST SUCCESSFUL **OLYMPIC NATIONS**

Including the results of the 2018 Winter Olympics in Pyeongchang, South Korea, this is how the international Olympics leader board looks...

	COUNTRY / TEAM	TOTAL SUMMER GAMES MEDALS	TOTAL WINTER GAMES MEDALS	TOTAL MEDALS
1	USA	2,522	305	2,827
2	RUSSIA (INCL. SOVIET UNION ERA)	1,436	314	1,750
3	GERMANY (INCL. EAST & WEST ERA)	1,228	389	1,617
4	GREAT BRITAIN	849	31	880
5	FRANCE	716	124	840
6	ITALY	577	124	701
7	SWEDEN	494	158	652
8	CHINA	546	62	608
9	NORWAY	152	368	520
10	AUSTRALIA	497	15	512

7 SWEDEN

Over the years, the Swedish Olympic teams have notched up a total of 145 gold medals in the Summer Olympics, and an additional 57 golds in the Winter Games. At the 2018 Winter Olympics in Pyeongchang, South Korea, Sweden took home 7 golds, 6 silvers, and 1 bronze, placing the country in sixth place overall.

9 NETHERLANDS

The 2018 Winter Paralympics ran for 10 days: March 9–18. Out of the 49 competing nations, the Netherlands placed 10th, with a combination of 3 gold, 3 silver, and 1 bronze medal.

TOP 10

MOST SUCCESSFUL
PARALYMPIC NATIONS

The winners at 2018's Winter Paralympics, in Pyeongchang, South Korea, saw numerous additional medals added to the chart totals in this epic sports Top 10...

	COUNTRY / TEAM	TOTAL SUMMER GAMES MEDALS	TOTAL WINTER GAMES MEDALS	TOTAL MEDALS
1	USA	2,054	314	2,368
2	GREAT BRITAIN	1,789	34	1,823
3	GERMANY (INCL. EAST & WEST ERA)	1,447	364	1,807
4	CANADA	1,059	163	1,222
5	AUSTRALIA	1,125	34	1,159
6	FRANCE	949	171	1,120
7	CHINA	1,033	1	1,034
8	SWEDEN	637	100	737
9	NETHERLANDS	714	18	732
10	SPAIN	661	43	704

COUNTRIES WHO'VE HOSTED THE MOST

USA
11
8 OLYMPICS +
3 PARALYMPICS

FRANCE
6
5 OLYMPICS +
1 PARALYMPICS

JAPAN
5
3 OLYMPICS +
2 PARALYMPICS

UK
5
3 OLYMPICS +
2 PARALYMPICS

SPEED **MASTERS**

7 ▷ SOPHIE PASCOE

Born January 8, 1993, in Christchurch (the largest city in New Zealand's South Island), Sophie Pascoe holds four world records, in 100 m butterfly (S10), 400 m individual medley (SM10), 50 m butterfly (S10), and 200 m individual medley (SM10).

FIRST EVER PARALYMPIC GAMES WERE HELD IN ROME, ITALY.

SEPTEMBER 18–25, 1960

TOP 10

QUICKEST **FEMALE PARA ATHLETES**

As comparing the different classifications is unfair, the below chart is not designed to be a definitive Top 10, but to convey the fastest speeds achieved by para athletes...

	SPORT	DISTANCE	FASTEST ATHLETE	CLASS	COUNTRY	YEAR	TIME	SPEED (MPH)	(KPH)
1	RUNNING	100 M	OMARA DURAND	T12	CUBA	2016	0:11.4	19.62	31.58
2	RUNNING	200 M	OMARA DURAND	T12	CUBA	2015	0:23.03	19.43	31.26
3	WHEELCHAIR RACING	800 M	TATYANA MCFADDEN	T54	USA	2015	1:42.72	17.42	28.03
4	WHEELCHAIR RACING	1500 M	TATYANA MCFADDEN	T53 / 54	USA	2015	3:13.27	17.36	27.94
5	RUNNING	400 M	OMARA DURAND	T12	CUBA	2016	0:51.77	17.28	27.82
6	SWIMMING: FREESTYLE	50 M	OXANA SAVCHENKO	S12	RUSSIA	2009	0:26.54	4.21	6.78
7	SWIMMING: BUTTERFLY*	50 M	SOPHIE PASCOE	S10	NEW ZEALAND	2013	0:28:38	3.94	6.34
8	SWIMMING: FREESTYLE	100 M	ANNA STETSENKO	S13	UKRAINE	2016	0:58.05	3.85	6.2
9	SWIMMING: BACKSTROKE	50 M	SOPHIE PASCOE	S10	NEW ZEALAND	2013	0:30.49	3.67	5.9
10	SWIMMING: FREESTYLE	200 M	SOPHIE PASCOE	S10	NEW ZEALAND	2017	2:06.58	3.53	5.68

*LONG COURSE; REST OF SWIMMING EVENTS ARE FROM SHORT COURSES.

TOP 10

QUICKEST **MALE PARA ATHLETES**

The top speeds achieved by para athletes of different classifications cannot be fairly compared. This Top 10 is a collection of the fastest speeds attained in "sprint" sports to date...

	SPORT	DISTANCE	FASTEST ATHLETE	CLASS	COUNTRY	YEAR	TIME	SPEED (MPH)	(KPH)
1	RUNNING	200 M	ALAN FONTELES CARDOSO OLIVEIRA	T43	BRAZIL	2013	0:20:66	21.65	34.85
2	RUNNING	100 M	JASON SMYTH	T13	IRELAND	2012	0:10.46	21.39	34.42
3	WHEELCHAIR RACING	400 M	LIXIN ZHANG	T54	CHINA	2008	0:45.07	19.85	31.95
4	WHEELCHAIR RACING	800 M	MARCEL HUG	T54	SWITZERLAND	2010	1:31.12	19.64	31.61
5	WHEELCHAIR RACING	1500 M	BRENT LAKATOS	T53 / 54	CANADA	2017	2:51.84	19.53	31.43
6	SWIMMING: FREESTYLE	50 M	ANDRE BRASIL	S10	BRAZIL	2009	0:22.44	4.98	8.02
7	SWIMMING: FREESTYLE	100 M	ANDRE BRASIL	S10	BRAZIL	2009	0:48.7	4.59	7.39
8	SWIMMING: BUTTERFLY	50 M	TIMOTHY ANTALFY	S13	AUSTRALIA	2014	0:24.6	4.55	7.32
9	SWIMMING: BACKSTROKE	50 M	MICHAEL ANDERSON	S10	AUSTRALIA	2015	0:26.97	4.15	6.68
10	SWIMMING: BUTTERFLY	100 M	ANDRE BRASIL	S10	BRAZIL	2009	0:54.76	4.08	6.57

SPEED MASTERS

FASTEST 100 M FEMALE SPRINTERS

You may know some of the 100 m times made by these incredibly fast sportswomen, but do you know the actual speed that they travel? It's a lot faster than you might think...

	ATHLETE	COUNTRY	YEAR	TIME (SECS)	AVERAGE SPEED (MPH)	(KPH)
1	FLORENCE GRIFFITH JOYNER	USA	1988	10.49	21.32	34.31
2	CARMELITA JETER	USA	2009	10.64	21.02	33.83
3	MARION JONES	USA	1998	10.65	21	33.8
4	SHELLY-ANN FRASER-PRYCE	JAMAICA	2012	10.7	20.91	33.65
=	ELAINE THOMPSON	JAMAICA	2016	10.7	20.91	33.65
6	CHRISTINE ARRON	FRANCE	1998	10.73	20.85	33.56
7	MERLENE OTTEY	JAMAICA	1996	10.74	20.83	33.52
=	ENGLISH GARDNER	USA	2016	10.74	20.83	33.52
9	KERRON STEWART	JAMAICA	2009	10.75	20.81	33.49
10	EVELYN ASHFORD / VERONICA CAMPBELL-BROWN	USA / JAMAICA	1984 / 2011	10.76	20.79	33.46

= 4 ELAINE THOMPSON

Elaine Thompson was born in the Parish of Manchester in Middlesex, Jamaica, on June 28, 1992. As well as winning silver in the 4 x 100 m relay, she won gold for both the 100 m and 200 m at the 2016 Summer Olympics. Thompson is the first woman to achieve this double-gold win since Florence Griffith Joyner did at the 1988 Olympic Games in Seoul, South Korea.

AVERAGE FEMALE SPEED **20.93 MPH (33.68 KPH)**

AVERAGE MALE SPEED **22.96 MPH (36.95 KPH)**

= 9 CHRISTIAN COLEMAN

Born in Atlanta, Georgia, Christian Coleman holds the world record for the indoor 60 m (6.34 secs). He achieved his personal best 100 m time (on the chart) at the 2017 NCAA Division I Outdoor Track and Field Championships, held June 7–10, 2017.

TOP 10

FASTEST 100 M MALE SPRINTERS

Will anyone ever be able to take Usain Bolt's crown as the fastest human on Earth? Some sprinters have come close to his world record speed, but not close enough...

	ATHLETE	COUNTRY	YEAR	TIME (SECS)	AVERAGE SPEED (MPH)	(KPH)
1	USAIN BOLT	JAMAICA	2009	9.58	23.35	37.58
2	TYSON GAY	USA	2009	9.69	23.08	37.14
=	YOHAN BLAKE	JAMAICA	2012	9.69	23.08	37.14
4	ASAFA POWELL	JAMAICA	2008	9.72	23.01	37.03
5	JUSTIN GATLIN	USA	2015	9.74	22.97	36.96
6	NESTA CARTER	JAMAICA	2010	9.78	22.87	36.81
7	MAURICE GREENE	USA	1999	9.79	22.85	36.77
8	STEVE MULLINGS	JAMAICA	2011	9.8	22.83	36.74
9	RICHARD THOMPSON	TRINIDAD & TOBAGO	2014	9.82	22.78	36.66
=	CHRISTIAN COLEMAN	USA	2017	9.82	22.78	36.66

8 ▶ CATE CAMPBELL

Swimmer Cate Campbell is the world-record holder for the 100 m freestyle (short course). She achieved her time of 50.25 seconds on October 26, 2017, at the annual Australian Short Course Swimming Championships. She also shares the world record for the 4 x 100 m freestyle relay (long course) with her younger sister, Bronte Campbell, and Brittany Elmslie and Emma McKeon.

TOTAL FLORENCE GRIFFITH JOYNER CAREER MEDALS AT OLYMPIC AND WORLD CHAMPIONSHIP LEVEL:

4 GOLD AND 3 SILVER (1984–1988)

HER SPEED RECORD HAS REMAINED UNBEATEN FOR OVER 31 YEARS

TOP 10

QUICKEST **SPORTSWOMEN**

The Top 10 takes a collection of sporting disciplines that require a burst of energy to complete them, then presents the fastest sportswomen from each event, with the average speed that they achieve...

	SPORT	DISTANCE	FASTEST ATHLETE	COUNTRY	YEAR	TIME	AVERAGE SPEED (MPH)	(KPH)
1	RUNNING	100 M	FLORENCE GRIFFITH JOYNER	USA	1988	0:10.49	21.32	34.32
2	RUNNING	200 M	FLORENCE GRIFFITH JOYNER	USA	1988	0:21.34	20.96	33.74
3	RUNNING	400 M	MARITA KOCH	GERMANY	1985	0:47.6	18.8	30.25
4	RUNNING	800 M	JARMILA KRATOCHVÍLOVÁ	CZECH REPUBLIC	1983	1:53.28	15.8	25.42
5	RUNNING	1000 M	SVETLANA MASTERKOVA	RUSSIA	1996	2:28.98	15.02	24.16
6	SWIMMING: FREESTYLE	50 M	RANOMI KROMOWIDJOJO	NETHERLANDS	2017	0:22.93	4.88	7.85
7	SWIMMING: BUTTERFLY	50 M	THERESE ALSHAMMAR	SWEDEN	2009	0:24.38	4.59	7.39
8	SWIMMING: FREESTYLE	100 M	CATE CAMPBELL	AUSTRALIA	2017	0:50.25	4.45	7.16
9	SWIMMING: BACKSTROKE	50 M	ETIENE MEDEIROS	BRAZIL	2014	0:25.67	4.36	7.02
10	SWIMMING: BUTTERFLY	100 M	SARAH SJÖSTRÖM	SWEDEN	2014	0:54.61	4.1	6.59

NOAH NGENY

Born on November 2, 1978, Noah Ngeny has held the world record for the 1000 m since September 5, 1999. At the 2000 Summer Olympics in Sydney, Australia, he won gold in the 1500 m. Ngeny officially retired from athletics on November 22, 2006.

QUICKEST **SPORTSMEN**

Examining all of the male events that involve an explosive burst of energy, these 10 sportsmen are the fastest athletes in each of these "sprint" sports...

	SPORT	DISTANCE	FASTEST ATHLETE	COUNTRY	YEAR	TIME	AVERAGE SPEED (MPH)	(KPH)
1	RUNNING	100 M	USAIN BOLT	JAMAICA	2009	0:09.58	23.35	37.58
2	RUNNING	200 M	USAIN BOLT	JAMAICA	2009	0:19.19	23.31	37.52
3	RUNNING	400 M	WAYDE VAN NIEKERK	SOUTH AFRICA	2016	0:43.03	20.79	33.47
4	RUNNING	800 M	DAVID RUDISHA	KENYA	2012	1:40.91	17.73	28.54
5	RUNNING	1000 M	NOAH NGENY	KENYA	1999	2:11.96	16.95	27.28
6	SWIMMING: FREESTYLE	50 M	FLORENT MANAUDOU	FRANCE	2014	0:20.26	5.52	8.88
7	SWIMMING: BUTTERFLY	50 M	STEFFEN DEIBLER	GERMANY	2009	0:21.8	5.13	8.26
8	SWIMMING: BACKSTROKE	50 M	FLORENT MANAUDOU	FRANCE	2014	0:22.22	5.03	8.1
9	SWIMMING: FREESTYLE	100 M	AMAURY LEVEAUX	FRANCE	2008	0:44.94	4.98	8.01
10	SWIMMING: BUTTERFLY	100 M	CHAD LE CLOS	SOUTH AFRICA	2016	0:48.08	4.65	7.49

TOP 10

FEMALE **MARATHON CHAMPIONS**

A marathon is a long-distance footrace that is 26.219 miles (42.195 km) long, and these 10 female athletes are the fastest marathon runners on the planet...

	ATHLETE	COUNTRY	YEAR	TIME	AVERAGE SPEED (MPH)	(KPH)
1	PAULA RADCLIFFE	UK	2003	2:15:25	11.617	18.696
2	MARY JEPKOSGEI KEITANY	KENYA	2017	2:17:01	11.481	18.478
3	TIRUNESH DIBABA	ETHIOPIA	2017	2:17:56	11.405	18.354
4	CATHERINE NDEREBA	KENYA	2001	2:18:47	11.335	18.242
5	TIKI GELANA	ETHIOPIA	2012	2:18:58	11.32	18.218
6	MIZUKI NOGUCHI	JAPAN	2005	2:19:12	11.301	18.188
7	IRINA MIKITENKO	GERMANY	2008	2:19:19	11.292	18.172
8	GLADYS CHERONO	KENYA	2015	2:19:25	11.284	18.159
9	ASELEFECH MERGIA	ETHIOPIA	2012	2:19:31	11.276	18.146
10	LUCY KABUU	KENYA	2012	2:19:34	11.272	18.14

3 TIRUNESH DIBABA

Tirunesh Dibaba, 5000 m outdoor track world-record holder, has 21 career medals. These include 14 golds, three of which are from Olympic Games and five from World Championships.

26.219 MI (42.195 KM)

50 KM (31.07 MI)

100 KM (62.14 MI)

50 MI (80.47 KM)

100 MI (160.93 KM)

MARATHON AND ULTRA-MARATHON DISTANCES

7 ⟩ GUYE ADOLA

This Ethiopian runner's first time competing, in the 2017 Berlin Marathon, is captured on the chart below. It is the fastest time for an athlete's marathon debut. Before this event, Adola had competed in half-marathons. His international debut was at the 2014 IAAF World Half Marathon Championships in Copenhagen, Denmark.

MALE **MARATHON CHAMPIONS**

TOP 10

As a companion chart to the one opposite, here are the 10 male marathon runners who have achieved the fastest speeds during their endurance races...

	ATHLETE	COUNTRY	YEAR	TIME	AVERAGE SPEED (MPH)	(KPH)
1	DENNIS KIPRUTO KIMETTO	KENYA	2014	2:02:57	12.795	20.591
2	KENENISA BEKELE	ETHIOPIA	2016	2:03:03	12.784	20.575
3	ELIUD KIPCHOGE	KENYA	2016	2:03:05	12.781	20.569
4	EMMANUEL MUTAI	KENYA	2014	2:03:13	12.767	20.547
=	WILSON KIPSANG KIPROTICH	KENYA	2016	2:03:13	12.767	20.547
6	PATRICK MAKAU MUSYOKI	KENYA	2011	2:03:38	12.724	20.478
7	GUYE ADOLA	ETHIOPIA	2017	2:03:46	12.712	20.456
8	STANLEY BIWOTT	KENYA	2016	2:03:51	12.702	20.442
9	HAILE GEBRSELASSIE	ETHIOPIA	2008	2:03:59	12.688	20.42
10	TAMIRAT TOLA	ETHIOPIA	2017	2:04:11	12.667	20.387

SOLO EVENTS

= 9 ▸ BRITTNEY REESE

Seven-time long jump world champion Brittney Reese was born in California, USA, on September 9, 1986. Although Reese is joint ninth on the chart, she is the indoor long jump world champion with a distance of 23.7 ft (7.23 m).

FEMALE LONG JUMP CHAMPIONS

TOP 10

When you consider that a one-story building averages at around 10 ft (3.05 m) high, the distances that these female athletes achieve in the long jump are truly extraordinary...

	ATHLETE	COUNTRY	YEAR	DISTANCE (FT)	(M)
1	GALINA CHISTYAKOVA	RUSSIA	1988	24.67	7.52
2	JACKIE JOYNER-KERSEE	USA	1994	24.57	7.52
3	HEIKE DRECHSLER	GERMANY	1988	24.54	7.48
4	ANISOARA CUSMIR	ROMANIA	1983	24.38	7.43
5	TATYANA KOTOVA	RUSSIA	2002	24.34	7.42
6	YELENA BELEVSKAYA	RUSSIA	1987	24.25	7.39
7	INESSA KRAVETS	UKRAINE	1992	24.18	7.37
8	TATYANA LEBEDEVA	RUSSIA	2004	24.05	7.33
9	OLENA KHLOPOTNOVA	RUSSIA	1985	23.98	7.31
=	MARION JONES / BRITTNEY REESE	USA	1998 / 2016	23.98	7.31

TOP 10

MALE **LONG JUMP CHAMPIONS**

In the past 10 years, only two male long-jumpers have managed to attain distances to get them into this Top 10, but the top spot has remained unchanged for nearly three decades...

	ATHLETE	COUNTRY	YEAR	DISTANCE (FT)	(M)
1	MIKE POWELL	USA	1991	29.36	8.95
2	BOB BEAMON	USA	1968	29.2	8.9
3	CARL LEWIS	USA	1991	29.1	8.87
4	ROBERT EMMIYAN	RUSSIA (SOVIET UNION ERA)	1987	29.07	8.86
5	LARRY MYRICKS	USA	1988	28.67	8.74
=	ERICK WALDER	USA	1994	28.67	8.74
=	DWIGHT PHILLIPS	USA	2009	28.67	8.74
8	IRVING SALADINO	PANAMA	2008	28.64	8.73
9	IVÁN PEDROSO	CUBA	1995	28.58	8.71
=	SEBASTIAN BAYER	GERMANY	2009	28.58	8.71

1 MIKE POWELL

Mike Powell's long jump world record has not been bested in 28 years. His daughter, Micha Powell, officially joined the Canadian Olympic team in 2016. Her mother is former Olympic athlete Rosey Edeh.

FEMALE PARA ATHLETE SHOT-PUTTERS

It is not fair to compare the distance achievements of different classes, so rather than this being a definitive Top 10, it merely collects together the greatest distances achieved by para athlete shot-putters, overall...

	ATHLETE	CLASS	COUNTRY	YEAR	DISTANCE (FT)	(M)
1	ASSUNTA LEGNANTE	F11	ITALY	2014	56.82	17.32
2	SAFIYA BURKHANOVA	F12	UZBEKISTAN	2016	49.38	15.05
3	EWA DURSKA	F20	POLAND	2016	46.26	14.1
4	FRANZISKA LIEBHARDT	F37	GERMANY	2016	45.8	13.96
5	JUN WANG	F35	CHINA	2016	45.64	13.91
6	JUAN YAO	F44	CHINA	2015	43.11	13.14
7	TAMARA SIVAKOVA	F13	BELARUS	1998	42.81	13.05
8	ALDONA GRIGALIUNIENE	F38	LITHUANIA	2008	41.27	12.58
9	YUKIKO SAITO	F46	JAPAN	2015	40.91	12.47
=	BIRGIT KOBER	F36	GERMANY	2016	37.8	11.52

2 SAFIYA BURKHANOVA

Safiya Burkhanova was born on December 1, 1989, in Uzbekistan. She competes in both shot put (F12) and discus (F12). On July 21, 2017, Burkhanova finished in second place in the women's discus throw (F12) at the 2017 World Para Athletics Championships, held in London, England.

TOP 10

MALE **PARA ATHLETE SHOT-PUTTERS**

The year 2017 saw five shot-putters from different classes achieve new record distances. This chart does not compare classifications: it simply shows the 10 greatest distances...

	ATHLETE	CLASS	COUNTRY	YEAR	DISTANCE (FT)	(M)
1	AKEEM STEWART	F43	TRINIDAD & TOBAGO	2017	62.6	19.08
2	JACKIE CHRISTIANSEN	F44	DENMARK	2011	60.3	18.38
3	XIA DONG	F37	CHINA	2012	57.48	17.52
=	ALED DAVIES	F42	UK	2017	57.48	17.52
5	MUHAMMAD ZIYAD ZOLKEFLI	F20	MALAYSIA	2017	56.73	17.29
6	ROMAN DANYLIUK	F12	UKRAINE	2015	54.59	16.64
7	HAITAO SUN	F13	CHINA	2000	54	16.46
8	WEI GUO	F35	CHINA	2008	53.22	16.22
9	JOSHUA CINNAMO	F46	USA	2017	52.43	15.98
10	CAMERON CROMBIE	F38	AUSTRALIA	2017	52.33	15.95

THE 2017 WORLD PARA ATHLETICS CHAMPIONSHIPS WERE HELD AT THE LONDON STADIUM IN LONDON, UK **JULY 14–23, 2017**

1 AKEEM STEWART

When Trinidad & Tobago's Akeem Stewart threw his world-record setting distance on July 23, 2017, he beat the previous F43 record by 16 ft (4.87 m). When he's not competing, Stewart's hobbies include swimming and fishing.

= 2 ILKE WYLUDDA

In December 2010, after an operation, Wyludda needed to have her right leg amputated as septicemia had set in. After returning to the sport she loves, Wyludda represented Germany in both the 2012 Olympic and Paralympic Games—a first for her nation.

TOP 10

FEMALE **DISCUS CHAMPIONS**

The first competitive discus competition was held in ancient Greece more than 2,700 years ago. No female athlete has gotten into this Top 10 in 30 years...

	ATHLETE	COUNTRY	YEAR	DISTANCE (FT)	(M)
1	GABRIELE REINSCH	GERMANY	1988	251.97	76.8
2	ZDENKA ŠILHAVÁ	CZECHOSLOVAKIA	1984	244.62	74.56
=	ILKE WYLUDDA	GERMANY	1989	244.62	74.56
4	DIANA SACHSE	GERMANY	1987	243.04	74.08
5	DANIELA COSTIAN	ROMANIA	1988	242.26	73.84
6	IRINA MESZYNSKI	GERMANY	1984	240.68	73.36
7	GALINA SAVINKOVA	RUSSIA (SOVIET UNION ERA)	1984	240.42	73.28
8	TSVETANKA KHRISTOVA	BULGARIA	1987	240.22	73.22
9	GISELA BEYER	GERMANY	1984	239.83	73.1
10	MARTINA HELLMANN	GERMANY	1987	239.24	72.92

Sainsbury's
1188

TOP 10

MALE **DISCUS CHAMPIONS**

Unlike the female discus champions chart opposite, male competitors of more recent years have managed to throw distances far enough to earn a place in this chart...

	ATHLETE	COUNTRY	YEAR	DISTANCE (FT)	(M)
1	JÜRGEN SCHULT	GERMANY	1986	243.04	74.08
2	VIRGILIJUS ALEKNA	LITHUANIA	2000	242.39	73.88
3	GERD KANTER	ESTONIA	2006	240.75	73.38
4	YURIY DUMCHEV	RUSSIA (SOVIET UNION ERA)	1983	235.76	71.86
5	PIOTR MAŁACHOWSKI	POLAND	2013	235.7	71.84
6	RÓBERT FAZEKAS	HUNGARY	2002	235.24	71.7
7	LARS RIEDEL	GERMANY	1997	234.58	71.5
8	BEN PLUCKNETT	USA	1983	233.99	71.32
9	DANIEL STÅHL	SWEDEN	2017	233.89	71.29
10	RICKARD BRUCH / IMRICH BUGÁR / JOHN POWELL	SWEDEN / CZECHOSLOVAKIA / USA	1984 / 1985 / 1984	233.79	71.26

9 DANIEL STÅHL

As well as being an expert at discus throwing, 6.6 ft (2.01 m) tall Daniel Ståhl has also made a sporting career from the shot put. At the 2017 World Athletics Championships in London, England, Ståhl finished in second place with a throw of 227 ft (69.19 m).

2 ▷ HOLLIE ARNOLD

Hollie Arnold was born June 26, 1994. Her first gold medal for the javelin (F46) was achieved at the 2013 IPC Athletics World Championships in Lyon, France. The distance on the below chart was achieved at the 2017 World Para Athletics Championships in London, England.

TOP 10

FEMALE **PARA ATHLETE JAVELIN MASTERS**

The javelin is another ancient sport, dating back over 2,700 years. At the original Olympics in ancient Greece, there was a distance as well as a target challenge event for the javelin...

	ATHLETE	CLASS	COUNTRY	YEAR	DISTANCE (FT)	(M)
1	NOZIMAKHON KAYUMOVA	F13	UZBEKISTAN	2016	146.26	44.58
2	HOLLIE ARNOLD	F46	GREAT BRITAIN	2017	141.14	43.02
3	YUPING ZHAO	F12	CHINA	2016	140.19	42.73
4	JUAN YAO	F44	CHINA	2008	132.91	40.51
5	MARTINA WILLING	F11	GERMANY	1992	126.71	38.62
6	SHIRLENE COELHO	F37	BRAZIL	2012	124.21	37.86
7	RAMUNE ADOMAITIENE	F38	LITHUANIA	2010	107.84	32.87
8	CLAUDIA BIENE	F42	GERMANY	2008	103.38	31.51
9	QING WU	F36	CHINA	2011	96.95	29.55
10	JUN WANG	F35	CHINA	2017	93.31	28.44

MALE **PARA ATHLETE JAVELIN MASTERS**

Like the chart opposite, this Top 10 doesn't aim to compare the different classifications of para athlete javelin competitors, it just collects together the furthest throws to date...

	ATHLETE	CLASS	COUNTRY	YEAR	DISTANCE (FT)	(M)
1	ALEKSANDR SVECHNIKOV	F13	UZBEKISTAN	2017	232.97	71.01
2	ZHU PENGKAI	F12	CHINA	2012	211.22	64.38
3	DEVENDRA JHAJHARIA	F46	INDIA	2016	209.88	63.97
4	GAO MINGJIE	F44	CHINA	2011	196.26	59.82
5	HELGI SVEINSSON	F42	ICELAND	2017	196.1	59.77
6	XIA DONG	F37	CHINA	2008	189.67	57.81
7	AKEEM STEWART	F43	TRINIDAD & TOBAGO	2017	189.01	57.61
8	GUO WEI	F35	CHINA	2008	183.96	56.07
9	BIL MARINKOVIC	F11	AUSTRIA	2010	177.13	53.99
10	JAYDEN SAWYER	F38	AUSTRALIA	2017	173.75	52.96

5 ▸ HELGI SVEINSSON

Hailing from Reykjavík, Iceland, javelin athlete Helgi Sveinsson also competes in the 100 m sprint and long jump. Sveinsson was the flag-bearer for the Icelandic team at the London 2012 Summer Paralympics. The rest of the team featured Matthildur Ylfa Þorsteinsdóttir, and swimmers Jón Margeir Sverrisson and Kolbrún Alda Stefánsdóttir.

8 ▷ BRYANT-DENNY STADIUM

Its home is the city of Tuscaloosa, and construction took less than a year. Originally called the Denny Stadium when it opened in 1929, it became the Bryant-Denny Stadium in 1975. The additional name was to honor the work of University of Alabama coach Paul "Bear" Bryant.

TOP 10

BIGGEST STADIUMS

For the sporting events that require a massive number of attendees, sometimes the only way to cater to the demand of the fans is to host them at a stadium...

	STADIUM	LOCATION	CAPACITY CROWD
1	RUNGNADO 1ST OF MAY STADIUM	PYONGYANG (NORTH KOREA)	150,000
2	MICHIGAN STADIUM	MICHIGAN (USA)	107,601
3	BEAVER STADIUM	PENNSYLVANIA (USA)	107,572
4	OHIO STADIUM	OHIO (USA)	104,944
5	KYLE FIELD	TEXAS (USA)	102,733
6	NEYLAND STADIUM	TENNESSEE (USA)	102,455
7	TIGER STADIUM	LOUISIANA (USA)	102,321
8	BRYANT-DENNY STADIUM	ALABAMA (USA)	101,821
9	DARRELL K ROYAL-TEXAS MEMORIAL STADIUM	TEXAS (USA)	100,119
10	MELBOURNE CRICKET GROUND	MELBOURNE (AUSTRALIA)	100,024

TOP 10

LARGEST **INDOOR ARENAS**

Although these buildings seem small in comparison to the stadiums chart opposite, they can still hold a huge number of people for sporting events and often concerts for touring music artists...

	ARENA	LOCATION	CAPACITY CROWD
1	PHILIPPINE ARENA	BOCAUE (PHILIPPINES)	55,000
2	SAITAMA SUPER ARENA	SAITAMA (JAPAN)	37,000
3	SC OLIMPIYSKIY	MOSCOW (RUSSIA)	35,000
4	GWANGMYEONG VELODROME	GWANGMYEONG (SOUTH KOREA)	30,000
5	BAKU CRYSTAL HALL	BAKU (AZERBAIJAN)	27,000
6	TELENOR ARENA	BÆRUM (NORWAY)	26,000
7	MINEIRINHO	BELO HORIZONTE (BRAZIL)	25,000
=	SMART ARANETA COLISEUM	QUEZON CITY (PHILIPPINES)	25,000
9	RUPP ARENA	KENTUCKY (USA)	24,500
10	GREENSBORO COLISEUM COMPLEX	NORTH CAROLINA (USA)	23,000

2 ▸ SAITAMA SUPER ARENA

This arena first opened its doors in September 2000. It is in Chou-ku, which is located in the northern region of the city of Saitama. As well as for a wide range of sports, including mixed martial arts and basketball, Saitama Super Arena has been used as a music venue for major artists including Babymetal and Ariana Grande.

EPIC **STRUCTURES** 05

1 HIGH ROLLER

This ferris wheel features 2,000 lights and 28 cabins. Each weighs 44,000 lb (19,958.1 kg) and can accommodate up to 40 people. It takes 30 minutes to complete one full rotation. The High Roller first opened March 31, 2014. The now-retired roller coaster that was atop Las Vegas's Stratosphere Tower (1996–2005) was also called the High Roller.

TOP 10

BIGGEST FERRIS WHEELS

As well as being an entertaining ride, ferris wheels also provide unique views and information about the surrounding landscape, and often become globally recognized structures in their own right...

	FERRIS WHEEL	LOCATION	COUNTRY	YEAR COMPLETED	HEIGHT (FT)	(M)
1	HIGH ROLLER	LAS VEGAS, NEVADA	USA	2014	550	167.6
2	SINGAPORE FLYER	MARINA CENTRE	SINGAPORE	2008	541	164.9
3	STAR OF NANCHANG	NANCHANG, JIANGXI	CHINA	2006	525	160
4	LONDON EYE	SOUTH BANK, LONDON	UK	2000	443	135
5	REDHORSE OSAKA WHEEL	EXPOCITY, SUITA, OSAKA	JAPAN	2016	403.5	123
6	ORLANDO EYE	ORLANDO, FLORIDA	USA	2015	400	121.9
7	MELBOURNE STAR	DOCKLANDS, MELBOURNE	AUSTRALIA	2008	394	120
=	SUZHOU FERRIS WHEEL	SUZHOU, JIANGSU	CHINA	2009	394	120
=	TIANJIN EYE	YONGLE BRIDGE, TIANJIN	CHINA	2008	394	120
=	ZHENGZHOU FERRIS WHEEL	CENTURY AMUSEMENT PARK, HENAN	CHINA	2003	394	120

TOP 10

OLDEST **OPERATIONAL THEME PARKS**

If you had to guess what the longest-running theme park is, which would it be? And how old would you guess it is? The reality is very surprising...

	THEME PARK	LOCATION	COUNTRY	FIRST OPENED	TOTAL YEARS OPERATIONAL
1	DYREHAVSBAKKEN	KLAMPENBORG	DENMARK	1583	436
2	WURSTELPRATER	VIENNA	AUSTRIA	1766	253
3	BLACKGANG CHINE	ISLE OF WIGHT	UK	1843	176
=	TIVOLI GARDENS	COPENHAGEN	DENMARK	1843	176
5	LAKE COMPOUNCE	CONNECTICUT	USA	1846	173
6	HANAYASHIKI	TOKYO	JAPAN	1853	166
7	CEDAR POINT	OHIO	USA	1870	149
=	SIX FLAGS NEW ENGLAND	MASSACHUSETTS	USA	1870	149
9	IDLEWILD PARK	PENNSYLVANIA	USA	1878	141
10	SEABREEZE AMUSEMENT PARK	ROCHESTER, NEW YORK	USA	1879	140

1 ▶ **DYREHAVSBAKKEN**

This Danish theme park's name translates as "the Animal Park's Hill." It still attracts millions of visitors each year. Known to locals simply as Bakken ("the Hill"), it has a total of 32 rides. The park's oldest wooden roller coaster was completed on May 16, 1932.

4 RED FORCE

This roller coaster is part of Ferrari Land, which opened April 7, 2017, as part of Spain's PortAventura Park. The Red Force ride was built by Intamin, the company behind Cedar Point's Millennium Force (in Ohio, USA) and Colossos in Heide Park (Soltau, Germany).

TOP 10

FASTEST ROLLER COASTERS

When you consider that the legal limit on many freeways is 70 mph (112.7 kph), the speeds that these roller coasters can achieve is truly something that is not for the faint of heart...

	ROLLER COASTER	LOCATION	COUNTRY	TOP SPEED (MPH)	(KPH)
1	FORMULA ROSSA	FERRARI WORLD	UNITED ARAB EMIRATES	149.1	240
2	KINGDA KA	SIX FLAGS	USA	128	206
3	TOP THRILL DRAGSTER	CEDAR POINT	USA	120	193.1
4	RED FORCE	FERRARI LAND	SPAIN	112	180
5	DODONPA	FUJI-Q HIGHLAND	JAPAN	106.9	172
6	SUPERMAN: ESCAPE FROM KRYPTON	SIX FLAGS	USA	100.8	162.2
7	TOWER OF TERROR II	DREAMWORLD	AUSTRALIA	100	160.9
8	STEEL DRAGON 2000	NAGASHIMA SPA LAND	JAPAN	95	152.9
=	FURY 325	CAROWINDS	USA	95	152.9
10	MILLENNIUM FORCE	CEDAR POINT	USA	93	149.7

3 SUPERMAN: ESCAPE FROM KRYPTON

This roller coaster was originally called Superman: The Escape, between its 1997 opening and closure in 2010. It then reopened in 2011 as Superman: Escape From Krypton. Lasting 28 seconds, it has the capacity to take more than 1,000 riders every hour.

TOP 10

TALLEST ROLLER COASTERS

You need to have a strong stomach for roller coasters' neck-bracing speeds, but you also need to be able to cope with being up four fifths the height of the Washington Monument...

	ROLLER COASTER	LOCATION	COUNTRY	HIGHEST DROP (FT)	(M)
1	KINGDA KA	SIX FLAGS	USA	456	139
2	TOP THRILL DRAGSTER	CEDAR POINT	USA	426.5	130
3	SUPERMAN: ESCAPE FROM KRYPTON	SIX FLAGS	USA	415	126.5
4	TOWER OF TERROR II	DREAMWORLD	AUSTRALIA	377.3	115
5	RED FORCE	FERRARI LAND	SPAIN	367.4	112
6	FURY 325	CAROWINDS	USA	324.8	99
7	STEEL DRAGON 2000	NAGASHIMA SPA LAND	JAPAN	318.2	97
8	MILLENNIUM FORCE	CEDAR POINT	USA	308.4	94
9	LEVIATHAN	CANADA'S WONDERLAND	CANADA	305.1	93
=	INTIMIDATOR 305	KING'S DOMINION	USA	305.1	93

2 LEGOLAND, MERLIN ENTERTAINMENTS GROUP

The first ever Legoland opened in Billund, Denmark, in 1968. All of the Legolands across the world are owned and operated by Merlin Entertainments, a British company founded in 1998. It has 127 different attractions worldwide, including in Denmark, Germany, Japan, Italy, and the USA. Merlin Entertainments is based in Poole, Dorset, home to The Lighthouse, one of the biggest arts centers in the UK.

TOTAL DISNEY PARKS (GLOBAL) = 11

TOTAL LEGO PARKS (GLOBAL) = 9

TOP 10

MOST POPULAR THEME PARKS

This Top 10 isn't about comparing individual parks; instead, we're examining the total visitors who attend all the parks owned by the companies who operate them...

	PARK CORPORATION	(PRIME) LOCATION	ANNUAL ATTENDANCE (MILLIONS)
1	WALT DISNEY PARKS & RESORTS	USA	140.4
2	MERLIN ENTERTAINMENTS GROUP	UK	61.2
3	UNIVERSAL STUDIOS RECREATION GROUP	USA	47.4
4	OCT PARKS CHINA	CHINA	32.3
5	FANTAWILD GROUP	CHINA	31.6
6	SIX FLAGS INC.	USA	30.1
7	CHIMELONG GROUP	CHINA	27.4
8	CEDAR FAIR ENTERTAINMENT COMPANY	USA	25.1
9	SEAWORLD PARKS & ENTERTAINMENT	USA	22.5
10	PARQUES REUNIDOS	SPAIN	20.8

3 ## ROYAL ARMOURIES MUSEUM, THE TOWER OF LONDON

The Tower of London is part of the Royal Armouries family of museums. Its full name, Her Majesty's Royal Palace and Fortress of the Tower of London, is a UNESCO (United Nations Educational, Scientific and Cultural Organization) World Heritage Site. Its White Tower dates back to 1078.

TOP 10

OLDEST OPERATIONAL MUSEUMS

How many museums do you have access to? And have you visited any of these that make it into this chart, all of which have had their doors open to the public for hundreds of years?...

	MUSEUM	CITY	COUNTRY	YEAR OFFICIALLY OPENED TO THE PUBLIC
1	CAPITOLINE MUSEUMS	ROME	ITALY	1471
2	VATICAN MUSEUMS	VATICAN CITY	VATICAN CITY	1506
3	ROYAL ARMOURIES MUSEUM, THE TOWER OF LONDON	LONDON	UK	1660
4	KUNSTMUSEUM BASEL (FORMERLY AMERBACH CABINET)	BASEL	SWITZERLAND	1671
5	MUSÉE DES BEAUX-ARTS ET D'ARCHÉOLOGIE DE BESANÇON	BESANÇON	FRANCE	1694
6	KUNSTKAMERA	SAINT PETERSBURG	RUSSIA	1727
7	BRITISH MUSEUM	LONDON	UK	1759
8	UFFIZI GALLERY	FLORENCE	ITALY	1769
9	MUSEUM OF THE HISTORY OF RIGA AND NAVIGATION	OLD RIGA	LATVIA	1773
10	TEYLERS MUSEUM	HAARLEM	NETHERLANDS	1784

ChocoNut

ART & ENTERTAINMENT

 2 NATIONAL AIR & SPACE MUSEUM

Part of the Smithsonian Institution, the NASM first began its life in 1946 as the National Air Museum. Among its most popular attractions are the Apollo 11 command module (which put man on the Moon for the first time in 1969) and the first airplane (devised and constructed by the Wright Brothers in 1903).

TOP 10

MOST POPULAR MUSEUMS

When you go to a museum, what are you most interested in? Dinosaur bones, ancient art, and landmark moments in technology are all on display in these 10...

	MUSEUM	CITY	COUNTRY	ANNUAL ATTENDANCE (MILLIONS)
1	NATIONAL MUSEUM OF CHINA	BEIJING	CHINA	7.6
2	NATIONAL AIR & SPACE MUSEUM	WASHINGTON, D.C.	USA	7.5
3	LOUVRE	PARIS	FRANCE	7.4
4	NATIONAL MUSEUM OF NATURAL HISTORY	WASHINGTON, D.C.	USA	7.1
5	THE METROPOLITAN MUSEUM OF ART	NEW YORK CITY	USA	7
6	BRITISH MUSEUM	LONDON	UK	6.4
7	SHANGHAI SCIENCE & TECHNOLOGY MUSEUM	SHANGHAI	CHINA	6.3
8	NATIONAL GALLERY	LONDON	UK	6.26
9	NATIONAL PALACE MUSEUM	TAIPEI	TAIWAN	6.1
10	VATICAN MUSEUMS	VATICAN CITY	VATICAN CITY	6.06

600 BILLION LEGO BRICKS
HAVE BEEN MADE
SINCE 1949

A MINI-FIGURE (WITH NO
ACCESSORIES / HAIR) WEIGHS ONE
TENTH OF AN OUNCE (2.8 GRAMS)

1 ULTIMATE COLLECTOR'S SERIES: STAR WARS MILLENNIUM FALCON (75192) – 2017 EDITION

Released on October 1, 2017, this *Millennium Falcon* build comes with 10 mini-figures (including BB-8 and two Porgs). It has seven landing legs, two escape pod hatches, and it can be switched between looking like the *Star Wars: Episode VII* and *VIII* versions of the famous Corellian ship.

TOP 10

MOST LEGO BRICKS **IN A MODEL SET**

LEGO have been making their construction bricks since 1949. Of the millions of pieces they've manufactured over the past 70 years, these 10 sets contain more pieces than any others...

	MODEL SET	SET CODE	YEAR RELEASED	NUMBER OF LEGO BRICKS
1	ULTIMATE COLLECTOR'S SERIES: STAR WARS MILLENNIUM FALCON	75192	2017	7,541
2	CREATOR: TAJ MAHAL	10256	2017 (REISSUE FROM 2008)	5,923
3	ULTIMATE COLLECTOR'S SERIES: STAR WARS MILLENNIUM FALCON	10179	2007	5,195
4	THE NINJAGO MOVIE: NINJAGO CITY	70620	2017	4,867
5	GHOSTBUSTERS FIREHOUSE HEADQUARTERS	75827	2016	4,634
6	CREATOR: TOWER BRIDGE	10214	2010	4,295
7	CREATOR: BIG BEN	10253	2016	4,163
8	DISNEY CASTLE	71040	2016	4,080
9	STAR WARS DEATH STAR	75159	2016	4,016
10	CREATOR: ASSEMBLY SQUARE	10255	2017	4,002

UNDERGROUND

1 **LONDON UNDERGROUND**

The underground railway of the United Kingdom's capital city serves 270 stations across 11 lines. Nearly 1.5 billion people annually use what is commonly known as "the Tube." The average speed of Tube trains is 21 mph (33.8 kph).

TOP 10

OLDEST **METRO SYSTEMS**

Some underground railway systems have been in use for more than 120 years. Check out this Top 10 and count how many you have traveled on...

	NAME	CITY	COUNTRY	YEAR OPENED
1	LONDON UNDERGROUND	LONDON	UK	1890
2	BUDAPEST METRO	BUDAPEST	HUNGARY	1896
=	GLASGOW SUBWAY	GLASGOW	UK	1896
4	CHICAGO L	CHICAGO	USA	1897
5	PARIS MÉTRO	PARIS	FRANCE	1900
6	MBTA SUBWAY	BOSTON	USA	1901
7	BERLIN U-BAHN	BERLIN	GERMANY	1902
8	ATHENS METRO	ATHENS	GREECE	1904
=	NEW YORK CITY SUBWAY	NEW YORK CITY	USA	1904
10	MARKET–FRANKFORD LINE	PHILADELPHIA	USA	1907

TOTAL STATIONS IN UK METRO SYSTEMS FEATURED = 285

TOTAL STATIONS IN U.S. METRO SYSTEMS FEATURED = 778

TOP 10

BIGGEST **LIBRARIES**

There are almost 120,000 libraries across the United States alone, and these eight countries are home to the most expansive collections on the planet...

	LIBRARY	CITY	COUNTRY	NUMBER OF BOOKS (MILLIONS)
1	THE BRITISH LIBRARY	LONDON	UK	170
2	LIBRARY OF CONGRESS	WASHINGTON, D.C.	USA	164
3	LIBRARY AND ARCHIVES	OTTAWA	CANADA	54
4	NEW YORK PUBLIC LIBRARY	NEW YORK CITY	USA	53.1
5	RUSSIAN STATE LIBRARY	MOSCOW	RUSSIA	44.4
6	NATIONAL DIET LIBRARY	TOKYO / KYOTO	JAPAN	41.9
7	BIBLIOTHÈQUE NATIONALE DE FRANCE	PARIS	FRANCE	40
8	NATIONAL LIBRARY OF RUSSIA	SAINT PETERSBURG	RUSSIA	36.5
9	NATIONAL LIBRARY OF CHINA	BEIJING	CHINA	36.4
10	ROYAL DANISH LIBRARY	COPENHAGEN	DENMARK	35.4

3 LIBRARY AND ARCHIVES

This building has grown its collection over 140 years. Aside from its vast number of books, it has more than 90,000 archived films, with the oldest dating back to 1897. It also preserves the largest collection of Canadian sheet music in the world, with 550,000 pieces.

EPIC BUILDS

BUILDINGS **WITH THE MOST FLOORS**

If you prefer to take the stairs instead of the elevator, you may want to avoid a visit to any of these truly epic buildings, the "smallest" of which still has more than 100 floors...

	BUILDING	CITY	COUNTRY	YEAR COMPLETED	TOTAL FLOORS
1	BURJ KHALIFA	DUBAI	UNITED ARAB EMIRATES	2010	163
2	SHANGHAI TOWER	SHANGHAI	CHINA	2015	128
3	LOTTE WORLD TOWER	SEOUL	SOUTH KOREA	2017	123
4	MAKKAH ROYAL CLOCK TOWER HOTEL	MECCA	SAUDI ARABIA	2012	120
5	PING AN FINANCE CENTER	SHENZHEN	CHINA	2017	115
6	GUANGZHOU CTF FINANCE CENTRE	GUANGZHOU	CHINA	2016	111
7	INTERNATIONAL COMMERCE CENTRE	HONG KONG	CHINA	2010	108
=	WILLIS TOWER	CHICAGO	USA	1974	108
9	ONE WORLD TRADE CENTER	NEW YORK CITY	USA	2014	104
10	GUANGZHOU INTERNATIONAL FINANCE CENTER	GUANGZHOU	CHINA	2010	103

3 ▶ LOTTE WORLD TOWER

As well as its 123 floors above ground, the Lotte World Tower—the tallest building in South Korea—also has six floors below ground. It has 58 elevators that can travel up to 32.8 ft (10 m) per second. The hotel, office, residential, and retail combination has 260 hotel rooms.

EAST PACIFIC CENTER TOWER A

The East Pacific Center Tower A in Shenzhen, China, just misses out on a place in this Top 10 chart. Completed in 2013, it has 85 floors and measures 1,004 ft (306 m) high.

TOP 10

LARGEST **ALL-RESIDENTIAL BUILDINGS**

A lot of skyscrapers are built to be multipurpose, providing office space, floors for retail businesses, as well as homes for people. This chart compares the tallest that are exclusively residential...

	BUILDING	CITY	COUNTRY	YEAR COMPLETED	FLOORS	HEIGHT (FT)	(M)
1	432 PARK AVENUE	NEW YORK CITY	USA	2015	85	1,396	425.5
2	PRINCESS TOWER	DUBAI	UNITED ARAB EMIRATES	2012	101	1,356	413.4
3	23 MARINA	DUBAI	UNITED ARAB EMIRATES	2012	88	1,287	392.4
4	BURJ MOHAMMED BIN RASHID TOWER	ABU DHABI	UNITED ARAB EMIRATES	2014	88	1,251	381.2
5	ELITE RESIDENCE	DUBAI	UNITED ARAB EMIRATES	2012	87	1,248	380.5
6	THE TORCH	DUBAI	UNITED ARAB EMIRATES	2011	86	1,155	352
7	Q1 TOWER	GOLD COAST	AUSTRALIA	2005	78	1,058	322.5
8	HHHR TOWER	DUBAI	UNITED ARAB EMIRATES	2010	72	1,042	317.6
9	OCEAN HEIGHTS	DUBAI	UNITED ARAB EMIRATES	2010	83	1,017	310
10	CAYAN TOWER	DUBAI	UNITED ARAB EMIRATES	2013	73	1,005	306.4

TOP 10

BIGGEST **AQUARIUMS**

The best kinds of aquariums in the world are the ones that actively engage in learning about sea life in an effort to help save and maintain it...

	AQUARIUM	LOCATION	TOTAL WATER (MILLIONS)	
			(U.S. GAL)	(LTR)
1	GEORGIA AQUARIUM	USA	6.3	23.85
2	DUBAI AQUARIUM & UNDERWATER ZOO	DUBAI	2.64	10
3	OKINAWA CHURAUMI AQUARIUM	JAPAN	1.98	7.5
4	THE OCEANOGRÀFIC OF THE CITY OF ARTS AND SCIENCES	SPAIN	1.85	7
5	TURKUAZOO	TURKEY	1.32	5
6	MONTEREY BAY AQUARIUM	USA	1.2	4.54
7	USHAKA MARINE WORLD	SOUTH AFRICA	0.98	3.71
8	SHANGHAI OCEAN AQUARIUM	CHINA	0.92	3.48
9	AQUARIUM OF GENOA	ITALY	0.87	3.29
10	AQUARIUM OF WESTERN AUSTRALIA	AUSTRALIA	0.8	3.03

6 MONTEREY BAY AQUARIUM

Monterey Bay Aquarium is a nonprofit organization. It first opened its doors on October 20, 1984, and had 10,681 visitors. The following year, in March, the aquarium began its programs for schoolchildren. In 1987, MBARI (the Monterey Bay Aquarium Research Institute) was founded to develop new methods for studying our oceans.

1 ▶ **PING AN FINANCE CENTER**

Located in the city of Shenzhen, in the Guangdong Province of South China, Ping An Finance Center is made of 1,700 tons of stainless steel. This prevents the salt in the atmosphere from eroding and altering the aesthetic of the tower. The architects behind it are Kohn Pedersen Fox Associates.

TOP 10

BIGGEST **ALL-OFFICE BUILDINGS**

This popular Top 10 chart has a brand-new number one. With the vast number of skyscrapers being constructed every year, we wonder how long it will hold onto the top spot...

	BUILDING	CITY	COUNTRY	YEAR COMPLETED	FLOORS	HEIGHT (FT)	(M)
1	PING AN FINANCE CENTER	SHENZHEN	CHINA	2016	115	1,965	598.9
2	ONE WORLD TRADE CENTER	NEW YORK CITY	USA	2014	104	1,776	541.3
3	TAIPEI 101	TAIPEI	TAIWAN	2004	101	1,667	508.1
4	PETRONAS TOWERS	KUALA LUMPUR	MALAYSIA	1998	88	1,483	452
5	WILLIS TOWER	CHICAGO	USA	1974	108	1,451	442.3
6	AL HAMRA TOWER	KUWAIT CITY	KUWAIT	2011	80	1,354	412.7
7	TWO INTERNATIONAL FINANCE CENTRE	HONG KONG	CHINA	2003	88	1,352	412.1
8	CITIC PLAZA	GUANGZHOU	CHINA	1996	80	1,280	390.1
9	SHUN HING SQUARE	SHENZHEN	CHINA	1996	69	1,260	384
10	EMPIRE STATE BUILDING	NEW YORK CITY	USA	1931	102	1,250	381

TALLEST CONSTRUCTIONS

TALLEST COMPLETED BUILDINGS

Architects are constantly finding ways to make skyscrapers bigger and more technologically advanced, and the number one on this chart towers over its city at more than half a mile (0.8 km) high...

	BUILDING	CITY	COUNTRY	YEAR COMPLETED	FLOORS	HEIGHT (FT)	(M)
1	BURJ KHALIFA	DUBAI	UNITED ARAB EMIRATES	2010	163	2,717	828
2	SHANGHAI TOWER	SHANGHAI	CHINA	2015	128	2,073	632
3	MAKKAH ROYAL CLOCK TOWER HOTEL	MECCA	SAUDI ARABIA	2012	120	1,972	601
4	PING AN FINANCE CENTER	SHENZHEN	CHINA	2017	115	1,965	598.9
5	LOTTE WORLD TOWER	SEOUL	SOUTH KOREA	2017	123	1,819	554.5
6	ONE WORLD TRADE CENTER	NEW YORK CITY	USA	2014	104	1,776	541.3
7	GUANGZHOU CTF FINANCE CENTRE	GUANGZHOU	CHINA	2016	111	1,739	530
8	TAIPEI 101	TAIPEI	TAIWAN	2004	101	1,667	508.1
9	SHANGHAI WORLD FINANCIAL CENTER	SHANGHAI	CHINA	2008	101	1,614	492
10	INTERNATIONAL COMMERCE CENTRE	HONG KONG	CHINA	2010	108	1,588	484

7 GUANGZHOU CTF FINANCE CENTRE

To accommodate its mixture of hotel room and permanent resident occupants, this building has capacity for 1,705 parking spaces. After being initially proposed in 2009, Guangzhou CTF Finance Centre was constructed over a six-year period that began in 2010. It is the third tallest building in China.

5 **BAIYOKE TOWER II**

The construction of Baiyoke Tower II, in Bangkok, began in 1990 and finished in 1997. Part of the Baiyoke Group of Hotels, it is the second tallest tower in Thailand, features 673 rooms, and is the 108th tallest building in the world.

TOP 10
TALLEST **ALL-HOTEL BUILDINGS**

At first glance, the buildings in this chart do seem massive, but when you compare it with the list opposite, you'll notice that many of the entries are less than half the height of their counterparts...

	BUILDING	COUNTRY	YEAR COMPLETED	FLOORS	HEIGHT (FT)	(M)
1	JW MARRIOTT MARQUIS HOTEL DUBAI TOWERS	UNITED ARAB EMIRATES	2012 & 2013	82	1,166	355.4
2	ROSE RAYHAAN BY ROTANA	UNITED ARAB EMIRATES	2007	71	1,093	333
3	BURJ AL ARAB	UNITED ARAB EMIRATES	1999	56	1,053	321
4	EMIRATES TOWER TWO	UNITED ARAB EMIRATES	2000	56	1,014	309
5	BAIYOKE TOWER II	THAILAND	1997	85	997	304
6	WUXI MAOYE CITY – MARRIOTT HOTEL	CHINA	2014	68	996.7	303.8
7	KHALID AL ATTAR TOWER 2	UNITED ARAB EMIRATES	2011	66	965	294
8	ABRAJ AL BAIT ZAMZAM TOWER	SAUDI ARABIA	2012	58	915	279
9	ABRAJ AL BAIT HAJAR TOWER	SAUDI ARABIA	2012	54	906	276
10	FOUR SEASONS HOTEL	BAHRAIN	2015	50	885	269.4
BONUS	RADISSON ROYAL HOTEL DUBAI	UNITED ARAB EMIRATES	2010	60	883	269

TOP 10

COUNTRIES WITH THE
MOST 300M+ BUILDINGS

The top four countries on this chart have all increased their total number of skyscrapers taller than 984 ft since the last *Top 10 of Everything* annual, with China alone adding 10 more...

	COUNTRY	NUMBER OF 300M+ BUILDINGS
1	CHINA	57
2	UNITED ARAB EMIRATES	25
3	USA	18
4	RUSSIA	5
5	MALAYSIA	3
=	SAUDI ARABIA	3
=	SOUTH KOREA	3
8	KUWAIT	2
=	TAIWAN	2
=	THAILAND	2

AUSTRALIA, JAPAN, UK, INDIA, QATAR, VIETNAM, CHILE, AND SWITZERLAND
ALL HAVE 1 X 300M+ BUILDING

2 ▶ UNITED ARAB EMIRATES

Dubai's The Address stands 991 ft (302.2 m) tall. It was completed in 2008. A combination of 626 apartments and 196 hotel rooms make up the building, with 895 parking spaces. Although it is a gigantic skyscraper, it is the 21st tallest building in Dubai.

6 INDONESIA

Gama Tower, located in Indonesia's capital city, Jakarta, is the country's tallest skyscraper. It is 937 ft (285.5 m) tall, has 272 hotel rooms, and ranks as the 93rd tallest building in Asia, and the 163rd tallest in the world. Construction began in 2011 and finished in 2016.

TOP 10

COUNTRIES WITH THE
MOST 200M+ BUILDINGS

The minimum height required for a building to qualify for this Top 10 is 656.2 ft, and one country is way ahead of the other nine here...

	COUNTRY	NUMBER OF 200M+ BUILDINGS
1	CHINA	579
2	USA	185
3	UNITED ARAB EMIRATES	95
4	SOUTH KOREA	64
5	JAPAN	39
6	INDONESIA	35
7	AUSTRALIA	33
8	SINGAPORE	32
9	PHILIPPINES	27
10	CANADA	26

TOP 10

MOST COMMUNICATIONS TOWERS

Telecom ("telecommunications") towers around the world are crucial for the transmission of all different kinds of communications signals, including radio and television signals...

	COUNTRY	NUMBER OF TELECOM TOWERS
1	NETHERLANDS	88
2	CHINA	33
3	USA	26
4	GERMANY	16
5	UK	14
6	JAPAN	9
7	INDIA	7
8	CANADA	6
9	RUSSIA	5
=	ITALY	5

2 CHINA

China Tower is the biggest telecom company in the country. It came to be when, in 2014, the three largest telephone companies in China—Mobile, China Telecom, and China Unicom—joined forces and combined all their telecom towers under a single banner.

1 JEDDAH TOWER

Construction began on April 1, 2013.
By February 2018, 63 floors of this
new building were completed.
If it is completed to the current
specifications, it will become the
tallest building in the world, exceeding
Dubai's Burj Khalifa by 564 ft (171.9 m).

TOP 10

TALLEST FUTURE BUILDINGS (UNDER CONSTRUCTION)

Look back over the height charts featured in this Top 10 zone and compare them to the insane proposed
measurements for these upcoming skyscrapers...

	BUILDING	CITY	COUNTRY	YEAR TO BE COMPLETED	FLOORS	HEIGHT (FT)	(M)
1	JEDDAH TOWER	JEDDAH	SAUDI ARABIA	2020	167	3,281	1,000
2	DUBAI ONE	DUBAI	UNITED ARAB EMIRATES	2021	161	2,333	711
3	TIANFU CENTER	CHENGDU	CHINA	2023	157	2,218	676
4	WUHAN CTF FINANCE CENTER	WUHAN	CHINA	2022	121	2,126	648
5	SIGNATURE TOWER JAKARTA	JAKARTA	INDONESIA	2022	113	2,093	638
6	MERDEKA PNB118	KUALA LUMPUR	MALAYSIA	2021	118	2,067	630
7	WORLD CAPITAL CENTRE	COLOMBO	SRI LANKA	2023	117	2,051	625
8	GRAND RAMA 9 TOWER	BANGKOK	THAILAND	2021	125	2,018	615
9	BAONENG BINHU CENTER T1	HEFEI	CHINA	2024	119	1,929	588
10	HYUNDAI GLOBAL BUSINESS CENTER	SEOUL	SOUTH KOREA	2022	105	1,867	569

LONGEST **DESIGNS**

TOP 10

LONGEST
UNDERGROUND TRAIN SYSTEMS

If you were able to line up all of the different train tracks that make up every component of these complete underground railways, these are the world's longest...

	NAME	LOCATION	COUNTRY	TOTAL LENGTH (MI)	(KM)
1	SHANGHAI METRO	SHANGHAI	CHINA	365	587.4
2	BEIJING SUBWAY	BEIJING	CHINA	357	574.5
3	LONDON UNDERGROUND	LONDON	UK	250	402.3
4	NEW YORK CITY SUBWAY	NEW YORK CITY	USA	236.2	380.1
5	MOSCOW METRO	MOSCOW	RUSSIA	215.1	346.2
6	SEOUL SUBWAY (LINE 1-9)	SEOUL	SOUTH KOREA	206	331.5
7	GUANGZHOU METRO	GUANGZHOU	CHINA	191.8	308.7
8	NANJING METRO	NANJING	CHINA	183	294.5
9	MADRID METRO	MADRID	SPAIN	183	294.5
10	SHENZHEN METRO	SHENZHEN	CHINA	177.8	286.1

4 NEW YORK CITY SUBWAY

The first underground element of the New York City Subway debuted on October 27, 1904. It utilizes 6,418 subway cars, 472 stations, and employs more than 50,000 people. More than 2 billion people ride the New York City Subway every year.

LONGEST **U.S. INTERSTATE HIGHWAYS**

If a highway is classified as "interstate" it means that it crosses a state line in the USA as part of the country's National Highway System...

	HIGHWAY	NUMBER OF STATES IT SERVES	LENGTH (MI)	(KM)
1	I-90	13	3,020.5	4,861
2	I-80	11	2,899.5	4,666.3
3	I-40	8	2,555.1	4,112
4	I-10	8	2,460.3	3,959.5
5	I-70	10	2,153.1	3,465.1
6	I-95	15	1,925.7	3,099.1
7	I-75	6	1,786.5	2,875.1
8	I-94	7	1,585.2	2,551.1
9	I-35	6	1,568.4	2,524.1
10	I-20	6	1,539.4	2,477.4

1   I-90

Interstate 90 connects and passes through: Idaho, Illinois, Indiana, Massachusetts, Minnesota, Montana, New York, Ohio, Pennsylvania, South Dakota, Washington, Wisconsin, and Wyoming.

NUMBER OF "I" HIGHWAYS FOUNDED BY YEAR

1956 = 7

1957 = 11

1958 = 7

1959 = 4

1960 = 4

TOP 10

LONGEST ROLLER COASTERS

If you ride the number one roller coaster on this Top 10, you will travel more than 1.5 miles (2.4 km), and even the 10th entry covers more than 1.1 miles (1.8 km)...

	ROLLER COASTER	LOCATION	COUNTRY	LENGTH (FT)	(M)
1	STEEL DRAGON 2000	NAGASHIMA SPA LAND	JAPAN	8,133	2,479
2	THE ULTIMATE	LIGHTWATER VALLEY	UK	7,442	2,268
3	THE BEAST	KINGS ISLAND	USA	7,359	2,243
4	FUJIYAMA	FUJI-Q HIGHLAND	JAPAN	6,709	2,045
5	FURY 325	CAROWINDS	USA	6,602	2,012
6	MILLENNIUM FORCE	CEDAR POINT	USA	6,595	2,010
7	FORMULA ROSSA	FERRARI WORLD	UNITED ARAB EMIRATES	6,562	2,000
8	THE VOYAGE	HOLIDAY WORLD & SPLASHIN' SAFARI	USA	6,442	1,964
9	CALIFORNIA SCREAMIN'	DISNEY CALIFORNIA ADVENTURE	USA	6,072	1,851
10	DESPERADO	BUFFALO BILL'S	USA	5,843	1,781

2 THE ULTIMATE

This roller coaster takes a total of 40 riders at speeds of up to 50 mph (80.5 kph). Its home, the Lightwater Valley theme park, is based in North Yorkshire, England. It first opened in 1969. The Ultimate is one of the park's 35 rides, which also include an underground ride called Raptor Attack.

6 | HONG KONG–ZHUHAI–MACAU BRIDGE

Completed in 2017, the Hong Kong–Zhuhai–Macau Bridge is a bridge and tunnel system that was eight years in the making. It officially opened on July 1, 2018. The massive structure required three man-made islands to be built. The idea behind the bridge dates back to 1983.

TOP 10

LONGEST BRIDGES

If you love bridges, and want to travel on one that is more than 102.4 miles (164.8 km) long, make plans to visit the top spot on this chart...

	BRIDGE	COUNTRY	LENGTH (FT)	(M)
1	DANYANG–KUNSHAN GRAND BRIDGE	CHINA	540,700	164,800
2	THSR CHANGHUA–KAOHSIUNG VIADUCT	TAIWAN	516,132	157,317
3	TIANJIN GRAND BRIDGE	CHINA	373,000	113,700
4	CANGDE GRAND BRIDGE	CHINA	347,146	105,810
5	WEINAN WEIHE GRAND BRIDGE	CHINA	261,588	79,732
6	HONG KONG–ZHUHAI–MACAU BRIDGE	CHINA	180,446	55,000
7	BANG NA EXPRESSWAY	THAILAND	177,000	54,000
8	BEIJING GRAND BRIDGE	CHINA	157,982	48,153
9	LAKE PONTCHARTRAIN CAUSEWAY	USA	126,122	38,442
10	MANCHAC SWAMP BRIDGE	USA	120,440	36,710

MECHANICAL
CREATIONS **06**

TOP 10

FASTEST
ELECTRIC / HYBRID CARS

Exclusively gasoline-powered cars are fast becoming a thing of the past, and these 10 innovations in road travel are the fastest in their class...

	MODEL	TOP SPEED (MPH)	(KPH)
1	VENTURI BUCKEYE BULLET 3	342.14	550.63
2	LUCID AIR	235	378.2
3	RIMAC CONCEPT ONE	221	355.67
4	GENOVATION GXE	220	354.06
5	VANDA DENDROBIUM	200	321.87
6	NIO EP9	194	312.21
7	ZOMBIE 222	178	286.46
8	TESLA MODEL S P100D	155	249.45
=	ASTON MARTIN RAPIDE	155	249.45
10	TOROIDION 1MW	100	160.93

1 VENTURI BUCKEYE BULLET 3

This electric vehicle was developed by engineering students at The Ohio State University in Columbus, Ohio, USA. The project is a collaboration with electric automotive manufacturer Venturi. The previous version, the Buckeye Bullet 2.5, reached 307.7 mph (495.1 kph). The Bullet 3 achieved its world record on September 19, 2016.

THE TESLA MODEL S CAN ACCELERATE FROM ZERO TO 60 MPH (96.6 KPH) IN... **2.5 SECONDS**

WORLD'S FASTEST EV's

VENTURI

TOP 10

FIRST iPHONES

It may feel like smartphones have always been a part of our daily lives, but they first entered the market in 2007 when Apple invented the iPhone...

	MODEL	RELEASED
1	iPHONE	JUN 29, 2007
2	iPHONE 3G	JUL 11, 2008
3	iPHONE 3GS	JUN 19, 2009
4	iPHONE 4	JUN 24, 2010
5	iPHONE 4S	OCT 14, 2011
6	iPHONE 5	SEP 21, 2012
7	iPHONE 5S / 5C	SEP 20, 2013
8	iPHONE 6 / 6 PLUS	SEP 19, 2014
9	iPHONE 6S / 6S PLUS	SEP 25, 2015
10	iPHONE SE	MAR 31, 2016

IPHONE X

The iPhone X was released November 3, 2017, to celebrate the 10th anniversary of the original iPhone. On launch, the iPhone X cost $999. Instead of a user pressing the home key and entering a pass code to unlock the iPhone X, the phone uses Face ID, facial recognition technology.

INNOVATIONS

TOP 10

FASTEST VEHICLES OF ALL

Looking at all the different kinds of vehicles there are—from rocket ships to seafaring craft—these are the models, in each category, that have world records in speed...

	TYPE	NAME	COUNTRY	TOP SPEED (MPH)	(KPH)
1	ROCKET	APOLLO 10	USA	24,791	39,897
2	HYPERSONIC CRUISE VEHICLE	FALCON HTV-2	USA	13,000	20,921.47
3	ROCKET PLANE	NORTH AMERICAN X-15	USA	4,520	7,274.24
4	PLANE	LOCKHEED SR-71 BLACKBIRD	USA	2,193.6	3,529.6
5	JET-ENGINE CAR	THRUSTSSC	USA	763.04	1,227.98
6	UNMANNED AERIAL VEHICLE	BARRACUDA	GERMANY / SPAIN	647	1,041.3
7	CAR	BLUEBIRD CN7	AUSTRALIA	440	710
8	MOTORCYCLE	TOP 1 ACK ATTACK	USA	376.36	605.7
9	TRAIN	L0 SERIES SCMAGLEV	JAPAN	375	603.5
10	BOAT	SPIRIT OF AUSTRALIA	AUSTRALIA	345	555.21

1 APOLLO 10

NASA's Apollo 10 launched May 18, 1969. Its world-record speed was achieved during its return journey from orbiting the moon. Apollo 10 collected the final data necessary for what would become the first moon landing mission (Apollo 11, on July 16, 1969). Apollo 10 splashed back down into the Pacific Ocean on May 26, 1969.

142

TOP 10

BIGGEST **VEHICLES OF ALL**

You may be familiar with the more traditional modes of transportation, but to really get the giants of travel involved in this Top 10, we included every type of construction that provides movement for humankind...

	TYPE	NAME	COUNTRY	SIZE (FT)	(M)
1	TRAIN	BHP IRON ORE	AUSTRALIA	24,124	7,353
2	LAND TRANSPORTER	F60 OVERBURDEN CONVEYOR	GERMANY	1,647	502.01
3	SHIP	SEAWISE GIANT OIL TANKER	JAPAN	1,504.1	458.46
4	AIRCRAFT CARRIER	USS ENTERPRISE	USA	1,122	342
5	AIRSHIP	HINDENBURG & GRAF ZEPPELIN II	GERMANY	803.8	245
6	SUBMARINE	TYPHOON-CLASS	RUSSIA	574.15	175
7	SPACE STATION	INTERNATIONAL SPACE STATION	USA, CANADA, RUSSIA, JAPAN, EUROPE	356*	108.5*
8	PLANE	HUGHES H4 HERCULES	USA	319.92**	97.51**
9	HELICOPTER	MIL V-12	RUSSIA (SOVIET UNION ERA)	121.39	37
10	TANK	CHAR 2C / FCM 2C	FRANCE	33.69	10.27

ALL MEASUREMENTS ARE VEHICLE LENGTHS EXCEPT: *WIDTH AND **WINGSPAN.

9 ▶ MIL V-12

The largest helicopter ever built is on display at Central Air Force Museum, in Monino, Moscow Oblast, Russia. Its first successful test flight was on July 10, 1968. However impressive its length is (on the above chart), its width—including the rotor blades—measures 219.8 ft (67 m).

TOP 10

WORLD CUP
SAILING NATIONS (MOST MEDALS)

Learning how to sail is as much about figuring out how to control a sailboat as it is about understanding how to manipulate the natural force of the wind. These nations have produced the greatest sailing champions of them all...

	COUNTRY	GOLD	SILVER	BRONZE	TOTAL MEDALS
1	GREAT BRITAIN	108	98	81	287
2	AUSTRALIA	94	75	72	241
3	FRANCE	55	56	52	163
4	USA	35	30	47	112
5	NETHERLANDS	47	31	32	110
6	NEW ZEALAND	27	36	22	85
7	CHINA	29	25	28	82
8	SPAIN	26	25	29	80
9	GERMANY	27	20	17	64
10	CROATIA	16	20	18	54

6 NEW ZEALAND

The national sailing team, called Team New Zealand, is based in Auckland, a city in New Zealand's North Island. TNZ was established in 1993. Their wins include the 2017 America's Cup, skippered by Glenn Ashby, who holds 15 career gold medals, 5 silver (including one from the 2008 Summer Olympic Games held in Beijing, China), and 1 bronze.

3 ❯ BLUEBIRD K7

This seacraft is a type of hydroplane. *Bluebird K7* was powered by jet engines. Between July 23, 1955, and December 31, 1964, Donald Campbell achieved a total of seven world water-speed records with *Bluebird K7*. Campbell was tragically killed during another record attempt on January 4, 1967.

FASTEST ON-WATER RECORD HOLDERS

TOP 10

Pay close attention to the dates on this chart to really get a sense of how long the world-record speed for traveling on water has remained unbeaten...

	SKIPPER	VESSEL	COUNTRY	YEAR	BEST SPEED ACHIEVED (MPH)	(KPH)
1	KEN WARBY	SPIRIT OF AUSTRALIA	AUSTRALIA	1978	317.6	511.12
2	LEE TAYLOR	HUSTLER	USA	1967	285.22	459.02
3	DONALD CAMPBELL	BLUEBIRD K7	UK	1964	276.33	444.71
4	STANLEY SAYRES, ELMER LENINSCHMIDT	SLO-MO-SHUN IV	USA	1952	178.5	287.26
5	MALCOLM CAMPBELL	BLUEBIRD K4	UK	1939	141.74	228.11
6	GAR WOOD	MISS AMERICA X	USA	1932	124.86	200.94
7	KAYE DON	MISS ENGLAND III	ITALY	1932	119.81	192.82
8	HENRY SEGRAVE	MISS ENGLAND II	UK	1930	98.76	158.94
9	GEORGE WOOD	MISS AMERICA II	USA	1928	92.84	149.41
10	JULES FISHER	FARMAN HYDROGLIDER	USA	1924	87.39	140.64

OCEANIC CRAFT

7 ▶ VIKRANT

This craft's name means "courageous." It is the first ship of the *Vikrant* class of aircraft carriers for the Indian navy, Bharatiya Nau Sena. The Indian navy dates back to 1612. INS *Vikrant*'s completion date of December 2018 will be followed by two years of sea trials.

TOP 10

LARGEST **ACTIVE AIRCRAFT CARRIERS / WARSHIPS**

Aircraft carriers are among the most expensive military constructions, costing billions of dollars in R&D (research and development) and construction...

	NAME / CLASS	COUNTRY	LENGTH (FT)	(M)
1	GERALD R. FORD	USA	1,105.6	337
2	NIMITZ	USA	1,092.5	333
3	TYPE 001A	CHINA	1,033.5	315
4	ADMIRAL KUZNETSOV	RUSSIA	990.8	302
5	QUEEN ELIZABETH	UK	931.8	284
6	VIKRAMADITYA	INDIA	930.1	283.5
7	VIKRANT	INDIA	860	262.1
8	CHARLES DE GAULLE	FRANCE	858	261.5
9	AMERICA	USA	844	257.3
10	WASP	USA	843	256.9

TOP 10

BIGGEST **DECOMMISSIONED AIRCRAFT CARRIERS / WARSHIPS**

When aircraft carriers are decommissioned, they are stripped of all their artillery, taken out of service, and no longer used as part of a nation's naval fleet...

	NAME / CLASS	COUNTRY	LENGTH (FT)	(M)
1	ENTERPRISE	USA	1,122	342
2	KITTY HAWK	USA	1,072.8	327
3	FORRESTAL	USA	1,066.3	325
4	JOHN F. KENNEDY	USA	1,049.9	320
5	MIDWAY	USA	1,003.9	306
6	ESSEX	USA	888	270.7
7	IOWA	USA	885.8	270
8	SÃO PAULO	BRAZIL	869	264.9
9	TARAWA	USA	834	254.2
10	AUDACIOUS / EAGLE	UK	811.8	247.4

8   SÃO PAULO

This vessel began its life as an aircraft carrier named *Foch* for the Marine Nationale (French navy). It became the flagship of Marinha do Brasil (Brazilian navy) in September 2000. *São Paulo* was taken out of commission on February 14, 2017.

OCEANIC CRAFT

NATIONS WITH THE MOST DECOMMISSIONED AIRCRAFT CARRIERS

Aircraft carriers have been around for more than 100 years and, even though they are extremely costly, more than 100 of them have been decommissioned...

	COUNTRY	TOTAL DECOMMISSIONED
1	USA	55
2	UK	40
3	FRANCE	7
4	JAPAN	4
=	NETHERLANDS	4
6	SPAIN	3
=	AUSTRALIA	3
=	CANADA	3
9	INDIA	2
=	ARGENTINA / BRAZIL	2

1 › USS TARAWA

The USS *Tarawa* launched May 12, 1945. It was decommissioned on May 13, 1960, and later sold for scrap in 1968. The vessel was named after the US victory at the Battle of Tarawa (between the United States and Japan) that took place November 20–23, 1943.

ONLY THE FOLLOWING COUNTRIES HAVE AIRCRAFT CARRIERS IN ACTIVE SERVICE:

- UK = 1
- THAILAND = 1
- RUSSIA = 1
- INDIA = 1
- FRANCE = 1
- CHINA = 2
- ITALY = 2
- USA = 11

TOP 10

LONGEST SUBMARINES

Submarines can cost up to around $3 billion to develop and complete, and these are the longest deep-diving vessels ever made...

	CLASS	COUNTRY	LENGTH (FT)	(M)
1	TYPHOON	RUSSIA	574.1	175
2	BOREI	RUSSIA	557.7	170
=	OHIO	USA	557.7	170
4	DELTA III	RUSSIA	544.6	166
5	OSCAR II	RUSSIA	508.5	155
6	VANGUARD	UK	491.8	149.9
7	TRIOMPHANT	FRANCE	452.8	138
8	YASEN	RUSSIA	393.7	120
9	VIRGINIA	USA	377.3	115
10	SIERRA II	RUSSIA	364.2	111

6 VANGUARD

This class of submarine is owned and operated by the Royal Navy, the naval force of the UK. All four *Vanguard*-class submarines that were built are active. They have been part of the Royal Navy's fleet since 1993. The *Dreadnought* class is planned to replace the *Vanguard* class from 2028.

TOP 10

FASTEST CARS

Team Top 10 looked at all cars—be they concept cars, or ones in production and available to the public—to discover the fastest in the world...

	MODEL	TOP SPEED (MPH)	(KPH)
1	HENNESSEY VENOM F5	301	484.4
2	BUGATTI CHIRON	288	463.5
3	KOENIGSEGG ONE:1	273	439.35
4	HENNESSEY VENOM GT	270.49	435.31
5	KOENIGSEGG AGERA R	270	434.5
6	KOENIGSEGG AGERA S	268	431.3
7	BUGATTI VEYRON 16.4 SUPER SPORT WORLD RECORD EDITION	267.85	431.07
8	KOENIGSEGG AGERA RS	267	429.7
9	KOENIGSEGG AGERA	260	418.42
10	SSC ULTIMATE AERO	257.44	414.31

BONUS

FIVE OTHER SUPER-FAST CARS

MODEL	MPH	KPH
9FF GT9-R	257	413.59
KOENIGSEGG REGERA	255	410.4
BUGATTI VEYRON GRAND SPORT VITESSE	254.04	408.84
SALEEN S7 TWIN TURBO	248	399.11
KOENIGSEGG CCX	245	394.28

1 — HENNESSEY VENOM F5

This car was first publicly shown at the SEMA (Specialty Equipment Market Association) show in Las Vegas, Nevada, USA, on November 1, 2017. It can achieve 0–186 mph (299 kph) in under 10 seconds. The base price for the Hennessey Venom F5 will be $1.6 million. Its predecessor is the Hennessey Venom GT.

TOP 10

FASTEST **MOTORCYCLES**

Some of the vehicles featured on this chart are far from being traditional-looking motorcycles, but they all qualify as motorbikes, and all reach incredible speeds...

	MODEL	TOP SPEED (MPH)	(KPH)
1	TOP 1 ACK ATTACK	394.1	634.2
2	BUB SEVEN STREAMLINER	367.4	591.2
3	LIGHTNING BOLT	333.1	536.1
4	EASYRIDERS	322.9	519.6
5	SILVER BIRD	303.8	488.9
6	GYRONAUT X-1	279.6	450
7	YAMAHA BIG RED	265.5	427.3
8	HARLEY-DAVIDSON GODZILLA SPORTSTER	255	410.4
9	KAWASAKI NINJA H2R	249	400.7
10	MTT TURBINE SUPERBIKE Y2K	227	365.3

2 BUB SEVEN STREAMLINER

This peculiar-looking motorcycle is a streamliner, meaning it has a specially designed outer shell to maximize its aerodynamics. The BUB Seven is 21 ft (6.4 m) long and weighs 1,600 lb (730 kg).

5 ▸ FUXING HAO

This train is 686 ft (209.1 m) long and is operated by the China Railway Corporation. The CR400AF model (pictured left) is colloquially known as the Blue / Red Dolphin, due to its appearance. It can carry more than 550 passengers.

TOP 10

FASTEST WHEEL-AND-TRACK TRAINS

Have you traveled on any of the trains listed on these two pages? If so, then you have been on one of the 20 fastest trains in the world...

	TRAIN	COUNTRY	TOP SPEED* (MPH)	(KPH)
1	TGV POS	FRANCE	357.2	574.8
2	TGV ATLANTIQUE	FRANCE	320.2	515.3
3	CRH380BL	CHINA	302.8	487.3
4	CRH380A	CHINA	302	486.1
5	FUXING HAO	CHINA	261	420
6	AVE CLASS 103	SPAIN	250.8	403.7
7	CRH3	CHINA	244.9	394.2
8	ETR.400	ITALY	244.7	393.8
9	ZEFIRO 380	CHINA	236.1	380
10	ICE 3	GERMANY / NETHERLANDS	228.7	368

*DURING TESTS, NOT NECESSARILY DURING OPERATIONAL COMMERCIAL JOURNEYS.

SPAIN'S AVE CLASS 102 WHEEL-AND-TRACK TRAIN CAN TRAVEL AT
226.8 MPH (365 KPH)

TOP 10

FASTEST
MAGNETIC LEVITATION TRAINS

You may have heard the phrase "mag-lev," which is the shortened way of describing trains that literally float, or levitate, above the tracks by way of the power of magnetic forces...

	TRAIN	COUNTRY	TOP SPEED* (MPH)	(KPH)
1	L0 SERIES	JAPAN	374.7	603
2	MLX01	JAPAN	361	581
3	JNR ML500	JAPAN	321.2	517
4	SHANGHAI MAGLEV TRAIN	CHINA	311.3	501
5	TR-07	GERMANY	279.6	450
6	MLU002N	JAPAN	267.8	431
7	TR-06	GERMANY	256.6	413
8	MLU001	JAPAN	249.2	401
=	KOMET	GERMANY	249.2	401
10	HSST-04-1	JAPAN	191.4	308

*DURING TESTS, NOT NECESSARILY DURING OPERATIONAL COMMERCIAL JOURNEYS.

4 ▸ SHANGHAI MAGLEV TRAIN

This magnetic levitation train has been in operation in China since 2004. Construction took three years, and began in March 2001. It connects Shanghai Pudong International Airport and Longyang Road station in Shanghai, so that passengers can then take the metro to the heart of the city.

Air Canada

COMMERCIAL / PASSENGER AIRLINES
THAT VISIT THE MOST PLACES

If you've ever been on an airplane, statistically the chances are high that it was run and operated by one of these airlines. The data on this chart includes routes operated by their subsidiaries...

	AIRLINE	COUNTRY	TOTAL DESTINATIONS
1	AIR CANADA	CANADA	350
=	AMERICAN AIRLINES	USA	350
3	UNITED	USA	342
4	DELTA	USA	325
5	TURKISH AIRLINES	TURKEY	302
6	SKYWEST	USA	233
7	LUFTHANSA	GERMANY	220
8	CHINA EASTERN AIRLINES	CHINA	217
9	CHINA SOUTHERN AIRLINES	CHINA	208
10	RYANAIR	IRELAND	205

= 1 AIR CANADA

This airline's first flight, in its previous incarnation as Trans-Canada Air Lines, was on September 1, 1937. Air Canada employs more than 30,000 people. Its fleet is one of the youngest and most environmentally friendly collections of aircraft in the world.

HUGHES H-4 SPRUCE GOOSE

1

This colossal aircraft, made entirely of wood, was manufactured by the Hughes Aircraft Company, founded by American inventor and film director Howard Hughes. It is 218.7 ft (66.7 m) long and 79.3 ft (24.2 m) high at the tail-end, which exceeds the height of a seven-story building. It is the centerpiece display at Evergreen Aviation & Space Museum in McMinnville, Oregon, USA.

TOP 10

PLANES **WITH THE LARGEST WINGSPANS**

To give you a comparison to show just how huge these planes' wingspans are, consider that New York City's Statue of Liberty is 305.5 ft (93.1 m) tall...

	PLANE	COUNTRY	DEBUT FLIGHT	WINGSPAN (FT)	(M)
1	HUGHES H-4 SPRUCE GOOSE	USA	NOV 2, 1947	319.8	97.5
2	ANTONOV AN-225 MRIYA	RUSSIA (SOVIET UNION ERA)	NOV 21, 1988	290	88.4
3	AIRBUS A380-800	EUROPE (VARIOUS)	APR 21, 2005	261.8	79.8
4	ANTONOV AN-124	RUSSIA (SOVIET UNION ERA)	DEC 26, 1982	240.5	73.3
5	CONVAIR B-36J-III	USA	AUG 8, 1946	230	70.1
=	CONVAIR XC-99	USA	NOV 23, 1947	230	70.1
7	BOEING 747-8F	USA	FEB 8, 2010	224.7	68.5
8	LOCKHEED C-5B	USA	JUN 30, 1968	222.7	67.9
9	BOEING 747-400	USA	FEB 9, 1969	211.3	64.4
=	ANTONOV AN-22	RUSSIA (SOVIET UNION ERA)	FEB 27, 1965	211.3	64.4

7 › LOCKHEED F-104C STARFIGHTER

Howard C. Johnson broke the altitude world record in the Lockheed F-104C Starfighter. The US Air Force major achieved a height of 91,243 ft (27,811 m) at Edwards Air Force Base, located in Kern County, California.

TOP 10

FASTEST MANNED AIRCRAFT

For an aircraft to qualify for this Top 10 chart, it must be one that requires a human pilot. When studying the speeds, remember that a bullet travels at around 1,700 mph (2,735.9 kph)...

	AIRCRAFT	PILOT(S)	DATE	TOP SPEED (MPH)	(KPH)
1	NORTH AMERICAN X-15	WILLIAM J. "PETE" KNIGHT	OCT 3, 1967	4,519	7,273
2	LOCKHEED SR-71 BLACKBIRD	ELDON W. JOERSZ & GEORGE T. MORGAN	JUL 28, 1976	2,193.2	3,529.6
3	LOCKHEED YF-12A	ROBERT L. STEPHENS & DANIEL ANDRE	MAY 1, 1965	2,070.1	3,331.5
4	MIKOYAN-GUREVICH YE-166	GEORGI MOSOLOV	JUL 7, 1962	1,665.9	2,681
5	McDONNELL DOUGLAS F-4 PHANTOM II	ROBERT G. ROBERTSON	NOV 22, 1961	1,606.3	2,585.1
6	CONVAIR F-106 DELTA DART	JOSEPH ROGERS	DEC 15, 1959	1,525.9	2,455.7
7	LOCKHEED F-104C STARFIGHTER	W. W. IRWIN	MAY 16, 1958	1,404	2,259.5
8	McDONNELL F-101A VOODOO	ADRIAN DREW	DEC 12, 1957	1,207.6	1,943.5
9	FAIREY DELTA 2	PETER TWISS	MAR 10, 1956	1,139.2	1,833.31
10	F-100C SUPER SABRE	HORACE A. HANES	AUG 20, 1955	822.1	1,323

TOP 10

LARGEST **COMMERCIAL / PASSENGER AIRLINES BY FLEET**

Ever wondered which commercial airlines have the most planes? The Top 10 on this chart encompass companies from all over the world, including one that specializes in delivering mail...

	AIRLINE	COUNTRY	NUMBER OF CRAFT
1	AMERICAN AIRLINES	USA	1,536
2	DELTA	USA	860
3	UNITED	USA	749
4	SOUTHWEST	USA	718
5	FEDEX EXPRESS	USA	650
6	CHINA SOUTHERN AIRLINES	CHINA	552
7	CHINA EASTERN AIRLINES	CHINA	489
8	RYANAIR	IRELAND	426
9	AIR CHINA	CHINA	400
10	TURKISH AIRLINES	TURKEY	329

5 FEDEX EXPRESS

This company debuted its overnight delivery option in 1973, and 14 planes served 25 American cities. By 1976, they were delivering nearly 20,000 packages every day. Nowadays, that figure exceeds 13 million parcels.

TOP 10

FASTEST HELICOPTERS OF ALL TIME

Combining military, commercial, and experimental helicopters, these are the choppers that can tear through the clouds the fastest...

	HELICOPTER	COUNTRY	SPEED (MPH)	(KPH)
1	EUROCOPTER X³	FRANCE	303	487.6
=	SIKORSKY S-69	USA	303	487.6
3	SIKORSKY X2	USA	300	482.8
4	SIKORSKY S-97 RAIDER	USA	270	434.5
5	BELL AH-1Z VIPER	USA	255	410.4
6	MI-24LL PSV	RUSSIA	251.7	405.1
7	A-10	RUSSIA	228.9	368.4
8	MIL MI-24	RUSSIA	208	334.7
9	MIL MI-28 HAVOC	RUSSIA	201.3	324
10	KAMOV KA-50 BLACK SHARK	RUSSIA	195.7	315

10 KAMOV KA-50 BLACK SHARK

This military helicopter's debut flight in the 1980s led to its production the following decade. It is a single-seater aircraft. Variants include Kamov Ka-52K Katran, which has folding rotary blades and wings, and the Kamov Ka-52 Alligator, which is a two-seater.

1 NEW ZEALAND'S HUMANITY STAR

This satellite remained in orbit for just over two months. It reentered Earth's atmosphere on March 22, 2018. The carbon-fiber geodesic sphere, made with 76 reflective panels, was developed by aerospace manufacturer Rocket Lab. It could be seen by the naked eye anywhere on Earth. The makers of the Star describe its purpose as "a bright symbol and reminder to all on Earth about our fragile place in the Universe."

TOP 10

NATIONS'
MOST RECENT ORBITAL LAUNCHES

The launch of satellites and other technologies is more frequent than you might think, and these countries have sent up devices in the past few years...

	COUNTRY	SATELLITE	DATE LAUNCHED
1	NEW ZEALAND	HUMANITY STAR	JAN 21, 2018
2	ANGOLA	ANGOSAT 1	DEC 26, 2017
3	LATVIA	VENTA 1	JUN 23, 2017
=	SLOVAKIA	SKCUBE	JUN 23, 2017
5	BANGLADESH	BRAC ONNESHA	JUN 3, 2017
=	GHANA	GHANASAT-1	JUN 3, 2017
=	MONGOLIA	MAZAALAI	JUN 3, 2017
8	FINLAND	AALTO-2	APR 18, 2017
9	LAOS	LAOSAT-1	NOV 20, 2015
10	TURKMENISTAN	TÜRKMENÄLEM 52°E / MONACOSAT	APR 27, 2015

OUTER **SPACE** 07

FIRST **WOMEN IN SPACE**

When it comes to the history of space exploration, these 10 women played a vital part in humankind's journey to the stars...

	ASTRONAUT	COUNTRY	MISSION	LAUNCH DATE
1	VALENTINA TERESHKOVA	RUSSIA (SOVIET UNION ERA)	VOSTOK 6	JUN 16, 1963
2	SVETLANA SAVITSKAYA	RUSSIA (SOVIET UNION ERA)	SOYUZ T-5	JUL 19, 1982
3	SALLY RIDE	USA	STS-7	JUN 18, 1983
4	JUDITH RESNIK	USA	STS-41-D	AUG 30, 1984
5	KATHRYN D. SULLIVAN	USA	STS-41-G	OCT 5, 1984
6	ANNA LEE FISHER	USA	STS-51-A	NOV 8, 1984
7	MARGARET RHEA SEDDON	USA	STS-51-D	APR 12, 1985
8	SHANNON LUCID	USA	STS-51-G	JUN 17, 1985
9	BONNIE J. DUNBAR	USA	STS-61-A	OCT 30, 1985
10	MARY L. CLEAVE	USA	STS-61-B	NOV 26, 1985

1 VALENTINA TERESHKOVA

Born March 6, 1937, Valentina Tereshkova was 26 when she was chosen to become the first ever woman in space. Her many awards include Russia's Order of Friendship, "for outstanding contribution to the development and strengthening of international scientific, cultural, and social ties." In 2013, Tereshkova expressed her interest in being part of a one-way trip to Mars, should the opportunity arise.

| 1 | ANNE McCLAIN |

US Army major and astronaut Anne McClain studied in West Point, New York, USA, as well as in Bath and Bristol in the UK. In 2013 she became the youngest active NASA astronaut. Her first mission was an expedition to the International Space Station in November 2018 as part of Soyuz MS-11.

TOP 10

MOST RECENT **WOMEN IN SPACE**

Space missions take a long time to study, plan, and train for, something these 10 female astronauts are more than familiar with...

	ASTRONAUT	COUNTRY	MISSION	LAUNCH DATE
1	ANNE McCLAIN	USA	SOYUZ MS-11	NOV 15, 2018
2	SERENA M. AUÑÓN-CHANCELLOR	USA	SOYUZ MS-09	JUN 6, 2018
3	JEANETTE J. EPPS	USA	SOYUZ MS-09	APR 28, 2018
4	PEGGY WHITSON	USA	SOYUZ MS-03	NOV 17, 2016
5	KATHLEEN RUBINS	USA	SOYUZ MS-01	JUL 7, 2016
6	SAMANTHA CRISTOFORETTI	ITALY	SOYUZ TMA-15M	NOV 23, 2014
7	YELENA SEROVA	RUSSIA	SOYUZ TMA-14M	SEP 25, 2014
8	WANG YAPING	CHINA	SHENZHOU 10	JUN 11, 2013
9	KAREN L. NYBERG	USA	SOYUZ TMA-09M	MAY 28, 2013
10	SUNITA WILLIAMS	USA	SOYUZ TMA-05M	JUL 15, 2012

TOP 10

FIRST **MEN IN SPACE**

You may be familiar with the astronauts involved with the 1969 moon landing, but several years before touchdown, these were the first 10 humans in space...

	ASTRONAUT	COUNTRY	MISSION	LAUNCH DATE
1	YURI GAGARIN	RUSSIA (SOVIET UNION ERA)	VOSTOK 1	APR 12, 1961
2	ALAN SHEPARD	USA	MERCURY 3	MAY 5, 1961
3	GUS GRISSOM	USA	MERCURY 4	JUL 21, 1961
4	GHERMAN TITOV	RUSSIA (SOVIET UNION ERA)	VOSTOK 2	AUG 6, 1961
5	JOHN GLENN	USA	MERCURY 6	FEB 20,1962
6	SCOTT CARPENTER	USA	MERCURY 7	MAY 24, 1962
7	ANDRIAN NIKOLAYEV	RUSSIA (SOVIET UNION ERA)	VOSTOK 3	AUG 11, 1962
8	PAVEL POPOVICH	RUSSIA (SOVIET UNION ERA)	VOSTOK 4	AUG 12, 1962
9	WALTER SCHIRRA	USA	MERCURY 8	OCT 3, 1962
10	GORDON COOPER	USA	MERCURY 9	MAY 15, 1963

4 GHERMAN TITOV

The Vostok 2 mission was Gherman Titov's only expedition into space. At 25, he holds the record for being the youngest person in space. He was also the first person to film Earth from space, and his footage lasted 10 minutes. His many accolades include appearing on a Russian postage stamp.

= 9 JOSEPH M. ACABA

Born on May 17, 1967, in Inglewood, California, USA, astronaut Joseph M. Acaba's debut mission was the STS-119 trip to the ISS. The expedition launched March 15, 2009, and the crew returned to Earth on March 28, 2009.

ESA EMPLOYEES = 2,000

NASA EMPLOYEES = 18,000

TOP 10

MOST RECENT **MEN IN SPACE**

Space exploration is an ongoing, but very expensive, endeavor. These are the 10 male astronauts who have most recently traveled to the stars...

	ASTRONAUT	COUNTRY	MISSION	LAUNCH DATE
1	SERGEI PROKOPYEV	RUSSIA	SOYUZ MS-09	JUN 6, 2018
=	ALEXANDER GERST	GERMANY	SOYUZ MS-09	JUN 6, 2018
3	OLEG ARTEMYEV	RUSSIA	SOYUZ MS-08	MAR 21, 2018
=	ANDREW J. FEUSTEL	USA	SOYUZ MS-08	MAR 21, 2018
=	RICHARD R. ARNOLD	USA	SOYUZ MS-08	MAR 21, 2018
6	ANTON SHKAPLEROV	RUSSIA	SOYUZ MS-07	DEC 17, 2017
=	SCOTT D. TINGLE	USA	SOYUZ MS-07	DEC 17, 2017
=	NORISHIGE KANAI	JAPAN	SOYUZ MS-07	DEC 17, 2017
9	JOSEPH M. ACABA	USA	SOYUZ MS-06	SEP 12, 2017
=	ALEXANDER MISURKIN / MARK T. VANDE HEI	RUSSIA / USA	SOYUZ MS-06	SEP 12, 2017

TOP 10

NATIONS WITH
THE MOST SPACEWALKERS

Spacewalks are one type of EVA (extra-vehicular activity), where an astronaut needs to carry out a task outside of a space station or craft...

	NATION	TOTAL SPACEWALKERS
1	USA	130
2	RUSSIA (INCL. SOVIET UNION ERA)	65
3	FRANCE	4
4	CANADA	3
=	JAPAN	3
=	GERMANY	3
7	CHINA	2
8	SWEDEN	1
=	ITALY	1
=	SWITZERLAND / UK	1

2 ALEXEY LEONOV

On March 18, 1965, Russian cosmonaut Alexey Leonov became the first person to perform a spacewalk. His second (of two) career missions was the historic Apollo–Soyuz Test Project of July 1975, the first collaboration between the American and Russian space agencies.

3 ► EUGENE CERNAN

This NASA astronaut was the 11th person to walk on the moon. He experienced this as part of the Apollo 17 mission of December 1972. His prior missions were Apollo 10 (May 1969), and Gemini 9A, the latter mission (in the below chart) being Cernan's first.

TOP 10

FIRST SPACEWALKS

It was almost four years after the first man traveled into space that the first astronaut bravely stepped outside of his spacecraft...

	ASTRONAUT	COUNTRY	MISSION	SPACEWALK TIME (MINS)	DATE
1	ALEXEY LEONOV	RUSSIA (SOVIET UNION ERA)	VOSKHOD 2	12	MAR 18, 1965
2	EDWARD WHITE	USA	GEMINI 4	20	JUN 3, 1965
3	EUGENE CERNAN	USA	GEMINI 9A	127	JUN 5, 1966
4	MICHAEL COLLINS	USA	GEMINI 10	49	JUL 19, 1966
5	MICHAEL COLLINS	USA	GEMINI 10	39	JUL 20, 1966
6	RICHARD GORDON	USA	GEMINI 11	33	SEP 13, 1966
7	RICHARD GORDON	USA	GEMINI 11	128	SEP 14, 1966
8	BUZZ ALDRIN	USA	GEMINI 12	149	NOV 12, 1966
9	BUZZ ALDRIN	USA	GEMINI 12	126	NOV 13, 1966
10	BUZZ ALDRIN	USA	GEMINI 12	55	NOV 14, 1966

1 PEGGY WHITSON

Born in Iowa, USA, NASA astronaut Peggy Whitson has broken several records in space exploration. These include becoming the first female commander of the ISS in 2007, and, in 2017, becoming the first to command it twice. Her three NASA missions include 10 spacewalks.

TOP 10

MOST TIME SPENT IN SPACE (WOMEN – SINGLE SPACE FLIGHT)

This chart is dedicated to female astronauts who have completed the longest mission time in space during one there-and-back journey...

	ASTRONAUT	COUNTRY	TOTAL TIME IN SPACE (DAYS)
1	PEGGY WHITSON	USA	289.2
2	SAMANTHA CRISTOFORETTI	ITALY	199.6
3	SUNITA WILLIAMS	USA	195
4	SHANNON LUCID	USA	188.2
5	TRACY CALDWELL DYSON	USA	176
6	YELENA KONDAKOVA	RUSSIA	169.2
7	KAREN NYBERG	USA	166.3
8	SHANNON WALKER	USA	163.3
9	SUSAN HELMS	USA	163
10	CATHERINE COLEMAN	USA	159.3

TOP 10

MOST TIME **SPENT IN SPACE** **(MEN – SINGLE SPACE FLIGHT)**

As an accompanying Top 10 to the chart opposite, here are the male astronauts who have spent the longest time in space during a single mission...

	ASTRONAUT	COUNTRY	TOTAL TIME IN SPACE (DAYS)
1	VALERI POLYAKOV	RUSSIA	437.75
2	SERGEI AVDEYEV	RUSSIA	379.6
3	VLADIMIR TITOV	RUSSIA*	365
=	MUSA MANAROV	RUSSIA*	365
5	SCOTT KELLY	USA	340.4
=	MIKHAIL KORNIENKO	RUSSIA	340.4
7	YURY ROMANENKO	RUSSIA*	326.5
8	SERGEI KRIKALEV	RUSSIA*	311.8
9	LEONID KIZIM	RUSSIA*	237
=	VLADIMIR SOLOVYOV / OLEG ATKOV	RUSSIA*	237

*INCLUDES MISSION(S) DURING SOVIET UNION ERA.

1 ▶ VALERI POLYAKOV

Russian cosmonaut Valeri Polyakov may have been part of only two space missions, but check out the data in the above chart. This shows the length of his second stay on the Mir space station. His first lasted more than 240 days between August 1988 and April 1989.

2 — SUNITA WILLIAMS

NASA's Sunita Williams was born September 19, 1965. Her seven EVAs total more than 50 hours. She made history on April 16, 2007, by becoming the first person to run a marathon in space.

TOP 10

MOST TIME **SPENT IN SPACE** (WOMEN – MULTIPLE MISSIONS)

For some astronauts, their careers will involve more than one trip off-planet, and these spacewomen have clocked up more mission time than any other women...

	ASTRONAUT	COUNTRY	TOTAL FLIGHTS	TOTAL TIME IN SPACE (DAYS)
1	PEGGY WHITSON	USA	3	665.9
2	SUNITA WILLIAMS	USA	2	321.7
3	SHANNON LUCID	USA	5	223.13
4	SUSAN HELMS	USA	5	210.9
5	TRACY CALDWELL DYSON	USA	2	188.8
6	CATHERINE COLEMAN	USA	3	180.2
7	KAREN NYBERG	USA	2	180
8	YELENA KONDAKOVA	RUSSIA	2	178.5
9	SANDRA MAGNUS	USA	3	157.3
10	NICOLE P. STOTT	USA	2	103.2

TOTAL TIME IN SPACE (MULTIPLE MISSIONS)

WOMEN = 2,409.63 DAYS

MEN = 7,006.6 DAYS

MOST TIME **SPENT IN SPACE (MEN – MULTIPLE MISSIONS)**

TOP 10

To travel into space just once is a dream for some trainee astronauts, but these spacemen have been up there on as many as six different occasions...

	ASTRONAUT	COUNTRY	TOTAL FLIGHTS	TOTAL TIME IN SPACE (DAYS)
1	GENNADY PADALKA	RUSSIA	5	879.5
2	YURI MALENCHENKO	RUSSIA	6	827.4
3	SERGEI KRIKALEV	RUSSIA*	6	803.4
4	ALEKSANDR KALERI	RUSSIA	5	769.3
5	SERGEI AVDEYEV	RUSSIA*	3	747.6
6	VALERIY POLYAKOV	RUSSIA*	2	678.7
7	ANATOLY SOLOVYEV	RUSSIA*	5	651.1
8	VIKTOR AFANASYEV	RUSSIA*	4	555.8
9	YURY USACHEV	RUSSIA	4	552.8
10	MUSA MANAROV	RUSSIA	2	541

*INCLUDES MISSION(S) DURING SOVIET UNION ERA.

2 YURI MALENCHENKO

Cosmonaut Yuri Malenchenko's first space mission was 1994's Soyuz TM-19. His astronaut career saw him spend time on board both the ISS and Mir space station. Prior to retiring, he performed a total of six EVAs that lasted almost 35 hours. He was also a trained fighter pilot for the Russian air force.

1 SERGEI AVDEYEV

Russian cosmonaut Sergei Avdeyev spent a total of 747 days, 14 hours and 14 minutes in space during his missions between 1992 and 1999, all on board the Mir space station. Avdeyev also achieved 10 spacewalks totaling more than 42 hours.

TOP 10

NATIONS WITH **LONGEST TOTAL TIME IN SPACE**

Top 10 charts on previous pages focused on individuals, but this one examines the amount of time countries' astronauts have spent in space...

	COUNTRY	TOTAL HUMAN DAYS IN SPACE
1	RUSSIA (INCL. SOVIET UNION ERA)	27,158+
2	USA	19,627+
3	JAPAN	1,294+
4	ITALY	765.9
5	GERMANY	658.97
6	FRANCE	628.92
7	CANADA	506.14
8	NETHERLANDS	210.69
9	BELGIUM	207.65
10	UK	193.81

TOP 10

FIRST LIVING **ORGANISMS IN SPACE**

Decades before humankind successfully traveled into space, various other organisms were sent up in rockets to see how they were affected by space...

	ORGANISM	ROCKET	DATE
1	FRUIT FLIES	V2	FEB 20, 1947
2	MOSS	V2	VARIOUS, 1947
3	RHESUS MONKEY (ALBERT II)	V2	JUN 14, 1949
4	MOUSE	V2	AUG 31, 1950
5	DOG (LAIKA)	SPUTNIK 2	NOV 3, 1957
6	SQUIRREL MONKEY (GORDO)	JUPITER IRBM AM-13	DEC 13, 1958
7	RABBIT (MARFUSHA)	R2	JUL 2, 1959
7	CHIMPANZEE (HAM)	MERCURY-REDSTONE 2	JAN 31, 1961
9	GUINEA PIGS, FROGS, MICE	VOSTOK-3A	MAR 1961
10	TORTOISE	ZOND 5	SEP 18, 1968

7 ▸ RABBIT (MARFUSHA)

Marfusha was the first rabbit ever to travel into space. Her mission allies were two dogs called Snezhinka and Otvazhnaya. All three animals survived the trip and were even honored on a special postage stamp.

173

TOP 10

MOST
ISS VISITS BY NATION

The biggest and most expensive space construction ever, the International Space Station is proof that nations around the world can work together...

	NATION	INDIVIDUAL(S)	ISS CREW MEMBER(S)
1	USA	143	51
2	RUSSIA	46	39
3	JAPAN	8	6
4	CANADA	7	2
5	ITALY	5	3
6	GERMANY	3	3
=	FRANCE	4	2
8	BELGIUM	1	1
=	NETHERLANDS	1	1
=	UK	1	1

1   SPACE SHUTTLE DISCOVERY

Discovery's debut mission was the STS-41-D, on August 30, 1984. Its final flight was the return-to-Earth journey from the STS-133 mission on March 9, 2011. During its active years, *Discovery* traveled into space and back 39 times, totaling more than a year, and transporting 252 crew members.

FIRST **ISS EXPEDITIONS**

It's coming up to the 20th anniversary of the first ever International Space Station expedition, and 10 missions were carried out in the ISS's first five years...

	MISSION	LAUNCH DATE	MISSION CONCLUDED
1	EXPEDITION 1	NOV 2, 2000	MAR 18, 2001
2	EXPEDITION 2	MAR 10, 2001	AUG 20, 2001
3	EXPEDITION 3	AUG 12, 2001	DEC 15, 2001
4	EXPEDITION 4	DEC 7, 2001	JUN 15, 2002
5	EXPEDITION 5	JUN 7, 2002	DEC 2, 2002
6	EXPEDITION 6	NOV 25, 2002	MAY 3, 2003
7	EXPEDITION 7	APR 28, 2003	OCT 27, 2003
8	EXPEDITION 8	OCT 20, 2003	APR 29, 2004
9	EXPEDITION 9	APR 21, 2004	OCT 23, 2004
10	EXPEDITION 10	OCT 16, 2004	APR 24, 2005

1 ISS EXPEDITION I CREW: WILLIAM SHEPHERD, YURI GIDZENKO, SERGEI K. KRIKALEV

All the members of the inaugural ISS expedition had prior experience of being in space. It was Shepherd's fourth mission, Gidzenko's second, and Krikalev's fifth. The total mission time was 22 minutes shy of 141 days. Since November 2, 2000, the ISS has been continuously occupied by astronauts.

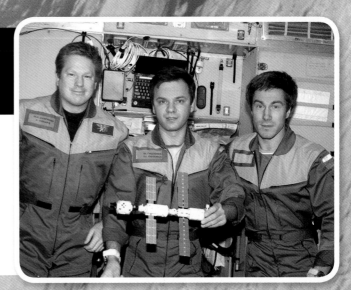

175

10 ▸ CSA

The first male Canadian in space was Marc Garneau on October 5, 1984, on mission STS-41-G. The first female Canadian, Roberta Bondar, followed nearly eight years later, on January 22, 1992. Bondar was Payload Specialist 1 for the STS-42 mission.

TOP 10

LONGEST-RUNNING
OPERATIONAL SPACE AGENCIES

Many space agencies have gone through different iterations over the years, but these are the longest-running ones in their current form...

	AGENCY	COUNTRY	YEAR FOUNDED
1	INTA (INSTITUTO NACIONAL DE TÉCNICA AEROESPACIAL)	SPAIN	1942
2	NASA (NATIONAL AERONAUTICS AND SPACE ADMINISTRATION)	USA	1958
3	CNES (CENTRE NATIONAL D'ÉTUDES SPATIALES)	FRANCE	1961
=	SUPARCO (SPACE AND UPPER ATMOSPHERE RESEARCH COMMISSION)	PAKISTAN	1961
5	DLR (GERMAN AEROSPACE CENTER)	GERMANY	1969
=	ISRO (INDIAN SPACE RESEARCH ORGANISATION)	INDIA	1969
7	SNSB (SWEDISH NATIONAL SPACE BOARD)	SWEDEN	1972
8	ESA (EUROPEAN SPACE AGENCY)	(EUROPEAN SYNDICATION)	1975
9	ASI (ITALIAN SPACE AGENCY)	ITALY	1988
10	CSA (CANADIAN SPACE AGENCY)	CANADA	1989
	KARI (KOREA AEROSPACE RESEARCH INSTITUTE)	SOUTH KOREA	1989*

*BEGAN SEVEN MONTHS LATER THAN THE CSA.

CSA ASC

OTHER **SPACE AGENCY ORIGINS**

Here is when five other space agencies began or took over from former versions of their nations' agencies...

AGENCY	COUNTRY	YEAR FOUNDED
CONAE (COMISIÓN NACIONAL DE ACTIVIDADES ESPACIALES)	ARGENTINA	1991
ROSCOSMOS (RUSSIAN FEDERAL SPACE AGENCY)	RUSSIA	1992
SSAU (STATE SPACE AGENCY OF UKRAINE)	UKRAINE	1992
CNSA (CHINA NATIONAL SPACE ADMINISTRATION)	CHINA	1993
JAXA (JAPAN AEROSPACE EXPLORATION AGENCY)	JAPAN	2003

TOP 10

MOST ASTRONAUTS **LAUNCHED BY A NATION**

How many people would you guess have been sent into space over the past 50+ years? The results may be fewer than you think...

	COUNTRY	TOTAL PEOPLE SENT INTO SPACE
1	USA	338
2	RUSSIA (INCL. SOVIET UNION ERA)	122
3	CHINA	11
=	GERMANY	11
=	JAPAN	11
6	FRANCE	10
7	CANADA	9
8	ITALY	7
9	BELGIUM / NETHERLANDS	2
=	BULGARIA / UK	2

1 ▶ OLYMPUS MONS

This natural formation is almost triple the height of Earth's Mount Everest. At more than 370 miles (595.5 km) wide, this shield volcano is comparable to the size of the USA's state of Arizona.

TOP 10

TALLEST **PLANET-BASED MOUNTAINS**

Of all the giant mountains that exist in our solar system, these are the ones that easily tower over all others (that we know of to date)...

	NAME	LOCATION	TALLEST POINT (MI)	(KM)
1	OLYMPUS MONS	MARS	16.2	26
2	ARSIA MONS	MARS	12.4	20
3	ASCRAEUS MONS	MARS	11.3	18.2
4	ELYSIUM MONS	MARS	9.9	16
5	HALEAKALA	EARTH	5.7	9.1
6	MAUNA KEA	EARTH	5.53	8.9
7	MOUNT EVEREST	EARTH	5.5	8.85
8	K2	EARTH	5.34	8.6
9	KANGCHENJUNGA	EARTH	5.33	8.59
10	LHOTSE	EARTH	5.29	8.52

TOP 10

LARGEST **IMPACT CRATERS**

When a celestial object strikes another, it leaves a deep impression in its surface. As the measurements on this chart show, these are far from small bumps...

	CRATER	CELESTIAL BODY	(WIDEST) DIAMETER (MI)	(KM)
1	UTOPIA	MARS	2,050.6	3,300
2	SOUTH POLE-AITKEN BASIN	THE MOON	1,553.4	2,500
3	HELLAS	MARS	1,429.2	2,300
4	CALORIS	MERCURY	963.1	1,550
5	IMBRIUM	THE MOON	711.5	1,145
6	SPUTNIK PLANITIA	PLUTO	683.5	1,100
7	REMBRANDT	MERCURY	444.3	715
8	TURGIS	IAPETUS	360.4	580
9	RHEASILVIA	VESTA	313.8	505
10	ENGELIER	IAPETUS	313.2	504

UTOPIA IS AS WIDE AS **68,041 NFL FOOTBALL FIELDS**

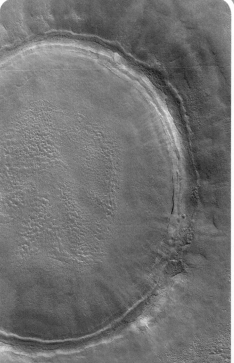

1 ▶ UTOPIA

This, the largest known impact crater, is home to the plains of Utopia Planitia. NASA reported subterranean ice had been found in Utopia Planitia on November 22, 2016. The groundbreaking discovery was recorded by SHARAD (the Shallow Radar device) on NASA's Mars Reconnaissance Orbiter.

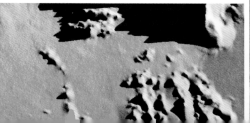

1 HAUMEA

No recognized astronomer(s) is registered as the official discoverer of Haumea, but the location of its finding is recorded as March 7, 2003, at the Sierra Nevada Observatory in Spain. It has two moons, named Hi'iaka and Namaka, that were discovered in January and June, respectively, of 2005.

TOP 10

COLDEST **PLANETS / DWARF PLANETS**

Where is the coldest place on Earth you've visited? Find out the lowest temperature on record for that town, and then compare it to these...

	NAME	TYPE	COLDEST EFFECTIVE TEMPERATURE RECORDED	
			(°F)	(°C)
1	HAUMEA	DWARF PLANET	-401.8	-241
2	MAKEMAKE	DWARF PLANET	-398.2	-239
3	PLUTO	DWARF PLANET	-387	-233
4	ERIS	DWARF PLANET	-383.8	-231
5	URANUS	PLANET	-357	-216
6	NEPTUNE	PLANET	-353	-214
7	SATURN	PLANET	-288	-178
8	JUPITER	PLANET	-234	-148
9	MARS	PLANET	-225	-143
10	CERES	DWARF PLANET	-157	-105

HOTTEST **PLANETS / DWARF PLANETS**

When you consider that the boiling point of water is 212ºF (100ºC), the vast range of these planetary temperatures is mind-boggling...

	NAME	TYPE	HOTTEST EFFECTIVE TEMPERATURE RECORDED	
			(ºF)	(ºC)
1	VENUS	PLANET	863.6	462
2	MERCURY	PLANET	800.6	427
3	EARTH	PLANET	136.4	58
4	MARS	PLANET	70	20
5	CERES	DWARF PLANET	-157	-105
6	JUPITER	PLANET	-234	-148
7	SATURN	PLANET	-288	-178
8	NEPTUNE	PLANET	-353	-214
9	URANUS	PLANET	-357	-216
10	PLUTO	DWARF PLANET	-369	-223

5 CERES

Previously referred to as an asteroid, Ceres was reclassified a dwarf planet in 2006. Scientists have discovered that Ceres's atmosphere contains water vapor. This dwarf planet does not have any rings or moons.

BIGGEST **MASSES IN OUR SOLAR SYSTEM**

The data in this chart is presented in pounds and kilograms, so you can compare the weights of these objects to others in this book. As a quick reference, our sun is 4.3 nonillion (30 zeroes) lb, and Earth is 13 septillion (24 zeroes) lb...

	NAME	TYPE	WEIGHT (LB)	(KG)
1	THE SUN	STAR	4,385,214,857,119,400,000,000,000,000,000	1,989,100,000,000,000,000,000,000,000,000
2	JUPITER	PLANET	4,184,660,337,117,234,000,000,000,000	1,898,130,000,000,000,000,000,000,000
3	SATURN	PLANET	1,252,928,923,798,754,200,000,000,000	568,319,000,000,000,000,000,000,000
4	NEPTUNE	PLANET	225,775,402,698,538,000,000,000,000	102,410,000,000,000,000,000,000,000
5	URANUS	PLANET	191,383,951,185,244,540,000,000,000	86,810,300,000,000,000,000,000,000
6	EARTH	PLANET	13,166,425,175,687,742,000,000,000	5,972,190,000,000,000,000,000,000
7	VENUS	PLANET	10,730,603,779,539,576,000,000,000	4,867,320,000,000,000,000,000,000
8	MARS	PLANET	1,414,690,904,050,707,400,000,000	641,693,000,000,000,000,000,000
9	MERCURY	PLANET	727,754,745,946,667,200,000,000	330,104,000,000,000,000,000,000
0	GANYMEDE	MOON	326,693,870,251,330,477,251,333.6	148,185,846,875,052,000,000,000

1 ▶ THE SUN

The sun is a yellow dwarf star. The position and orbit of everything in our solar system is caused by the sun's gravitational field. Its mass is comprised of 70.6 percent hydrogen and 27.4 percent helium. Scientists have discovered billions of stars just like our sun in the known universe.

64.3 MILLION MOONS COULD FIT INSIDE **THE SUN**

1.3 MILLION EARTHS COULD FIT INSIDE **THE SUN**

CELESTIAL BODIES
WITH THE LARGEST VOLUME

Although our planet makes it onto this Top 10, look carefully at its volume compared to the gigantic measurements of the five entries above it...

	NAME	TYPE	VOLUME (CUBIC MI)	(CUBIC KM)
1	THE SUN	STAR	338,102,469,632,763,000	1,409,272,569,059,860,000
2	JUPITER	PLANET	343,382,767,518,322	1,431,281,810,739,360
3	SATURN	PLANET	198,439,019,647,006	827,129,915,150,897
4	URANUS	PLANET	16,394,283,780,641	68,334,355,695,584
5	NEPTUNE	PLANET	15,000,714,125,712	62,525,703,987,421
6	EARTH	PLANET	259,875,159,532	1,083,206,916,846
7	VENUS	PLANET	222,738,686,740	928,415,345,893
8	MARS	PLANET	39,133,515,914	163,115,609,799
9	GANYMEDE	MOON	18,306,424,766	76,304,506,998
10	TITAN	MOON	17,152,879,380	71,496,320,086

MERCURY

Just missing out on a place in the above chart, Mercury has a volume of 14,593,223,446 cubic miles (60,827,208,742 cubic km). It is the planet closest to the sun, but it does not have the hottest surface temperature. It travels once around the sun every 88 Earth days.

2 ▶ MAKEMAKE

A relatively modern find, this dwarf planet was discovered on March 31, 2005, by a trio of American astronomers, Michael E. Brown, Chad Trujillo, and David L. Rabinowitz, at the Palomar Observatory in San Diego, California. At this point in time, scientists know very little about the structure of Makemake.

TOP 10

SMALLEST **PLANETS / DWARF PLANETS IN OUR SOLAR SYSTEM**

Our neighboring dwarf planets are a fascinating and eclectic collection of celestial bodies that are a lot smaller than Mercury, our tiniest planet...

	NAME	TYPE	EQUATORIAL RADIUS (MI)	(KM)
1	CERES	DWARF PLANET	295.9	476.2
2	MAKEMAKE	DWARF PLANET	445.523	717
3	HAUMEA	DWARF PLANET	471.621 TO 608.944*	759 TO 980*
4	PLUTO	DWARF PLANET	715.2	1,151
5	ERIS	DWARF PLANET	722.7	1,163
6	MERCURY	PLANET	1,516	2,439.7
7	MARS	PLANET	2,106.1	3,389.5
8	VENUS	PLANET	3,760.4	6,051.8
9	EARTH	PLANET	3,958.75	6,371
10	NEPTUNE	PLANET	15,299.4	24,622

*DUE TO ITS ELONGATED SHAPE.

PLANETS / DWARF PLANETS
WITH THE GREATEST ORBIT

So that you can see the best comparison of the orbital distances between the planets and dwarf planets, we've included the next three "off-the-chart" entries...

	NAME	TYPE	ORBIT SIZE AROUND THE SUN (MI)	(KM)
1	ERIS	DWARF PLANET	6,325,635,074	10,180,122,852
2	MAKEMAKE	DWARF PLANET	4,214,975,546	6,783,345,606
3	HAUMEA	DWARF PLANET	3,996,666,630	6,432,011,461
4	PLUTO	DWARF PLANET	3,670,092,055	5,906,440,628
5	NEPTUNE	PLANET	2,795,173,960	4,498,396,441
6	URANUS	PLANET	1,783,744,300	2,870,658,186
7	SATURN	PLANET	886,489,415	1,426,666,422
8	JUPITER	PLANET	483,638,564	778,340,821
9	CERES	DWARF PLANET	257,055,204	413,690,250
10	MARS	PLANET	141,637,725	227,943,824
EXTRA	EARTH	PLANET	92,956,050	149,598,262
	VENUS	PLANET	67,238,251	108,209,475
	MERCURY	PLANET	35,983,125	57,909,227

1 ERIS

This dwarf planet was discovered on October 21, 2003, by the same trio of American astronomers mentioned in the Makemake info box, and at the same San Diego observatory. It has a small moon named Dysnomia.

BIGGEST **MOONS**

Don't go thinking that because something is classified as a moon it means it's small—Jupiter's Ganymede is almost half the size of Mars...

	MOON	ORBITS	VOLUME (CUBIC MI)	(CUBIC KM)
1	GANYMEDE	JUPITER	18,306,424,766	76,304,506,998
2	TITAN	SATURN	17,152,879,380	71,496,320,086
3	CALLISTO	JUPITER	14,071,981,516	58,654,577,603
4	IO	JUPITER	6,074,366,707	25,319,064,907
5	THE MOON	EARTH	5,271,283,736	21,971,669,064
6	EUROPA	JUPITER	3,821,058,818	15,926,867,918
7	TRITON	NEPTUNE	2,491,268,118	10,384,058,491
8	TITANIA	URANUS	493,409,858	2,056,622,001
9	RHEA	SATURN	448,676,716	1,870,166,133
10	OBERON	URANUS	443,588,799	1,848,958,769

1 GANYMEDE

The biggest moon in our solar system is 2.4 times smaller than our planet, and is approximately three quarters the size of Mars. It was discovered on January 7, 1610, by groundbreaking Italian astronomer, scientist, and philosopher, Galileo Galilei.

TOP 10

TALLEST **MOON-BASED MOUNTAINS**

If you thought that gigantic mountains were only found on planets and dwarf planets, check out the miles-high formations on these moons...

	NAME / DESCRIPTION	LOCATION	TALLEST POINT (MI)	(KM)
1	EQUATORIAL RIDGE	IAPETUS	12.4	20
2	SOUTH BOÖSAULE	IO	11.3	18.2
3	EUBOEA MONTES	IO	8.3	13.4
4	EASTERN IONIAN MONS	IO	7.9	12.7
5	UNNAMED	OBERON	6.8	11
6	HERSCHEL	MIMAS	4.3	7
7	MONS HUYGENS	THE MOON	3.4	5.5
8	MONS HADLEY	THE MOON	2.6	4.2
9	MITHRIM MONTES	TITAN	2.1	3.3
10	UNNAMED	IO	1.6	2.5

RHEASILVIA

Rheasilvia is the name of a surface feature on Vesta, and its central peak measures 15.5 miles (25 km) in height. However, it doesn't qualify for the above chart because its home of Vesta isn't a moon—it is classified as a protoplanet. It has a minor-planet designation of "4 Vesta."

TOP 10

NEXT
LUNAR & SOLAR ECLIPSES

If you're a fan of tracking and observing eclipses, here are the need-to-know dates for your calendar for the next two years...

	TIME (UTC)	DATE	TYPE OF ECLIPSE
1	23:34	JAN 5, 2019	SOLAR (PARTIAL)
2	02:36	JAN 20, 2019	LUNAR (TOTAL)
3	16:55	JUL 2, 2019	SOLAR (TOTAL)
4	18:43	JUL 16, 2019	LUNAR (PARTIAL)
5	02:29	DEC 26, 2019	SOLAR (ANNULAR)
6	17:07	JAN 10, 2020	LUNAR (PENUMBRAL)
7	17:45	JUN 5, 2020	LUNAR (PENUMBRAL)
8	03:45	JUN 21, 2020	SOLAR (ANNULAR)
9	03:07	JUL 5, 2020	LUNAR (PENUMBRAL)
10	07:32	NOV 30, 2020	LUNAR (PENUMBRAL)

OREGON, USA
(AUG 21, 2017)

Tens of thousands of people flocked to Oregon, USA, to witness the 2017 total solar eclipse hit land. It plunged the area into darkness for almost two full minutes. It was the first total eclipse to be visible in the USA since 1979. It had been 99 years since an eclipse had crossed the entire USA, coast to coast.

10 ▸ CHARLES DUKE

NASA astronaut Charles Duke may have been the 10th person on the moon, but he is in the number one position in terms of age. Born October 3, 1935, at the age of 37 Duke was the youngest person to walk on the moon's surface. His many awards include the NASA Distinguished Service Medal.

TOP 10

FIRST HUMANS
TO WALK ON THE MOON

Only 12 people (all men) have walked on the surface of the moon. Do you think that humankind will ever set foot on the moon's surface again?

	ASTRONAUT	COUNTRY	MISSION	DATE WALKED ON THE MOON
1	NEIL ARMSTRONG	USA	APOLLO 11	JUL 21, 1969
2	BUZZ ALDRIN	USA	APOLLO 11	JUL 21, 1969
3	PETE CONRAD	USA	APOLLO 12	NOV 19–20, 1969
4	ALAN BEAN	USA	APOLLO 12	NOV 19–20, 1969
5	ALAN SHEPARD	USA	APOLLO 14	FEB 5–6, 1971
6	EDGAR MITCHELL	USA	APOLLO 14	FEB 5–6, 1971
7	DAVID SCOTT	USA	APOLLO 15	JUL 31–AUG 2, 1971
8	JAMES IRWIN	USA	APOLLO 15	JUL 31–AUG 2, 1971
9	JOHN W. YOUNG	USA	APOLLO 16	APR 21–23, 1972
10	CHARLES DUKE	USA	APOLLO 16	APR 21–23, 1972

VIDEO GAMES 08

PLATFORM **WARS**

8 | POKÉMON SUN / MOON

This game debuted on the Nintendo 3DS on November 18, 2016, more than two decades after the very first title in the franchise, *Pokémon Red / Blue / Green*, was released. On November 30, 2016, the complete soundtrack, *Pokémon Sun & Pokémon Moon: Super Music Collection*, was made available.

TOP 10

BIGGEST
CONSOLE GAMES SINCE 2010

Tallying up the sales of every console game released between 2010 and 2019, these are the bestsellers that shifted more copies than the rest...

	GAME	GENRE	RELEASED	PLATFORM	UNIT SALES (MILLIONS)
1	KINECT ADVENTURES!	PARTY	2010	XBOX 360	22.02
2	GRAND THEFT AUTO V	ACTION	2013	PS3	21.49
3	GRAND THEFT AUTO V	ACTION	2014	PS4	16.1
4	POKÉMON BLACK / WHITE	RPG	2010	DS	15.18
5	CALL OF DUTY: BLACK OPS 3	SHOOTER	2015	PS4	14.93
6	CALL OF DUTY: MODERN WARFARE 3	SHOOTER	2011	XBOX 360	14.81
7	CALL OF DUTY: BLACK OPS	SHOOTER	2010	XBOX 360	14.74
8	POKÉMON SUN / MOON	RPG	2016	3DS	14.69
9	MARIO KART 7	RACING	2011	3DS	14.11
10	CALL OF DUTY: BLACK OPS II	SHOOTER	2012	PS3	13.85

TOP 10

BIGGEST
CONSOLE GAMES OF ALL TIME

Looking at every single game ever released for a console, including handheld ones, these 10 games are the most popular, worldwide...

	GAME	GENRE	RELEASED	PLATFORM	UNIT SALES (MILLIONS)
1	WII SPORTS	SPORTS	2006	WII	82.62
2	SUPER MARIO BROS.	PLATFORM	1985	NES	40.24
3	MARIO KART WII	RACING	2008	WII	35.72
4	WII SPORTS RESORT	SPORTS	2009	WII	32.86
5	POKÉMON RED / BLUE / GREEN	RPG	1996	GAME BOY	31.37
6	TETRIS	PUZZLE	1989	GAME BOY	30.26
7	NEW SUPER MARIO BROS.	PLATFORM	2006	DS	29.85
8	WII PLAY	PARTY	2006	WII	28.92
9	NEW SUPER MARIO BROS. WII	PLATFORM	2009	WII	28.46
10	DUCK HUNT	SHOOTER	1984	NES	28.31

3 ▶ MARIO KART WII

The sixth game released in the *Mario Kart* series comes with a Wii Wheel. The accessory holds the Wii controller to enhance the car-racing style of game play. *Mario Kart 8 Deluxe* was released for Nintendo's latest console, the Switch, on April 28, 2017. The same year saw *Mario Kart Arcade GP VR* released into arcades in Japan.

PLATFORM **WARS**

4 ▶ SUPER NINTENDO ENTERTAINMENT SYSTEM

Released 27 years after the original 1990 Super Nintendo Entertainment System, the Super NES Classic Edition (pictured right) debuted on September 29, 2017. Although the unit is much smaller, its controllers are an exact replica of the original system's. Twenty-one games come pre-installed in the Classic Edition's hard drive. These include the brand-new *Star Fox 2*, a sequel to the original 1993 *Star Fox* that was developed but never completed or released.

TOP 10

LONGEST-RUNNING **PLATFORMS**

How many gaming consoles have you played on? Although it can feel like a brand-new system is released every few years, some stuck around for more than a decade...

	PLATFORM	MADE BY	YEARS IN PRODUCTION	TOTAL YEARS
1	NINTENDO ENTERTAINMENT SYSTEM	NINTENDO	1983–2003	20
2	NINTENDO DS / DS LITE / 3DS / 3DS XL	NINTENDO	2004–PRESENT	15
3	GAME BOY / GAME BOY COLOR	NINTENDO	1989–2003	14
4	SUPER NINTENDO ENTERTAINMENT SYSTEM	NINTENDO	1990–2003	13
=	PLAYSTATION	SONY	1994–2006	12
6	PLAYSTATION 2	SONY	2000–12	12
=	PLAYSTATION 3	SONY	2006–17	11
8	XBOX 360	MICROSOFT	2005–16	11
9	PLAYSTATION PORTABLE	SONY	2004–14	10
10	WII	NINTENDO	2006–13	7

TOP 10

BIGGEST-SELLING
GAMING PLATFORMS OF ALL TIME

Looking at sales data for every gaming platform, from Nintendo's latest, the Switch, all the way back to the first consoles ever made, these are the 10 bestsellers...

	PLATFORM	MADE BY	RELEASED	UNIT SALES (MILLIONS)
1	PLAYSTATION 2	SONY	2000	157.68
2	NINTENDO DS / DS LITE / DSI	NINTENDO	2004	154.9
3	GAME BOY / GAME BOY COLOR	NINTENDO	1989 / 1998	118.69
4	PLAYSTATION	SONY	1994	104.25
5	WII	NINTENDO	2006	101.64
6	PLAYSTATION 3	SONY	2006	86.9
7	XBOX 360	MICROSOFT	2005	85.8
8	GAME BOY ADVANCE	NINTENDO	2001	81.51
9	PLAYSTATION PORTABLE	SONY	2004	80.82
10	NINTENDO 3DS / 3DSI XL	NINTENDO	2011	68.15

3 ▶ GAME BOY / GAME BOY COLOR

The original handheld Nintendo game system was first released in Japan on April 21, 1989, to mark the centenary of the company. The Game Boy Color, as its name suggests, updated the Game Boy's "four shades of gray / green" screen to now handle color graphics. It was released October 21, 1998, but the Game Boy remained in production through to 2003.

TOP 10

BIGGEST-SELLING
GAMES OF THE 21ST CENTURY

Since January 1, 2001, thousands of games have been released, but these 10 titles prove that, whatever the platform or genre, Nintendo remains the market leader...

	GAME	GENRE	RELEASED	PLATFORM	UNIT SALES (MILLIONS)
1	WII SPORTS	SPORTS	2006	WII	82.62
2	MARIO KART WII	RACING	2008	WII	35.72
3	WII SPORTS RESORT	SPORTS	2009	WII	32.86
4	NEW SUPER MARIO BROS.	PLATFORM	2006	DS	29.85
5	WII PLAY	PARTY	2006	WII	28.92
6	NEW SUPER MARIO BROS. WII	PLATFORM	2009	WII	28.46
7	NINTENDOGS	SIMULATION	2005	DS	24.68
8	MARIO KART DS	RACING	2005	DS	23.26
9	WII FIT	SPORTS	2007	WII	22.7
10	KINECT ADVENTURES!	PARTY	2010	XBOX 360	22.02

6 NEW SUPER MARIO BROS. WII

This, the 15th *Super Mario* title, marked the first time four players could play a *Mario* title simultaneously. Imagine Games Network awarded the game 2009 Wii Game of the Year. In Japan, two years after this game's release, an arcade version called *New Super Mario Bros. Wii Coin World* was finished.

2 WII

The Wii was Nintendo's fifth home video game console. It followed 1983's NES (Nintendo Entertainment System), which began its life in Japan as the Famicom (Family Computer); 1990's Super NES; 1996's N64; and 2001's GameCube. Early versions of the Wii could play all GameCube game disks.

TOP 10

BIGGEST-SELLING
PLATFORMS OF THE 21ST CENTURY

When it comes to the sales of gaming platforms this century, Nintendo has a lot of entries in this chart, but so do fellow manufacturers Sony and Microsoft...

	PLATFORM	MADE BY	RELEASED	UNIT SALES (MILLIONS)
1	NINTENDO DS	NINTENDO	2004	154.9
2	WII	NINTENDO	2006	101.64
3	PLAYSTATION 3	SONY	2006	86.9
4	XBOX 360	MICROSOFT	2005	85.8
5	GAME BOY ADVANCE	NINTENDO	2001	81.51
6	PLAYSTATION PORTABLE	SONY	2004	80.82
7	NINTENDO 3DS	NINTENDO	2011	68.15
8	PLAYSTATION 4	SONY	2013	66.51
9	XBOX ONE	MICROSOFT	2013	31.73
10	XBOX	MICROSOFT	2001	24.65

PLATFORM **WARS**

BIGGEST-SELLING **PS4 GAMES**

TOP 10

Since the PlayStation 4 was first released in 2013, these are the games that have captured the imagination of its players the most...

	GAME	GENRE	RELEASED	UNIT SALES (MILLIONS)
1	GRAND THEFT AUTO V	ACTION	2014	16.1
2	CALL OF DUTY: BLACK OPS 3	SHOOTER	2015	14.93
3	FIFA 17	SPORTS	2016	10.84
4	UNCHARTED 4: A THIEF'S END	ACTION	2016	9.59
5	FIFA 16	SPORTS	2015	8.21
6	FIFA 18	SPORTS	2017	8.12
7	STAR WARS BATTLEFRONT	SHOOTER	2015	7.91
8	CALL OF DUTY: INFINITE WARFARE	SHOOTER	2016	7.67
9	FALLOUT 4	RPG	2015	7.57
10	CALL OF DUTY: ADVANCED WARFARE	SHOOTER	2014	7.53

7 STAR WARS BATTLEFRONT

An exclusive extra game component entitled *Rogue One: X-wing VR Mission* was released for the PlayStation 4 version of *Star Wars Battlefront*. Using the PlayStation VR (virtual reality) headset, players can experience a story that parallels that of the 2016 film *Rogue One: A Star Wars Story*.

MINECRAFT
XBOX-ONE EDITION

TOP 10

BIGGEST-SELLING **XBOX ONE GAMES**

As it did for the previous incarnations, the Xbox and Xbox 360, the shooter genre remains the most popular for Xbox One...

	GAME	GENRE	RELEASED	UNIT SALES (MILLIONS)
1	CALL OF DUTY: BLACK OPS III	SHOOTER	2015	7.23
2	GRAND THEFT AUTO V	ACTION	2014	7.08
3	CALL OF DUTY: ADVANCED WARFARE	SHOOTER	2014	5.22
4	HALO 5: GUARDIANS	SHOOTER	2015	4.89
5	BATTLEFIELD 1	SHOOTER	2016	4.86
6	FALLOUT 4	RPG	2015	4.60
7	CALL OF DUTY: INFINITE WARFARE	SHOOTER	2016	4.53
8	MINECRAFT	ADVENTURE	2014	4.2
9	STAR WARS BATTLEFRONT	SHOOTER	2015	4.08
10	FIFA 17	SPORTS	2015	3.67

8   MINECRAFT

The first *Minecraft* game was released on November 18, 2011. This Xbox One version debuted September 5, 2014, 10 months after the console was first released. The franchise has its own fan convention, MineCon, which has been running since 2011.

PLATFORM **WARS**

BIGGEST-SELLING
WII U GAMING GENRES

Wii U had a lifespan of just over four years (November 2012 to January 2017), and here is how the popularity of its gaming genres breaks down...

	GENRE	UNIT SALES (MILLIONS)
1	PLATFORM	23.77
2	ACTION	22
3	RACING	8.45
4	FIGHTING	6.8
5	SHOOTER	6.33
6	RPG	3.46
7	SPORTS	3.34
8	PUZZLE	1.48
9	STRATEGY	1.33
10	ADVENTURE	0.23

7 | SUPER MARIO MAKER (WII U)

This game puts video-gaming creativity in the hands of the player. Using levels from *Super Mario Bros.* (1985), *Super Mario Bros. 3* (1988), *Super Mario World* (1990), and *New Super Mario Bros. U* (2012), brand-new challenges and courses can be made. Fans can also download levels crafted by fellow players.

BESTSELLING **WII U GAMES**

...and as an accompanying, bonus chart, here are the 10 most successful titles that were released for the Nintendo Wii U, proving the *Mario* brand remains unstoppable...

	GAME	GENRE	RELEASED	UNIT SALES (MILLIONS)
1	MARIO KART 8	RACING	2014	7.62
2	NEW SUPER MARIO BROS. U	ACTION	2012	5.59
3	SUPER SMASH BROS. FOR WII U AND 3DS	FIGHTING	2014	5.06
4	SUPER MARIO 3D WORLD	PLATFORM	2013	4.88
5	SPLATOON	SHOOTER	2015	4.67
6	NINTENDO LAND	ACTION	2012	4.59
7	SUPER MARIO MAKER	PLATFORM	2015	3.38
8	NEW SUPER LUIGI U	PLATFORM	2013	2.4
9	THE LEGEND OF ZELDA: THE WIND WAKER	ACTION	2013	2.03
10	MARIO PARTY 10	PARTY	2015	1.92

10 | NINTENDO SWITCH

The Switch is Nintendo's seventh home gaming system. It was released on March 3, 2017. Unlike Nintendo's previous home-based consoles, the Switch can be transformed into a handheld, portable console. Its first 12 months on the market saw sales exceed 14 million units worldwide.

TOP 10

BIGGEST-SELLING
NINTENDO PLATFORMS

The year 2019 marks Nintendo's 130th anniversary, and these are the gaming consoles that have contributed the most to the company's legacy so far...

	PLATFORM	YEARS IN PRODUCTION	UNIT SALES (MILLIONS)
1	NINTENDO DS / DS LITE / DSI	2004–16	154.9
2	GAME BOY / GAME BOY COLOR	1989–2003	118.69
3	WII	2006–13	101.64
4	GAME BOY ADVANCE	2001–09	81.51
5	NINTENDO 3DS / 3DSI XL	2011–PRESENT	72.09
6	NINTENDO ENTERTAINMENT SYSTEM	1983–2003	61.91
7	SUPER NINTENDO ENTERTAINMENT SYSTEM	1993–2003	49.1
8	NINTENDO 64	1996–2003	32.93
9	GAMECUBE	2001–07	21.74
10	NINTENDO SWITCH	2017–PRESENT	16.89

TOP 10

BIGGEST-SELLING **3DS GAMES**

The original Nintendo DS handheld console debuted November 2004, with its successor, the 3DS, arriving on the market February 2011...

	GAME	GENRE	RELEASED	UNIT SALES (MILLIONS)
1	POKÉMON X / Y	RPG	2013	16.11
2	POKÉMON SUN / MOON	RPG	2016	14.69
3	MARIO KART 7	RACING	2011	14.11
4	POKÉMON OMEGA RUBY / ALPHA SAPPHIRE	RPG	2014	12.62
5	SUPER MARIO 3D LAND	PLATFORM	2011	11.04
6	NEW SUPER MARIO BROS. 2	PLATFORM	2012	10.66
7	ANIMAL CROSSING: NEW LEAF	SIMULATION	2012	10.17
8	SUPER SMASH BROS. FOR WII U AND 3DS	FIGHTING	2014	7.95
9	TOMODACHI LIFE	SIMULATION	2013	5.67
10	LUIGI'S MANSION: DARK MOON	ADVENTURE	2013	5.06

5 SUPER MARIO 3D LAND

Although *Super Mario 3D Land* is a sideward-scrolling platform game, as its name suggests it incorporates 3D open-world components too. It is the most successful platform game for the Nintendo 3DS.

TOP 10

BIGGEST-SELLING **GAME BOY & GAME BOY ADVANCE GAMES**

Nintendo's first-ever handheld platform, the Game Boy, was released in April 1989. Its cousin console, the Game Boy Advance, debuted March 2001...

	GAME	PLATFORM	RELEASED	UNIT SALES (MILLIONS)
1	POKÉMON RED / BLUE / GREEN	GAME BOY	1996	31.37
2	TETRIS	GAME BOY	1989	30.26
3	POKÉMON GOLD / SILVER	GAME BOY	1999	23.1
4	SUPER MARIO LAND	GAME BOY	1989	18.14
5	POKÉMON RUBY / SAPPHIRE	GBA	2002	15.85
6	POKÉMON YELLOW: SPECIAL PIKACHU EDITION	GAME BOY	1998	14.64
7	SUPER MARIO LAND 2: 6 GOLDEN COINS	GAME BOY	1992	11.18
8	POKÉMON FIRERED / LEAFGREEN	GBA	2004	10.49
9	POKÉMON EMERALD	GBA	2004	6.41
10	POKÉMON CRYSTAL	GAME BOY	2000	6.39

7 SUPER MARIO LAND 2: 6 GOLDEN COINS

Released three years after the Game Boy–exclusive *Super Mario Land*, this sequel saw the introduction of the villainous character Wario. On January 21, 1994, the antagonist headlined the third adventure in this series, *Wario Land: Super Mario Land 3*.

HANDHELD CONSOLES
WITH THE MOST GAME SALES

The unit sales of games on Nintendo handheld systems total more than 2 billion on this chart, which makes up 82.4 percent of the total sales shown here...

	PLATFORM	MADE BY	RELEASED	UNIT SALES OF ALL GAMES (MILLIONS)
1	NINTENDO DS / DS LITE	NINTENDO	2004	844.74
2	GAME BOY / GAME BOY COLOR	NINTENDO	1989 / 1998	501.11
3	GAME BOY ADVANCE	NINTENDO	2001	377.41
4	PLAYSTATION PORTABLE	SONY	2004	304.58
5	NINTENDO 3DS / 3DS XL	NINTENDO	2011	303.14
6	PLAYSTATION VITA	SONY	2011	68.03
7	GAME GEAR	SEGA	1990	38.26
8	LEAPSTER	LEAPFROG ENTERPRISES	2008	12
9	NEO GEO POCKET / POCKET COLOR	SNK	1998 / 1999	1.51
10	WONDERSWAN	BANDAI	1999	1.5

10 ▶ WONDERSWAN

Bandai, the toy company behind the likes of *Power Rangers* and *Ben 10*, was behind the WonderSwan. It was a Japan-only handheld console that was released on March 4, 1999. Production ceased in 2003. Unusually for a console launch, the platform was available in a choice of nine different colors.

6 PLAYSTATION VITA

Debuting in Japan on December 17, 2011, the PSV (PlayStation Vita) was the sequel handheld console to Sony's PSP (PlayStation Portable). The PSV has the ability to play PS4 games, so owners can continue their game play on the handheld device.

TOTAL NINTENDO HANDHELD CONSOLE SALES = 2.0264 BILLION

TOP 10
BIGGEST-SELLING
HANDHELD CONSOLES / PLATFORMS

Although Sony has had great success with its handheld platforms, Nintendo's innovations still dominate the portable gaming system market...

	PLATFORM	MADE BY	RELEASED	UNIT SALES (MILLIONS)
1	NINTENDO DS / DS LITE / DSI	NINTENDO	2004	154.9
2	GAME BOY / GAME BOY COLOR	NINTENDO	1989 / 1998	118.69
3	GAME BOY ADVANCE	NINTENDO	2001	81.51
4	PLAYSTATION PORTABLE	SONY	2004	80.82
5	NINTENDO 3DS / 3DS XL	NINTENDO	2011	68.15
6	PLAYSTATION VITA	SONY	2011	15.75
7	GAME GEAR	SEGA	1990	10.62
8	LEAPSTER	LEAPFROG ENTERPRISES	2008	4
9	NEO GEO POCKET / POCKET COLOR	SNK	1998 / 1999	2
10	TURBOEXPRESS	NEC	1990	1.5

GENRE **LEADERS**

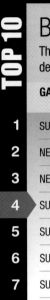

TOP 10

BIGGEST **PLATFORM GAMES**

There have been many successful platform franchises released over the past four decades, but none of them can touch the popularity of Mario and Luigi...

	GAME	PLATFORM	RELEASED	UNIT SALES (MILLIONS)
1	SUPER MARIO BROS.	NES	1985	40.24
2	NEW SUPER MARIO BROS.	DS	2006	29.85
3	NEW SUPER MARIO BROS. WII	WII	2009	28.46
4	SUPER MARIO WORLD	SNES	1990	20.61
5	SUPER MARIO LAND	GAME BOY	1989	18.14
6	SUPER MARIO BROS. 3	NES	1988	17.28
7	SUPER MARIO 64	N64	1996	11.89
8	SUPER MARIO GALAXY	WII	2007	11.39
9	SUPER MARIO LAND 2: 6 GOLDEN COINS	GAME BOY	1992	11.18
10	SUPER MARIO 3D LAND	3DS	2011	11.04

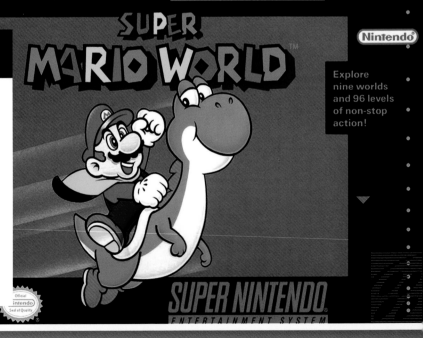

4   SUPER MARIO WORLD

This *Mario* game was developed specifically for the Super NES (Nintendo Entertainment System), and helped launch the console on November 21, 1990. The game features the debut of Yoshi, the dinosaur companion of Mario. *Super Mario World*, along with its sequel and two other *Mario* titles, come preinstalled on the SNES Classic Edition console.

Explore nine worlds and 96 levels of non-stop action!

TOP 10

BIGGEST **ADVENTURE GAMES**

The adventure genre covers a vast array of storytelling, from the covert spy missions of the *Metal Gear* series to the fantasy-led *Zelda* games...

	GAME	PLATFORM	RELEASED	UNIT SALES (MILLIONS)
1	MINECRAFT	XBOX 360	2013	9.71
2	THE LEGEND OF ZELDA: OCARINA OF TIME	N64	1998	7.6
3	THE LEGEND OF ZELDA: TWILIGHT PRINCESS	WII	2006	7.18
4	RED DEAD REDEMPTION	PS3	2010	6.56
5	THE LEGEND OF ZELDA	NES	1986	6.51
6	ASSASSIN'S CREED III	PS3	2012	6.48
7	RED DEAD REDEMPTION	XBOX 360	2010	6.41
8	METAL GEAR SOLID 2: SONS OF LIBERTY	PS2	2001	6.05
9	METAL GEAR SOLID	PS	1998	6.03
10	METAL GEAR SOLID 4: GUNS OF THE PATRIOTS	PS3	2008	6

FIRSTS

FIRST MARIO VIDEO GAME = JULY 9, 1981

FIRST ZELDA VIDEO GAME = FEBRUARY 21, 1986

3 THE LEGEND OF ZELDA: TWILIGHT PRINCESS

Although this game debuted on the Nintendo Wii on November 19, 2006, it was originally planned to be for the GameCube, Nintendo's previous console. The *Zelda* franchise began with *The Legend of Zelda* for the NES in 1986, and *Twilight Princess* was the 13th game. *The Legend of Zelda: Breath of the Wild* (2017) was one of the launch titles for Nintendo's latest console, the Switch.

GENRE **LEADERS**

BIGGEST **SHOOTER GAMES**

Accuracy and quick thinking drive the modern era of shooting games, but a 35-year-old target practice–style title is yet to be bested in sales...

	GAME	PLATFORM	RELEASED	UNIT SALES (MILLIONS)
1	DUCK HUNT	NES	1984	28.31
2	CALL OF DUTY: BLACK OPS III	PS4	2015	14.93
3	CALL OF DUTY: MODERN WARFARE 3	XBOX 360	2011	14.81
4	CALL OF DUTY: BLACK OPS	XBOX 360	2010	14.74
5	CALL OF DUTY: BLACK OPS II	PS3	2012	13.85
6	CALL OF DUTY: BLACK OPS II	XBOX 360	2012	13.82
7	CALL OF DUTY: MODERN WARFARE 2	XBOX 360	2009	13.51
8	CALL OF DUTY: MODERN WARFARE 3	PS3	2011	13.35
9	CALL OF DUTY: BLACK OPS	PS3	2010	12.67
10	HALO 3	XBOX 360	2007	12.13

1   DUCK HUNT

This 35-year-old game was played with a Nintendo Entertainment System light gun called the NES Zapper. One of the game modes is for clay pigeon shooting. An arcade version allowed two players to compete head to head with two Zappers.

9 STREET FIGHTER IV

There was a gap of 11 years between *Street Fighter III* and this sequel. The success of *IV* led to the release of 2010's *Super Street Fighter IV*, an *Arcade Edition*, as well as 2014's *Ultra Street Fighter IV*. The latter came with new characters and fighting abilities and additional combat stages.

TOP 10

BIGGEST **FIGHTING GAMES**

The disciplines featured in these titles range from capoeira and Muay Thai to ninjutsu, pro wrestling, and many more...

	GAME	PLATFORM	RELEASED	UNIT SALES (MILLIONS)
1	SUPER SMASH BROS. BRAWL	WII	2008	12.91
2	SUPER SMASH BROS. FOR WII U AND 3DS	3DS	2014	7.95
3	TEKKEN 3	PS	1998	7.16
4	SUPER SMASH BROS. MELEE	GAMECUBE	2001	7.07
5	STREET FIGHTER II: THE WORLD WARRIOR	SNES	1992	6.3
6	TEKKEN 2	PS	1996	5.74
7	SUPER SMASH BROS.	N64	1999	5.55
8	SUPER SMASH BROS. FOR WII U AND 3DS	WIIU	2014	5.06
9	STREET FIGHTER IV	PS3	2009	4.19
10	STREET FIGHTER II TURBO	SNES	1992	4.1

9 GRAND THEFT AUTO: LIBERTY CITY STORIES

This title began life as a PSP (PlayStation Portable)-only release on October 24, 2005, with a PS2 version following on June 6, 2006. Seven years later, a version was made available for the PS3. In late 2015 and early 2016, new editions were released for mobile and tablet platforms.

TOP 10

BIGGEST ACTION GAMES

The most popular component to modern action gaming is the non-linear construction, where players can veer away from the main storyline and do their own thing...

	GAME	PLATFORM	RELEASED	UNIT SALES (MILLIONS)
1	GRAND THEFT AUTO V	PS3	2013	21.49
2	GRAND THEFT AUTO: SAN ANDREAS	PS2	2004	20.81
3	GRAND THEFT AUTO V	XBOX 360	2013	16.85
4	GRAND THEFT AUTO: VICE CITY	PS2	2002	16.15
5	GRAND THEFT AUTO V	PS4	2014	16.1
6	GRAND THEFT AUTO III	PS2	2001	13.1
7	GRAND THEFT AUTO IV	XBOX 360	2008	11.07
8	GRAND THEFT AUTO IV	PS3	2008	10.55
9	GRAND THEFT AUTO: LIBERTY CITY STORIES	PSP	2005	7.72
10	GRAND THEFT AUTO V	XBOX ONE	2014	7.08

7 ▶ GRAN TURISMO 5

Up to and including 2017's *Gran Turismo Sport* for the PlayStation 4, there have been 13 titles released under the *Gran Turismo* franchise. *Gran Turismo 5* was the 11th, and provided the ability for 16 players to compete against one another online via the PlayStation 3's internet connectivity.

GAME TOTALS

GRAND THEFT AUTO = 15

GRAN TURISMO = 13

TOP 10

BIGGEST **RACING GAMES**

The first *Gran Turismo* title was released in December 1997 and, as this chart reveals, the franchise has remained strong ever since...

	GAME	PLATFORM	RELEASED	UNIT SALES (MILLIONS)
1	MARIO KART WII	WII	2008	35.72
2	MARIO KART DS	DS	2005	23.26
3	GRAN TURISMO 3: A-SPEC	PS2	2001	14.98
4	MARIO KART 7	3DS	2011	14.11
5	GRAN TURISMO 4	PS2	2004	11.66
6	GRAN TURISMO	PS	1997	10.95
7	GRAN TURISMO 5	PS3	2010	10.74
8	MARIO KART 64	N64	1996	9.87
9	GRAN TURISMO 2	PS	1999	9.49
10	SUPER MARIO KART	SNES	1992	8.76

BRAIN AGE 2: MORE TRAINING IN MINUTES A DAY!

2

Following the success of 2005's *Brain Age: Train Your Brain in Minutes a Day!*, this sequel debuted in Japan on December 29, 2005. Players must input their "brain age" before the puzzles begin, so that the challenges and points system match the user's age.

PROFESSOR LAYTON: TOTAL GAMES SALES OF FRANCHISE (7 TITLES)

18.43 MILLION UNITS SOLD

TOP 10

BIGGEST **PUZZLE GAMES**

The *Professor Layton* brand weaves mysterious storylines into its puzzling components. The franchise has released nine titles since 2007...

	GAME	PLATFORM	RELEASED	UNIT SALES (MILLIONS)
1	TETRIS	GAME BOY	1989	30.26
2	BRAIN AGE 2: MORE TRAINING IN MINUTES A DAY!	DS	2005	15.29
3	PAC-MAN	ATARI 2600	1982	7.81
4	TETRIS	NES	1988	5.58
5	DR. MARIO	GAME BOY	1989	5.34
6	PROFESSOR LAYTON AND THE CURIOUS VILLAGE	DS	2007	5.2
7	DR. MARIO	NES	1990	4.85
8	PROFESSOR LAYTON AND THE DIABOLICAL BOX	DS	2007	3.95
9	PROFESSOR LAYTON AND THE UNWOUND FUTURE	DS	2008	3.28
10	PAC-MAN COLLECTION	GBA	2001	2.94

9 ZUMBA FITNESS

Based on the fitness program created by Colombian dance choreographer Alberto Pérez, Zumba combines aerobic, dance, and martial arts moves. There are five different Zumba-related video games, including *Zumba Fitness: World Party*, a launch title for the Xbox One in 2013.

TOP 10

BIGGEST SPORTS GAMES

This chart includes games that feature a wide range of sports, from soccer and the Olympic events to fitness games that have a gymnastic or martial arts component...

	GAME	PLATFORM	RELEASED	UNIT SALES (MILLIONS)
1	WII SPORTS	WII	2006	82.62
2	WII SPORTS RESORT	WII	2009	32.86
3	WII FIT	WII	2007	22.7
4	WII FIT PLUS	WII	2009	21.81
5	FIFA 17	PS4	2016	10.84
6	FIFA 16	PS4	2015	8.21
7	FIFA 18	PS4	2017	8.12
8	MARIO & SONIC AT THE OLYMPIC GAMES	WII	2007	8
9	ZUMBA FITNESS	WII	2010	6.75
10	FIFA 12	PS3	2011	6.65

GENRE LEADERS

1 ▸ POKÉMON RED / BLUE / GREEN

This is the original Game Boy game(s) that launched the *Pokémon* brand. It led to an anime TV series that has over 1,000 episodes across 21 seasons, on air since April 1997. There have also been 21 *Pokémon* movies, including *Pokémon the Movie: Everyone's Story*, released July 2018.

TOP 10 — BIGGEST **RPG GAMES**

You'd be forgiven for thinking we forgot to include some other role-playing games but, truly, a singular franchise rules this genre...

	GAME	PLATFORM	RELEASED	UNIT SALES (MILLIONS)
1	POKÉMON RED / BLUE / GREEN	GAME BOY	1996	31.37
2	POKÉMON GOLD / SILVER	GAME BOY	1999	23.1
3	POKÉMON DIAMOND / PEARL	GAME BOY	2006	18.25
4	POKÉMON X / Y	3DS	2013	16.11
5	POKÉMON RUBY / SAPPHIRE	GBA	2002	15.85
6	POKÉMON BLACK / WHITE	DS	2010	15.18
7	POKÉMON SUN / MOON	3DS	2016	14.69
8	POKÉMON YELLOW: SPECIAL PIKACHU EDITION	GAME BOY	1998	14.64
9	POKÉMON HEARTGOLD / SOULSILVER	DS	2009	12.72
10	POKÉMON OMEGA RUBY / ALPHA SAPPHIRE	3DS	2014	12.62

THERE ARE MORE THAN 800 POKÉMON IN TOTAL

BIGGEST **STRATEGY GAMES**

TOP 10

Check out the years that these games were released. Very few modern strategy games have managed to get anywhere near the sales figures of these older titles...

	GAME	PLATFORM	RELEASED	UNIT SALES (MILLIONS)
1	POKÉMON STADIUM	N64	1999	5.45
2	WARZONE 2100	PS	1999	5.01
3	POKÉMON TRADING CARD GAME	GAME BOY	1998	3.7
4	POKÉMON STADIUM 2	N64	2000	2.73
5	HALO WARS	XBOX 360	2009	2.65
6	YU-GI-OH! THE ETERNAL DUELIST SOUL	GAME BOY	2001	2.07
7	PIKMIN	GAMECUBE	2001	1.63
8	YU-GI-OH! DUEL MONSTERS	GAME BOY	1998	1.61
9	LEGO BATTLES: NINJAGO	DS	2011	1.48
10	POCKET MONSTERS STADIUM	N64	1998	1.37

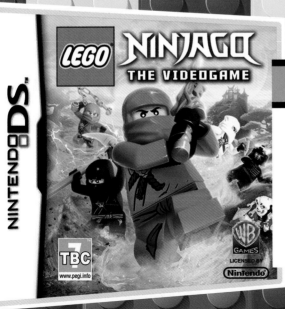

9 ▸ LEGO BATTLES: NINJAGO

LEGO's creator-owned Ninjago franchise launched as toy sets in 2010. An animated tie-in TV series called *Ninjago: Masters of Spinjitzu* began January 14, 2011. More than 80 episodes have been produced. The *LEGO Battles: Ninjago* game was released April 12, 2011. The first feature film for the franchise arrived in movie theaters September 2017.

TOP 10

BIGGEST **SIMULATION GAMES**

Whether you want to look after a virtual pet, learn to cook, or take care of an entire town, there is a simulation game out there for you...

	GAME	PLATFORM	RELEASED	UNIT SALES (MILLIONS)
1	NINTENDOGS	DS	2005	24.68
2	ANIMAL CROSSING: WILD WORLD	DS	2005	12.14
3	ANIMAL CROSSING: NEW LEAF	3DS	2012	10.17
4	TOMODACHI LIFE	3DS	2013	5.67
5	COOKING MAMA	DS	2006	5.65
6	ANIMAL CROSSING: CITY FOLK	WII	2008	4.64
7	NINTENDOGS + CATS	3DS	2011	4.07
8	MYSIMS	DS	2007	3.66
9	POKÉMON SNAP	N64	1999	3.63
10	COOKING MAMA 2: DINNER WITH FRIENDS	DS	2007	3.58

10 ▶ COOKING MAMA 2: DINNER WITH FRIENDS

This sequel was released just 20 months after the original *Cooking Mama* debuted (March 23, 2006). Both incorporate a multitude of mini games that simulate preparing food with touch-screen elements. Recipes range from pizza and steak to squid fried rice and apple pie.

NINTENDO DS™

cooking mama 2

LICENSED BY
Nintendo®

505 GAMES

3+
www.pegi.info

Dr. MARIO™
Miracle Cure

TOP 10
MOST SUCCESSFUL GENRES

Which genre of gaming do you and your friends most enjoy? See where it ranks in this chart, which shows just how popular action titles are...

	GENRE	ALL PLATFORMS' UNIT SALES (MILLIONS)
1	ACTION	1,824.25
2	SPORTS	1,373.37
3	SHOOTER	1,103.32
4	RPG	982.51
5	PLATFORM	846.49
6	PARTY	822.18
7	RACING	745.62
8	FIGHTING	457.85
9	SIMULATION	396.81
10	PUZZLE	245.7

DR. MARIO FRANCHISE

The Dr. Mario character has appeared in several of his own titles, with cameo appearances in many more, since his 1990 self-titled debut for the NES console. Like *Tetris*, the game's challenges fall into the category of tile matching. *Dr. Mario: Miracle Cure* was released on the Nintendo 3DS on May 31, 2015.

TOP 10

BIGGEST **LEGO GAMES**

LEGO is more than just the building-block toy giant: LEGO's video games—especially their official movie tie-ins—have shifted more than 30 million units...

	GAME	GENRE	PLATFORM	RELEASED	UNIT SALES (MILLIONS)
1	LEGO STAR WARS: THE COMPLETE SAGA	ACTION	WII	2007	5.66
2	LEGO STAR WARS: THE COMPLETE SAGA	ACTION	DS	2007	4.77
3	LEGO INDIANA JONES: THE ORIGINAL ADVENTURES	ADVENTURE	XBOX 360	2008	3.76
4	LEGO STAR WARS: THE VIDEO GAME	ACTION	PS2	2005	3.53
5	LEGO BATMAN: THE VIDEOGAME	ADVENTURE	XBOX 360	2008	3.42
6	LEGO BATMAN: THE VIDEOGAME	ADVENTURE	WII	2008	3.08
7	LEGO BATMAN: THE VIDEOGAME	ADVENTURE	DS	2008	3.06
8	LEGO STAR WARS II: THE ORIGINAL TRILOGY	ACTION	PS2	2006	2.69
9	LEGO STAR WARS: THE COMPLETE SAGA	ACTION	XBOX 360	2007	2.59
10	LEGO HARRY POTTER: YEARS 1–4	ADVENTURE	WII	2010	2.45

3 LEGO INDIANA JONES: THE ORIGINAL ADVENTURES

This game put a LEGO spin on the original trio of Indiana Jones adventures from the 1980s: *Raiders of the Lost Ark* (1981), *Indiana Jones and the Temple of Doom* (1984), and *Indiana Jones and the Last Crusade* (1989). A sequel game, *LEGO Indiana Jones 2: The Adventure Continues*, was released on November 17, 2009. Both games were directed by Jon Burton, the creative director of the *LEGO Star Wars* games.

8 ▶ RISE OF THE TOMB RAIDER

The 2013 *Tomb Raider* game marked a new beginning of the franchise, and 2015's *Rise of the Tomb Raider* is its sequel. Lead character Lara Croft is performed both vocally and physically (via motion-capture) by British actress Camilla Luddington. The next adventure, *Shadow of the Tomb Raider*, was released on April 27, 2018.

TOP 10

BIGGEST **TOMB RAIDER GAMES**

The first *Tomb Raider* title arrived in 1996, and a third movie adaptation (starring Oscar-winner Alicia Vikander playing Lara Croft for the first time) was released March 2018...

	GAME	PLATFORM	RELEASED	UNIT SALES (MILLIONS)
1	TOMB RAIDER II	PS	1997	5.24
2	TOMB RAIDER	PS	1996	4.63
3	TOMB RAIDER III: ADVENTURES OF LARA CROFT	PS	1997	3.54
4	TOMB RAIDER	PS3	2013	2.51
5	TOMB RAIDER: THE LAST REVELATION	PS	1998	2.48
6	TOMB RAIDER	XBOX 360	2013	1.9
7	RISE OF THE TOMB RAIDER	PS4	2016	1.7
8	RISE OF THE TOMB RAIDER	XBOX ONE	2015	1.57
9	TOMB RAIDER	PS4	2014	1.46
10	TOMB RAIDER: UNDERWORLD	PS3	2008	1.26

POWERFUL BRANDS

= 7 ▶ SILENT HILL: DOWNPOUR

The terrifying *Silent Hill* video game franchise began in 1999. *Silent Hill: Downpour* was the first title not to feature the work of Japanese composer Akira Yamaoka, who had been with the series since its beginning. American composer Daniel Licht (March 13, 1957–August 2, 2017) wrote *Downpour*'s score, and rock band Korn provided its theme song.

GAME TOTALS

SILENT HILL = 14

RESIDENT EVIL = 26

TOP 10

BIGGEST **SILENT HILL GAMES**

A total of 14 *Silent Hill* main games were released between 1999 and 2014, as well as several soundtracks, comics, and two feature films...

	GAME	PLATFORM	RELEASED	UNIT SALES (MILLIONS)
1	SILENT HILL	PS	1999	1.6
2	SILENT HILL 2	PS	2001	1.28
3	SILENT HILL 3	PS2	2003	0.71
4	SILENT HILL: SHATTERED MEMORIES	PS2	2010	0.59
5	SILENT HILL: ORIGINS	PSP	2007	0.52
6	SILENT HILL 4: THE ROOM	PS2	2004	0.51
7	SILENT HILL: DOWNPOUR	PS3	2012	0.47
=	SILENT HILL: SHATTERED MEMORIES	WII	2009	0.47
9	SILENT HILL: HOMECOMING	XBOX 360	2008	0.45
10	SILENT HILL: HOMECOMING	PS3	2008	0.39

TOP 10

BIGGEST **RESIDENT EVIL GAMES**

The *Resident Evil* games also spawned a successful movie franchise comprising six films released between 2002 and 2016...

	GAME	PLATFORM	RELEASED	UNIT SALES (MILLIONS)
1	RESIDENT EVIL 2	PS	1998	5.82
2	RESIDENT EVIL 5	PS3	2009	5.1
3	RESIDENT EVIL	PS	1996	5.05
4	RESIDENT EVIL: DIRECTOR'S CUT	PS	1996	3.77
5	RESIDENT EVIL 3	PS	1999	3.72
6	RESIDENT EVIL 4	PS2	2005	3.62
7	RESIDENT EVIL 5	XBOX 360	2009	3.51
8	RESIDENT EVIL 6	PS3	2012	3.12
9	RESIDENT EVIL VII: BIOHAZARD	PS4	2017	2.46
10	RESIDENT EVIL: CODE VERONICA X	PS2	2001	2.34

9 RESIDENT EVIL VII: BIOHAZARD

The title of this game should not be a surprise to *Resident Evil* fans, because in its Japan home, the franchise is known as *Biohazard*. *Resident Evil VII: Biohazard* was released in the 21st year of the brand, on January 24, 2017, and marked the 25th release of the survival horror series.

9   ASSASSIN'S CREED: UNITY

Unity marked the franchise's 15th video game release inside of just nine years. Its action is set in Paris, France, during the revolution of the late 18th century. The 20th game, *Assassin's Creed: Origins*, was released October 27, 2017.

TOP 10

BIGGEST **ASSASSIN'S CREED GAMES**

In December 2016, the first *Assassin's Creed* movie adaptation was released, with actor Michael Fassbender leading the cast...

	GAME	PLATFORM	RELEASED	UNIT SALES (MILLIONS)
1	ASSASSIN'S CREED III	PS3	2012	6.48
2	ASSASSIN'S CREED II	PS3	2009	5.57
3	ASSASSIN'S CREED	XBOX 360	2007	5.55
4	ASSASSIN'S CREED III	XBOX 360	2012	5.3
5	ASSASSIN'S CREED II	XBOX 360	2009	5.28
6	ASSASSIN'S CREED	PS3	2007	4.83
7	ASSASSIN'S CREED: REVELATIONS	PS3	2011	4.23
8	ASSASSIN'S CREED: REVELATIONS	XBOX 360	2011	4.21
9	ASSASSIN'S CREED: UNITY	PS4	2014	4.13
10	ASSASSIN'S CREED IV: BLACK FLAG	PS3	2013	3.93

8 STREET FIGHTER V

This is the eighth main title in the *Street Fighter* game franchise. In addition to including many classic characters, the base *Street Fighter V* game introduced four new ones: Laura, F.A.N.G., Necalli, and Rashid, with more available via DLC (downloadable content).

TOP 10

BIGGEST STREET FIGHTER GAMES

The *Street Fighter* game series has had a huge success in arcades, as well as home consoles, since the first title appeared in 1987...

	GAME	PLATFORM	RELEASED	UNIT SALES (MILLIONS)
1	STREET FIGHTER II	SNES	1992	6.3
2	STREET FIGHTER IV	PS3	2009	4.19
3	STREET FIGHTER II TURBO	SNES	1992	4.1
4	STREET FIGHTER IV	XBOX 360	2009	2.95
5	SUPER STREET FIGHTER II	SNES	1993	2
6	STREET FIGHTER II PLUS	GENESIS	1992	1.66
7	SUPER STREET FIGHTER IV 3D EDITION	3DS	2011	1.22
8	STREET FIGHTER V	PS4	2016	1.06
9	STREET FIGHTER ALPHA 3	PS	1998	1.03
10	STREET FIGHTER ZERO 2	PS	1996	0.85

MUSIC **09**

CHRIS CORNELL

Genre-defying songwriter Chris Cornell (July 20, 1964–May 18, 2017) wrote timeless anthems in the bands Temple of the Dog, Soundgarden, and Audioslave, and as a solo artist. He cowrote (with David Arnold) the award-winning theme song "You Know My Name" for the 2006 James Bond film *Casino Royale*.

CHRIS CORNELL: TOTAL STUDIO ALBUMS

- SOLO ARTIST = 4
- SOUNDGARDEN = 6
- AUDIOSLAVE = 3
- TEMPLE OF THE DOG = 1

TOP 10

MOST POPULAR
GENRES OF ALBUM
(BY SHARE & GROWTH)

From crashing guitar riffs and splashy pianos, to electronic samples and film soundtracks, these are the most popular types of albums released...

	GENRE	% OF TOTAL CONSUMPTION
1	ROCK	22.2
2	HIP-HOP / RAP	17.5
3	POP	17.2
4	R&B	8.7
5	COUNTRY	8.1
6	LATIN	7.5
7	STAGE & SCREEN	3.9
=	EDM	3.9
9	RELIGIOUS	2.9
10	JAZZ	1.2

SHARON JONES

Funk and soul legend Sharon Jones (May 4, 1956–November 18, 2016) was the lead singer of Sharon Jones & The Dap-Kings. The feature documentary *Miss Sharon Jones!* (2015) charted her battle with cancer and her triumphant return with her band's fifth album, *Give the People What They Want*, nominated for a 2014 Grammy Award.

TOP 10

MOST POPULAR **GENRES OF INDIVIDUAL SONG (BY SHARE & GROWTH)**

As an accompaniment to the Top 10 opposite, this chart examines songs (instead of full-length albums) to reveal how genre popularity shakes down...

	GENRE	% OF TOTAL CONSUMPTION
1	HIP-HOP / RAP	20.9
2	ROCK	19.8
3	POP	16.4
4	LATIN	9.5
=	R&B	9.5
6	COUNTRY	6.8
7	EDM	4.7
8	STAGE & SCREEN	3.1
9	RELIGIOUS	2.4
10	WORLD MUSIC	1.3

MOST POPULAR
GENRES ON VINYL

It may not be as popular a music format as streaming, but the vinyl record is far from dead and forgotten. These genres are the most popular purchases for turntables...

	GENRE	% OF TOTAL SALES
1	ROCK	53.9
2	POP	14.4
3	HIP-HOP / RAP	7
4	R&B	6.4
5	STAGE & SCREEN	5.3
6	JAZZ	3.5
7	COUNTRY	3
8	EDM	1.9
9	REGGAE	1
10	BLUES	0.9

FATS DOMINO

Born in New Orleans, Louisiana, USA, singer-songwriter and rock 'n' roll pianist Antoine "Fats" Domino Jr. (February 26, 1928–October 24, 2017) had many hits, including his 1956 version of "Blueberry Hill." It has been recorded dozens of times since Gene Autry's original appeared in the 1941 movie *The Singing Hill*.

STORE DAY APRIL 22, 2017 SAW 6% INCREASE IN ALBUM SALES, AND 14% INCREASE IN VINYL SALES FROM THE PREVIOUS YEAR

MOST POPULAR
GENRES ON CD

Between 2016 and 2017, sales of compact discs dropped 9.4 percent, but still equate to more than 74 million CD sales in the United States alone...

GENRE	% OF TOTAL SALES
ROCK	26.9
POP	21.8
COUNTRY	15.1
R&B	6.9
STAGE & SCREEN	5.3
RELIGIOUS	5
HIP-HOP / RAP	4.3
HOLIDAY	2.5
JAZZ	2.4
CLASSICAL	2

AL JARREAU

Seven-time Grammy Award–winning jazz artist Al Jarreau (March 12, 1940–February 12, 2017) had a string of hits over the course of five decades. One of his most beloved songs is the theme to TV series *Moonlighting* (1985–89). Jarreau cowrote the song with Lee Holdridge and it was produced by Nile Rodgers.

TOP 10

MOST STREAMED
ALBUMS (AUDIO & VIDEO) 2017

In the United States, the total annual streams of music and video content (lyrics, video promos, official music videos, etc) exceed 600 billion...

	ARTIST	ALBUM	TOTAL STREAMS
1	KENDRICK LAMAR	DAMN.	2,861,233,403
2	POST MALONE	STONEY	2,553,447,347
3	DRAKE	MORE LIFE	2,491,329,414
4	MIGOS	CULTURE	2,465,126,943
5	ED SHEERAN	÷	2,401,521,155
6	FUTURE	FUTURE	1,790,917,420
7	LIL UZI VERT	LUV IS RAGE 2	1,780,045,706
8	THE WEEKND	STARBOY	1,740,375,409
9	KHALID	AMERICAN TEEN	1,666,833,042
10	BRUNO MARS	24K MAGIC	1,578,693,330

10 BRUNO MARS

Following *Doo-Wops & Hooligans* (2010) and *Unorthodox Jukebox* (2012), *24K Magic* is Bruno Mars's third album. Mars has won 92 international awards for his music. These include *24K Magic's* 2018 Grammy Award for Album of the Year.

5 ▶ P!NK

The *Beautiful Trauma* tour, in support of
P!nk's seventh album of the same name,
began on March 1, 2018, in Phoenix, Arizona,
USA. It continued through September
with more than 80 shows across the USA,
Canada, Australia, and New Zealand.

TOP 10

BIGGEST-SELLING
ALBUMS (ALL FORMATS) 2017

Whether fans shelled out for CD, vinyl, cassette, or a digital download of
an album, the sales of every format are included here to determine the
album-selling champions...

	ARTIST	ALBUM	TOTAL SALES
1	TAYLOR SWIFT	REPUTATION	1,899,772
2	ED SHEERAN	÷	1,042,255
3	KENDRICK LAMAR	DAMN.	766,434
4	VARIOUS	MOANA (ORIGINAL MOTION PICTURE SOUNDTRACK)	659,884
5	P!NK	BEAUTIFUL TRAUMA	648,149
6	CHRIS STAPLETON	FROM A ROOM: VOLUME 1	606,342
7	BRUNO MARS	24K MAGIC	603,598
8	VARIOUS	GUARDIANS OF THE GALAXY: AWESOME MIX, VOL. 2	550,613
9	VARIOUS	TROLLS (ORIGINAL MOTION PICTURE SOUNDTRACK)	497,043
10	VARIOUS	HAMILTON (ORIGINAL BROADWAY CAST RECORDING)	410,354

3 ED SHEERAN

The names of British artist Ed Sheeran's three studio albums to date follow a pattern of mathematical symbols. His 2011 debut is called + (plus), the 2014 follow-up is x (multiply), and 2017's is ÷ *(Divide)*. His 2015 collection called 5 combined all the EPs he released prior to his full-length debut.

BIGGEST-SELLING **VINYL ALBUMS 2017**

Although more contemporary artists than ever are releasing vinyl editions of their albums, this Top 10 reveals that it's the classic records of yesteryear that still rule this chart...

	ARTIST	ALBUM	TOTAL SALES
1	VARIOUS	GUARDIANS OF THE GALAXY: AWESOME MIX, VOL. 1	164,175
2	THE BEATLES	ABBEY ROAD	62,177
3	ED SHEERAN	÷	49,218
4	AMY WINEHOUSE	BACK TO BLACK	48,236
5	BOB MARLEY AND THE WAILERS	LEGEND	47,173
6	VARIOUS	LA LA LAND (ORIGINAL MOTION PICTURE SOUNDTRACK)	43,704
7	THE BEATLES	SGT. PEPPER'S LONELY HEARTS CLUB BAND	42,131
8	PINK FLOYD	THE DARK SIDE OF THE MOON	40,444
9	MICHAEL JACKSON	THRILLER	39,728
10	FLEETWOOD MAC	RUMOURS	38,096
	PRINCE AND THE REVOLUTION	PURPLE RAIN	37,333
	MILES DAVIS	KIND OF BLUE	36,454
	KENDRICK LAMAR	GOOD KID, M.A.A.D CITY	35,558
	HARRY STYLES	HARRY STYLES	31,318
	LANA DEL REY	BORN TO DIE EP	31,106

1 TAYLOR SWIFT

Reputation (2017) is Taylor Swift's sixth album in 11 years. The music video for the album's lead single, "Look What You Made Me Do," has more than 895 million views on Swift's official YouTube channel.

TOP 10

BIGGEST-SELLING
INDEPENDENT ALBUMS 2017

You may be surprised by some of the megastars that occupy this chart, but all of these performers truly are independent artists who release music via an independent record label...

	ARTIST	ALBUM	TOTAL SALES
1	TAYLOR SWIFT	REPUTATION	1,899,772
2	VARIOUS	MOANA (ORIGINAL MOTION PICTURE SOUNDTRACK)	659,884
3	VARIOUS	GUARDIANS OF THE GALAXY: AWESOME MIX, VOL. 2	550,613
4	ALAN MENKEN	BEAUTY AND THE BEAST (ORIGINAL MOTION PICTURE SOUNDTRACK)	370,251
5	VARIOUS	GUARDIANS OF THE GALAXY: AWESOME MIX, VOL. 1	360,523
6	METALLICA	HARDWIRED...TO SELF-DESTRUCT	335,314
7	GARTH BROOKS	THE ANTHOLOGY, PART 1	230,889
8	THOMAS RHETT	LIFE CHANGES	188,447
9	REBA McENTIRE	SING IT NOW: SONGS OF FAITH & HOPE	186,826
10	BRANTLEY GILBERT	THE DEVIL DON'T SLEEP	183,905

2 LUIS FONSI FT. DADDY YANKEE

"Despacito" was the first single to be released by Puerto Rican music artist Luis Fonsi since his 2015 song "Tentación." The featured guest rapper, Daddy Yankee, is also from Puerto Rico. The music video was directed by Carlos Pérez and shot on their island home.

TOP 10

BIGGEST-SELLING **SONGS 2017**

Whether it was released as a single, or is an album track made available as an individual download, these 10 songs outsold all others in 2017...

	ARTIST	SONG	TOTAL SALES
1	ED SHEERAN	SHAPE OF YOU	2,653,251
2	LUIS FONSI FT. DADDY YANKEE	DESPACITO	2,389,522
3	SAM HUNT	BODY LIKE A BACK ROAD	1,827,047
4	BRUNO MARS	THAT'S WHAT I LIKE	1,705,634
5	IMAGINE DRAGONS	BELIEVER	1,663,646
6	THE CHAINSMOKERS & COLDPLAY	SOMETHING JUST LIKE THIS	1,383,688
7	JAMES ARTHUR	SAY YOU WON'T LET GO	1,209,491
8	IMAGINE DRAGONS	THUNDER	1,188,138
9	ZAYN & TAYLOR SWIFT	I DON'T WANNA LIVE FOREVER (FIFTY SHADES DARKER)	1,125,257
10	KENDRICK LAMAR	HUMBLE.	1,118,214

MOST STREAMED **SONGS 2017**

As opposed to the chart opposite, this chart ignores sales data, and is interested only in tallying up the number of times a song was streamed...

	ARTIST	SONG	TOTAL STREAMS
1	LUIS FONSI FT. DADDY YANKEE	DESPACITO	1,095,331,085
2	ED SHEERAN	SHAPE OF YOU	979,337,555
3	MIGOS	BAD AND BOUJEE	912,738,788
4	LIL UZI VERT	XO TOUR LLIF3	871,618,319
5	KENDRICK LAMAR	HUMBLE.	860,567,298
6	POST MALONE	CONGRATULATIONS	857,162,572
7	BRUNO MARS	THAT'S WHAT I LIKE	799,244,296
8	FUTURE	MASK OFF	773,384,832
9	CARDI B	BODAK YELLOW	690,190,054
10	KYLE	ISPY	657,651,273

10 KYLE

Kyle's hit song "iSpy" features guest vocals from artist Lil Yachty, born in Georgia, USA. It features on Kyle's debut album, *Light of Mine*, released May 18, 2018. Kyle also performed at the 2018 Coachella Valley Music and Arts Festival alongside Chance the Rapper.

MOST STREAMED ARTISTS (AUDIO & VIDEO) 2017

Switching from the previous pages' charts on albums, songs, genres, and formats, this Top 10 reveals which artists are the biggest in the streaming world...

	ARTIST	TOTAL STREAMS
1	DRAKE	6,039,965,826
2	FUTURE	4,222,876,327
3	KENDRICK LAMAR	4,054,558,340
4	ED SHEERAN	3,504,746,082
5	POST MALONE	3,276,433,461
6	LIL UZI VERT	3,079,032,169
7	MIGOS	2,990,938,364
8	THE WEEKND	2,970,595,276
9	KODAK BLACK	2,753,303,619
10	EMINEM	2,561,444,951

8 ▶ THE WEEKND

The Weeknd is the stage name of Canadian Abel Makkonen Tesfaye. His 2016 album *Starboy* includes collaborations with Daft Punk, Kendrick Lamar, and Lana Del Rey. His previous 2015 album, *Beauty Behind the Madness,* included the hit song "Can't Feel My Face."

TOP 10

BIGGEST-SELLING ARTISTS 2017

Streaming may be the most convenient way to access and enjoy music, but this Top 10 examines the all-important sales across all formats, both digital and physical...

	ARTIST	TOTAL SALES
1	TAYLOR SWIFT	2,185,416
2	ED SHEERAN	1,247,589
3	CHRIS STAPLETON	1,191,854
4	METALLICA	1,083,345
5	KENDRICK LAMAR	939,172
6	PINK	765,557
7	BRUNO MARS	754,474
8	GARTH BROOKS	746,592
9	PENTATONIX	720,646
10	THE BEATLES	698,662

3 CHRIS STAPLETON

Country artist Chris Stapleton has won more than 37 awards, including seven Country Music Association Awards. He has achieved all this since his debut album, *Traveller*, appeared on May 5, 2015. His follow-ups were released within seven months of one another, *From A Room: Volume 1* in May 2017, and *From A Room: Volume 2* in December of the same year.

PLAYLISTS – DATA PROVES THE MOST POPULAR / LISTENED-TO PLAYLISTS ARE THE ONES WE CREATE FOR OURSELVES:

33% = PLAYLISTS CREATED BY THE PLATFORM

54% = PLAYLISTS CREATED BY AN INDIVIDUAL FOR THEM TO LISTEN TO

13% = PLAYLISTS CREATED BY SOMEONE ELSE

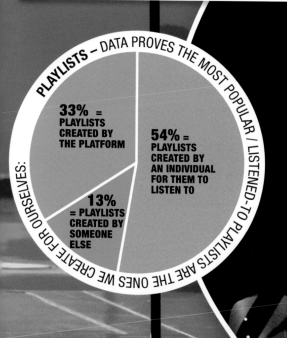

TOP 10

MOST POPULAR POP ALBUMS 2017

If you own copies of the *Top 10 of Everything* from the past few years, see how many artists pop up again and again in this music chart...

	ARTIST	ALBUM	TOTAL CONSUMPTION
1	ED SHEERAN	÷	2,645,600
2	TAYLOR SWIFT	REPUTATION	2,353,697
3	PINK	BEAUTIFUL TRAUMA	797,396
4	MAROON 5	RED PILL BLUES	769,017
5	SAM SMITH	THE THRILL OF IT ALL	703,122
6	SHAWN MENDES	ILLUMINATE	682,075
7	HARRY STYLES	HARRY STYLES	673,847
8	DEMI LOVATO	TELL ME YOU LOVE ME	626,529
9	RIHANNA	ANTI	613,880
10	NIALL HORAN	FLICKER	558,385

8 ▶ DEMI LOVATO

The 12-track studio album *Tell Me You Love Me*, Demi Lovato's sixth, was released on September 29, 2017. The Lovato-produced documentary, *Simply Complicated* (2017), charts the making of the album and shares Lovato's journey with her own mental health.

6 ▷ LINKIN PARK

Singer-songwriter Chester Bennington (March 20, 1976–July 20, 2017) gave Linkin Park a unique combination of cathartic and soulful vocals. *One More Light*, the band's seventh studio album, was released on May 19, 2017. The 16-track *One More Light Live* followed on December 15, 2017, released in honor of Bennington.

STUDIO ALBUMS = 7

LIVE ALBUMS = 3

REMIX ALBUMS = 2

EPS (STUDIO, COLLABORATIONS, LIVE) = 10

LP UNDERGROUND (FAN CLUB) EPS = 16

LINKIN PARK'S RELEASES TO DATE

TOP 10 — MOST POPULAR **ROCK ALBUMS 2017**

The rock genre has always been a place of experimentation, as proved by the metal, electronic, and genre-bending artists that make up this Top 10...

	ARTIST	ALBUM	TOTAL CONSUMPTION
1	IMAGINE DRAGONS	EVOLVE	1,129,981
2	TWENTY ONE PILOTS	BLURRYFACE	671,854
3	HALSEY	HOPELESS FOUNTAIN KINGDOM	610,614
4	PANIC! AT THE DISCO	DEATH OF A BACHELOR	438,267
5	METALLICA	HARDWIRED...TO SELF-DESTRUCT	432,524
6	LINKIN PARK	ONE MORE LIGHT	394,713
7	IMAGINE DRAGONS	NIGHT VISIONS	339,143
8	LED ZEPPELIN	LED ZEPPELIN	338,335
9	QUEEN	GREATEST HITS	335,426
10	TWENTY ONE PILOTS	VESSEL	333,171

TOP 10

MOST POPULAR **R&B ALBUMS 2017**

The nature of rhythm and blues has gone on a fascinating journey of invention and reinvention over the past 70 years...

	ARTIST	ALBUM	TOTAL CONSUMPTION
1	BRUNO MARS	24K MAGIC	1,488,815
2	THE WEEKND	STARBOY	1,309,978
3	KHALID	AMERICAN TEEN	1,129,978
4	SZA	CTRL	667,954
5	CHRIS BROWN	HEARTBREAK ON A FULL MOON	567,485
6	THE WEEKND	BEAUTY BEHIND THE MADNESS	464,617
7	CHILDISH GAMBINO	AWAKEN, MY LOVE!	455,356
8	BRYSON TILLER	TRAPSOUL	401,059
9	BRYSON TILLER	TRUE TO SELF	383,388
10	6LACK	FREE 6LACK	373,868

7 | CHILDISH GAMBINO

Childish Gambino is the name that actor Donald Glover performs under as a music artist. Glover first adopted the moniker for his 2011 debut five-track EP, co-produced by Ludwig Göransson, who also scored *Black Panther* (2018). Glover created and stars in the hit TV series *Atlanta*. He has won more than 20 awards for his acting.

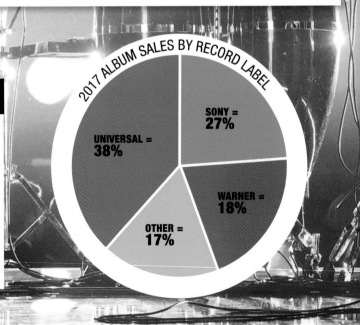

2017 ALBUM SALES BY RECORD LABEL

SONY = 27%

UNIVERSAL = 38%

WARNER = 18%

OTHER = 17%

1 KENDRICK LAMAR

Released April 14, 2017, *Damn.* made musical history by winning the 2018 Pulitzer Prize for Music (first awarded in 1943). *Damn.* was the first record to win that was not in the classical or jazz genre. On February 9, 2018, Lamar released *Black Panther: The Album*, the song-soundtrack for the movie *Black Panther.* Lamar curated the album and cowrote all 14 tracks.

TOP 10

MOST POPULAR
HIP-HOP / RAP ALBUMS 2017

Hip-hop and rap artistry has always pushed the envelope in the way music is created, the kinds of samples featured, the delivery of the lyrics, and, oftentimes, the important messages and statements artists make...

	ARTIST	ALBUM	TOTAL CONSUMPTION
1	KENDRICK LAMAR	DAMN.	2,562,942
2	DRAKE	MORE LIFE	2,182,282
3	POST MALONE	STONEY	1,446,491
4	MIGOS	CULTURE	1,291,968
5	FUTURE	FUTURE	1,058,383
6	LIL UZI VERT	LUV IS RAGE 2	938,838
7	DJ KHALED	GRATEFUL	901,185
8	BIG SEAN	I DECIDED.	836,632
9	DRAKE	VIEWS	818,775
10	LOGIC	EVERYBODY	796,264

TOP 10

MOST POPULAR EDM ALBUMS 2017

This electronic dance music Top 10 features relatively new artists of the past few years, such as duo The Chainsmokers, as well as veterans of the dance scene, such as Calvin Harris...

	ARTIST	ALBUM	TOTAL CONSUMPTION
1	THE CHAINSMOKERS	MEMORIES...DO NOT OPEN	981,850
2	CALVIN HARRIS	FUNK WAV BOUNCES VOL. 1	552,529
3	THE CHAINSMOKERS	COLLAGE EP	450,525
4	JONAS BLUE	JONAS BLUE: ELECTRONIC NATURE	287,342
5	THE CHAINSMOKERS	THE CHAINSMOKERS	205,068
6	DJ SNAKE	ENCORE	193,297
7	MARIAN HILL	ACT ONE (THE COMPLETE COLLECTION)	149,216
8	FLUME	SKIN	146,123
9	MAJOR LAZER	PEACE IS THE MISSION	132,386
10	ODESZA	IN RETURN	111,973

7 MARIAN HILL

Rather than being a solo artist, as the name suggests, Marian Hill is a duo, Samantha Gongol and Jeremy Lloyd. The band's name is a fusion of two character names from the 1957 musical *The Music Man*, namely Marian Paroo and Harold Hill. An extended version of their debut album *Act One (The Complete Collection)* includes 24 tracks across two discs.

EXTRA

FIVE BIGGEST EDM SONGS 2017

Here is a bonus extra chart, revealing the five EDM songs that dominated the sales, downloads, and stream charts of 2017...

	ARTIST	SONG	TOTAL CONSUMPTION
1	THE CHAINSMOKERS & COLDPLAY	SOMETHING JUST LIKE THIS	3,163,053
2	ZEDD & ALESSIA CARA	STAY	2,477,959
3	THE CHAINSMOKERS	CLOSER	2,162,071
4	THE CHAINSMOKERS	PARIS	2,113,746
5	CALVIN HARRIS	SLIDE	2,076,422

5   KANE BROWN

Kane Brown's debut EP, *Closer* (2014), was completed with the support of an online crowdfunding campaign. A follow-up EP, *Chapter 1*, arrived in 2016, with Brown's self-titled release coming in December of the same year. Its single "What Ifs" features Lauren Alaina, who was the runner-up on the 2011 season of *American Idol*.

TOP 10

MOST POPULAR
COUNTRY ALBUMS 2017

With the countless successful country artists out there, it's an amazing feat for one of them to make the top two spots on this chart, but that's exactly what Chris Stapleton has achieved...

	ARTIST	ALBUM	TOTAL CONSUMPTION
1	CHRIS STAPLETON	FROM A ROOM: VOLUME 1	750,883
2	CHRIS STAPLETON	TRAVELLER	709,721
3	KEITH URBAN	RIPCORD	567,759
4	FLORIDA GEORGIA LINE	DIG YOUR ROOTS	486,080
5	KANE BROWN	KANE BROWN	482,126
6	THOMAS RHETT	LIFE CHANGES	479,612
7	BRETT YOUNG	BRETT YOUNG	477,919
8	LUKE COMBS	THIS ONE'S FOR YOU	442,908
9	JON PARDI	CALIFORNIA SUNRISE	395,189
10	THOMAS RHETT	TANGLED UP	394,881

TOP 10

MOST POPULAR **FOLK ALBUMS 2017**

If you thought it was impressive that country artist Chris Stapleton appeared twice in the chart on the previous page, check out Gordon Lightfoot's presence below...

	ARTIST	ALBUM	TOTAL CONSUMPTION
1	TYLER CHILDERS	PURGATORY	24,851
2	GREGORY ALAN ISAKOV	THIS EMPTY NORTHERN HEMISPHERE	23,145
3	GORDON LIGHTFOOT	COMPLETE GREATEST HITS	19,534
4	DODIE	YOU EP	19,329
5	OLD CROW MEDICINE SHOW	O.C.M.S.	19,129
6	GORDON LIGHTFOOT	GORD'S GOLD	19,038
7	GORDON LIGHTFOOT	SUNDOWN	13,667
8	PETER, PAUL & MARY	THE VERY BEST OF PETER, PAUL & MARY	13,619
9	NICK DRAKE	PINK MOON	13,446
10	GREGORY ALAN ISAKOV	THAT SEA, THE GAMBLER	13,437

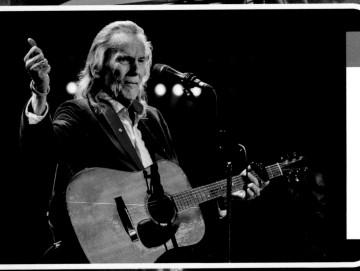

3 ▶ GORDON LIGHTFOOT

Canadian Gordon Lightfoot was born on November 17, 1938. He has been active in the music industry for more than 60 years. He has won 16 Juno Awards and has a star on Canada's Walk of Fame in Toronto, Ontario. Lightfoot's songs have also been recorded by the likes of Bob Dylan, Johnny Mathis, and Sarah McLachlan.

6 J BALVIN

Born in Medellín, Colombia, J Balvin's *Energía* is his fourth studio album. It followed *Real* (2010), *El Negocio* (2011), and *La Familia* (2016). His fifth, *Vibras*, was released May 25, 2018. Balvin is also known for 2012's *J Balvin Mix Tape*.

TOP 10

MOST POPULAR **LATIN ALBUMS 2017**

Shakira, who tops this chart, has been releasing records since she was just 13 years old, which means she is approaching her third decade as a music artist...

	ARTIST	ALBUM	TOTAL CONSUMPTION
1	SHAKIRA	EL DORADO	235,179
2	OZUNA	ODISEA	231,570
3	NICKY JAM	FÉNIX	177,262
4	ROMEO SANTOS	GOLDEN	139,502
5	ROMEO SANTOS	FORMULA VOL. 2	107,689
6	J BALVIN	ENERGÍA	100,050
7	PRINCE ROYCE	FIVE	88,905
8	OZUNA	ÉXITOS TRAP	79,105
9	CNCO	PRIMERA CITA	76,237
10	WISIN	VICTORY	70,877

CHART-TOPPERS

2 ETTA JAMES

Multi-award-winning California-born artist Etta James (January 25, 1938–January 20, 2012) released her debut studio album on November 15, 1960. Entitled *At Last!*, it contains the title track, one of her most famous songs. In 2003, James was given the Grammy Lifetime Achievement Award. Eight years later, she released her 28th album, *The Dreamer*.

TOP 10

MOST POPULAR **BLUES ALBUMS 2017**

From the rock-infused but soulful guitar sound of Gary Clark Jr. to the legend herself, Etta James, this chart is full of blues greats both contemporary and eternal...

	ARTIST	ALBUM	TOTAL CONSUMPTION
1	ERIC CLAPTON	ICON	74,482
2	ETTA JAMES	AT LAST!	55,404
3	TAJ MAHAL & KEB' MO'	TAJMO	34,136
4	ETTA JAMES	20TH CENTURY MASTERS: THE BEST OF ETTA JAMES (MILLENNIUM COLLECTION)	33,736
5	STEVIE RAY VAUGHAN	PLAYLIST: THE VERY BEST OF STEVIE RAY VAUGHAN	33,388
6	STEVIE RAY VAUGHAN AND DOUBLE TROUBLE	THE ESSENTIAL STEVIE RAY VAUGHAN AND DOUBLE TROUBLE	28,931
7	GARK CLARK JR.	LIVE NORTH AMERICA 2016	27,668
8	GARK CLARK JR.	GARK CLARK JR. LIVE	26,146
9	VARIOUS	ROOTS OF BLUES	23,483
10	KENNY WAYNE SHEPHERD BAND	LAY IT ON DOWN	23,406

FIVE BIGGEST LABELS: 2017 ALBUM SALES

INTERSCOPE = 9,300,452

COLUMBIA RECORDS = 8,278,173

RCA RECORDS = 7,517,562

ATLANTIC RECORDS = 6,620,596

CAPITOL = 4,917,681

1 NORAH JONES

Come Away With Me was nine-time Grammy Award–winner Norah Jones's debut album, released on February 26, 2002, and it topped this jazz chart all these years later. Its global sales approach 30 million copies. *Day Breaks* (2016) is her sixth studio album as a solo artist.

TOP 10

MOST POPULAR JAZZ ALBUMS 2017

The most striking aspect of this Top 10 is the staying power of its artists and their records. For example, Miles Davis's *Kind of Blue* was released in 1959...

	ARTIST	ALBUM	TOTAL CONSUMPTION
1	NORAH JONES	COME AWAY WITH ME	96,858
2	FRANK SINATRA	ULTIMATE SINATRA	78,122
3	DIANA KRALL	TURN UP THE QUIET	77,972
4	MILES DAVIS	KIND OF BLUE	73,769
5	MICHAEL BUBLÉ	NOBODY BUT ME	72,627
6	BING CROSBY	MERRY CHRISTMAS	59,212
7	FRANK SINATRA	NOTHING BUT THE BEST	41,429
8	CHUCK BERRY	20TH CENTURY MASTERS: THE BEST OF CHUCK BERRY (MILLENNIUM COLLECTION)	33,100
9	LOUIS ARMSTRONG	KEN BURNS JAZZ: LOUIS ARMSTRONG	25,419
10	NINA SIMONE	THE BEST OF NINA SIMONE	22,157

SOCIAL **NETWORKING**

2 ◢ ARIANA GRANDE

The hit single "No Tears Left to Cry" was the first track released (April 20, 2018) from Ariana Grande's fourth album. To date, Grande has been the lead artist or featured artist on more than 30 singles. On March 12, 2016, Grande hosted and performed on *Saturday Night Live*, including the sketch comedy song "This Is Not a Feminist Song."

FACEBOOK: FEB 4, 2004 (15 YEARS OLD)

TWITTER: JUL 15, 2006 (13 YEARS OLD)

INSTAGRAM: OCT 6, 2010 (9 YEARS OLD)

SOCIAL MEDIA RANKED BY ITS LAUNCH DATES

TOP 10 — MOST **INSTAGRAM FOLLOWERS (SOLO)**

If you enjoy seeing your favorite music artists post photography and videos related to their projects and everyday lives, it's likely you use the Instagram app...

	ARTIST	HANDLE	FOLLOWING	FOLLOWERS
1	SELENA GOMEZ	@SELENAGOMEZ	316	132,239,664
2	ARIANA GRANDE	@ARIANAGRANDE	1,339	116,644,488
3	BEYONCÉ	@BEYONCÉ	0	109,781,857
4	TAYLOR SWIFT	@TAYLORSWIFT	0	105,676,149
5	JUSTIN BIEBER	@JUSTINBIEBER	74	95,588,620
6	NICKI MINAJ	@NICKIMINAJ	1,029	85,279,074
7	MILEY CYRUS	@MILEYCYRUS	564	73,811,942
8	JENNIFER LOPEZ	@JLO	1,052	71,508,640
9	KATY PERRY	@KATYPERRY	335	68,365,331
10	DEMI LOVATO	@DDLOVATO	352	64,562,855

6 ▷ JUSTIN TIMBERLAKE

Justin Timberlake has released five studio albums. *Man of the Woods* arrived two days before his February 4, 2018, performance at the Super Bowl LII Halftime Show. His setlist concluded with his 2016 hit "Can't Stop the Feeling!" taken from the soundtrack to the animated film *Trolls*, in which Timberlake voices the character of Branch.

TOP 10

MOST **TWITTER FOLLOWERS (SOLO)**

If you compare the numbers of followers on both this chart and the one opposite, you can see that the audience sizes of Twitter and Instagram are similar...

	ARTIST	HANDLE	FOLLOWING	FOLLOWERS
1	KATY PERRY	@KATYPERRY	208	107,952,650
2	JUSTIN BIEBER	@JUSTINBIEBER	317,497	104,824,953
3	TAYLOR SWIFT	@TAYLORSWIFT13	0	85,827,866
4	RIHANNA	@RIHANNA	1,127	85,153,644
5	LADY GAGA	@LADYGAGA	128,366	75,791,764
6	JUSTIN TIMBERLAKE	@JTIMBERLAKE	254	64,650,737
7	ARIANA GRANDE	@ARIANAGRANDE	64,992	56,450,652
8	BRITNEY SPEARS	@BRITNEYSPEARS	388,813	56,423,799
9	SELENA GOMEZ	@SELENAGOMEZ	1,260	55,902,369
10	DEMI LOVATO	@DDLOVATO	551	53,570,126

TOP 10

MOST **FACEBOOK LIKES** (BANDS / GROUPS)

When you "like" an act on Facebook, that gives you the opportunity to receive updates on the band's activity...

	BAND / GROUP	"LIKES"
1	LINKIN PARK	62,113,481
2	THE BLACK EYED PEAS	43,224,843
3	THE BEATLES	41,618,350
4	COLDPLAY	39,380,944
5	MAROON 5	38,689,294
6	ONE DIRECTION	38,359,426
7	METALLICA	37,326,024
8	GREEN DAY	31,340,748
9	GUNS N' ROSES	30,466,817
10	AC / DC	30,071,880

10 ▶ AC / DC MALCOLM YOUNG

Although born in Scotland, Malcolm Young (January 6, 1953–November 18, 2017) moved to Australia with his family and grew up there. He cofounded rock band AC / DC with his younger brother Angus (born March 31, 1955) in 1973. AC / DC have released 16 albums. They won a Grammy in 2010 for the song "War Machine."

1 SHAKIRA

This Colombian artist's 11th studio album, *El Dorado*, was released on May 26, 2017. Her 55 singles include "Trap" (released January 26, 2018), which features fellow Colombian singer Maluma as a guest vocalist. Shakira herself has been a featured guest artist on numerous releases, including Black M's 2016 hit single "Comme Moi."

TOP 10

MOST **FACEBOOK LIKES (SOLO ARTISTS)**

As you can see, by examining the data on both charts shown here, solo music artists' official Facebook pages are a lot more popular with fans...

	SOLO ARTIST	"LIKES"
1	SHAKIRA	104,022,219
2	EMINEM	89,784,471
3	RIHANNA	81,234,412
4	JUSTIN BIEBER	78,616,320
5	WILL SMITH	74,898,558
6	MICHAEL JACKSON	74,346,375
7	TAYLOR SWIFT	73,839,689
8	BOB MARLEY	73,045,036
9	KATY PERRY	69,394,961
10	ADELE	65,306,161

2 | SEE YOU AGAIN—WIZ KHALIFA FT. CHARLIE PUTH

This song was written for the soundtrack to *Furious 7* (2015), the seventh release in *The Fast and the Furious* film franchise. "See You Again" is a tribute to the actor behind the franchise's character Brian O'Conner, Paul Walker (September 12, 1973–November 30, 2013), who tragically died in a car accident—not while filming, but during the period he was involved with making *Furious 7*.

TOP 10

OFFICIAL MUSIC VIDEOS WITH THE MOST VIEWS

Whether it's simply because the song is hugely popular, or because the video itself is inventive and demands watching more than once, these music videos have truly struck a chord with their fans...

	SONG	ARTIST	DATE UPLOADED	VIEWS
1	DESPACITO	LUIS FONSI FT. DADDY YANKEE	JAN 12, 2017	4,602,638,199
2	SEE YOU AGAIN	WIZ KHALIFA FT. CHARLIE PUTH	APR 6, 2015	3,304,946,999
3	GANGNAM STYLE	PSY	JUL 15, 2012	3,036,379,649
4	SHAPE OF YOU	ED SHEERAN	JAN 30, 2017	2,946,913,510
5	SORRY	JUSTIN BIEBER	OCT 22, 2015	2,857,799,094
6	UPTOWN FUNK	MARK RONSON FT. BRUNO MARS	NOV 19, 2014	2,849,150,561
7	SUGAR	MAROON 5	JAN 14, 2015	2,477,265,533
8	SHAKE IT OFF	TAYLOR SWIFT	AUG 18, 2014	2,461,857,343
9	BAILANDO	ENRIQUE IGLESIAS FT. DESCEMER BUENO & GENTE DE ZONA	APR 11, 2014	2,449,846,425
10	ROAR	KATY PERRY	SEP 5, 2013	2,381,598,448

THE TOP 95 MOST-WATCHED MUSIC VIDEOS ON YOUTUBE ALL EXCEED 1 BILLION VIEWS

4 ▶ KATY PERRY

Witness is the fourth studio album recorded under this artist's stage name of Katy Perry. (Her debut album as an artist, and her fifth overall, is 2001's self-titled *Katy Hudson*.) The global *Witness: The Tour* began in Montreal, Canada, on September 19, 2017, and featured more than 100 shows through 2018.

TOP 10 — MOST SUBSCRIBED YOUTUBE MUSIC CHANNELS

Video content doesn't just mean official music videos and live footage—your favorite artists frequently produce lyric videos and short films too...

	ARTIST	SUBSCRIBERS
1	JUSTIN BIEBER	33,226,400
2	TAYLOR SWIFT	26,771,992
3	RIHANNA	26,240,189
4	KATY PERRY	26,026,763
5	EMINEM	25,207,265
6	ONE DIRECTION	23,085,800
7	ARIANA GRANDE	18,708,827
8	SHAKIRA	18,373,404
9	LUIS FONSI	16,419,450
10	ADELE	15,792,585

MOVIES & TV **10**

MULTIPLE-OSCAR-WINNING ACTRESSES **WITH THE MOST MOVIE & TV CREDITS**

Of all the actresses who have won more than one Academy Award, these are the winners who have more film and television credits than any of their peers...

	ACTRESS	OSCAR WINS	TOTAL CREDITS
1	SHELLEY WINTERS	2	160
2	BETTE DAVIS	2	123
3	MERYL STREEP	3	81
4	JODIE FOSTER	2	79
5	ELIZABETH TAYLOR	2	77
6	SALLY FIELD	2	64
7	OLIVIA DE HAVILLAND	2	60
=	DIANNE WIEST	2	60
9	JANE FONDA	2	57
10	INGRID BERGMAN	3	55
	KATHARINE HEPBURN	4	52
	GLENDA JACKSON	2	51
	HILARY SWANK	2	47
	LUISE RAINER	2	24
	VIVIEN LEIGH	2	20

MOVIE AND TV DATA PROVIDED BY IMDb (HTTPS://WWW.IMDB.COM).

1 ▸ SHELLEY WINTERS

American actress Shelley Winters (August 18, 1920–January 14, 2006) won the Academy Award for Best Supporting Actress in 1960 for *The Diary of Anne Frank* (1959) and in 1966 for *A Patch of Blue* (1965), and was nominated for *The Poseidon Adventure* (1972). Winters was also nominated for Best Actress at the 1952 Oscars for *A Place in the Sun* (1951).

TOP 10

MULTIPLE-OSCAR-WINNING ACTORS **WITH THE MOST MOVIE & TV CREDITS**

As an accompaniment to the Top 10 chart opposite, this includes the multiple–Academy Award–winning actors who have notched up the most movie and television credits...

	ACTOR	OSCAR WINS	TOTAL CREDITS
1	WALTER BRENNAN	3	244
2	ANTHONY QUINN	2	169
3	MICHAEL CAINE	2	165
4	JASON ROBARDS	2	131
5	GARY COOPER	2	117
6	MELVYN DOUGLAS	2	113
=	CHRISTOPH WALTZ	2	113
8	PETER USTINOV	2	102
9	FREDRIC MARCH	2	86
10	TOM HANKS	2	85

MOVIE AND TV DATA PROVIDED BY IMDb (HTTPS://WWW.IMDB.COM).

10 TOM HANKS

California-born actor Tom Hanks has two Best Actor Oscars, for *Philadelphia* (1993) and *Forrest Gump* (1994). He has been nominated in the same category a further three times, for *Big* (1988), *Saving Private Ryan* (1998), and *Cast Away* (2000). He has won more than 80 other international film and TV awards.

LONGEST-RUNNING US TV SHOWS

Think that your favorite television program of all time had a great run?
Check out the number of decades these shows have been on air...

	SHOW	NETWORK	YEARS ON AIR
1	MEET THE PRESS	NBC	72
2	CBS EVENING NEWS	CBS	71
3	MUSIC & THE SPOKEN WORD	KSL / VARIOUS	70
4	HALLMARK HALL OF FAME	HALLMARK / VARIOUS	68
5	TODAY	NBC	67
6	ABC NEWS / WORLD NEWS	ABC	66
7	THE TONIGHT SHOW	NBC	65
=	FACE THE NATION	CBS	65
9	IT IS WRITTEN	VARIOUS	63
=	THE OPEN MIND	VARIOUS	63

MOVIE AND TV DATA PROVIDED BY IMDb (HTTPS://WWW.IMDB.COM).

7 ▶ JOHNNY CARSON

Multi-award-winning presenter, writer, and producer Johnny Carson (October 23, 1925–January 23, 2005) served in the US Navy prior to his TV career. Carson's time hosting *The Tonight Show* ran from October 1, 1962 through May 22, 1992.

9 ▶ **BLACK PANTHER**

Director Ryan Coogler's *Black Panther* is the 18th film in Marvel Studios' interconnected cinematic universe. It passed $1 billion at the worldwide box office in just four weeks. It also remained at number one in the US for five consecutive weeks—the only Marvel Studios movie to achieve this. T'Challa / Black Panther actor Chadwick Boseman has also directed two short films, *Heaven* (2012) and *Blood Over a Broken Pawn* (2008).

TOP 10

BIGGEST **MOVIES OF ALL TIME**

The year 2018 was epic for films passing the $1 billion box office mark, and at the time of going to press with this edition, these are the 10 films that rule the cinematic universe...

	MOVIE	YEAR OF RELEASE	BOX OFFICE ($ WORLDWIDE)
1	AVATAR	2009	2,787,965,087
2	TITANIC	1997	2,187,187,302
3	STAR WARS: EPISODE VII – THE FORCE AWAKENS	2015	2,068,223,624
4	AVENGERS: INFINITY WAR	2018	1,914,538,462
5	JURASSIC WORLD	2015	1,671,713,208
6	THE AVENGERS	2012	1,518,812,988
7	FURIOUS 7	2015	1,516,045,911
8	AVENGERS: AGE OF ULTRON	2015	1,405,403,694
9	BLACK PANTHER	2018	1,343,859,226
10	HARRY POTTER AND THE DEATHLY HALLOWS PART 2	2011	1,341,511,219

MOVIE AND TV DATA PROVIDED BY IMDb (HTTPS://WWW.IMDB.COM).

MULTIPLE-OSCAR-WINNING DIRECTORS **WITH THE MOST MOVIE & TV CREDITS**

If a film director has more than one Academy Award to his name, team Top 10 looked at their total number of credits to see if they qualified for this chart...

	DIRECTOR	OSCAR WINS	TOTAL CREDITS
1	JOHN FORD	4	146
2	FRANK LLOYD	2	135
3	FRANK BORZAGE	2	113
4	LEO McCAREY	3	104
5	WILLIAM WYLER	3	73
6	CLINT EASTWOOD	4	70
7	GEORGE STEVENS	2	59
8	FRANK CAPRA	3	58
9	STEVEN SPIELBERG	3	56
10	LEWIS MILESTONE	2	53

	FRED ZINNEMANN	4	47
	ROBERT WISE	4	41
	OLIVER STONE	3	31
	BILLY WILDER	6	27
	JOSEPH L. MANKIEWICZ	4	22
	ELIA KAZAN	2	21
	MILOŠ FORMAN	2	20
	DAVID LEAN	2	19
	ANG LEE	2	17
	ALEJANDRO G. IÑÁRRITU	4	15

MOVIE AND TV DATA PROVIDED BY IMDb (HTTPS://WWW.IMDB.COM).

9 STEVEN SPIELBERG

American filmmaker Steven Spielberg directed some of the most famous and influential films of all time, including *Jaws* (1975), *Raiders of the Lost Ark* (1981), *E.T.: The Extra-Terrestrial* (1982), and *Jurassic Park* (1993). In addition to his numerous director credits, Spielberg also has more than 170 credits as a producer.

COSTUME DESIGNERS
WITH THE MOST OSCAR WINS

If you think it's just the acting, writing, and directing aspects of filmmaking that can garner multiple Academy Award nominations and wins, think again...

	DESIGNER	OSCAR NOMINATIONS	TOTAL WINS
1	EDITH HEAD	35	8
2	IRENE SHARAFF	16	5
3	COLLEEN ATWOOD	12	4
=	MILENA CANONERO	9	4
5	CHARLES LeMAIRE	16	3
=	DOROTHY JEAKINS	12	3
=	SANDY POWELL	12	3
=	ANTHONY POWELL	6	3
=	ORRY-KELLY	4	3
=	JAMES ACHESON	3	3

MOVIE AND TV DATA PROVIDED BY IMDb (HTTPS://WWW.IMDB.COM).

1 EDITH HEAD

California-born Edith Head (October 28, 1897–October 24, 1981) has 441 credits as a costume designer. These include films from every decade from the 1920s to the 1980s. Her Academy Award wins include for iconic films *The Sting* (1973), *Roman Holiday* (1953), and *The Heiress* (1949).

2 THE LORD OF THE RINGS: THE RETURN OF THE KING

In 2004, this, the third and final part of filmmaker Peter Jackson's *The Lord of the Rings* trilogy, won all 11 of its Academy Award nominations. It also won a further 197 international film awards. Viggo Mortensen (pictured right) has two Oscar nominations for Best Actor, for *Eastern Promises* (2007) and *Captain Fantastic* (2016).

2018 BEST FILM OSCAR WINNER: *THE SHAPE OF WATER* (DIRECTED BY GUILLERMO DEL TORO)

TOP 10

BIGGEST-GROSSING BEST FILM OSCAR WINNERS

The productions that receive the coveted Best Film at the Academy Awards aren't chosen because they won at the box office, but here are the most commercially successful winners...

	MOVIE	YEAR OF BEST FILM WIN	BOX OFFICE ($ WORLDWIDE)
1	TITANIC	1997	2,187,187,302
2	THE LORD OF THE RINGS: THE RETURN OF THE KING	2003	1,119,929,521
3	FORREST GUMP	1994	677,945,399
4	GLADIATOR	2000	457,640,427
5	DANCES WITH WOLVES	1990	424,208,848
6	THE KING'S SPEECH	2010	414,211,549
7	SLUMDOG MILLIONAIRE	2008	377,910,544
8	RAIN MAN	1989	354,825,435
9	SCHINDLER'S LIST	1993	321,306,305
10	A BEAUTIFUL MIND	2001	313,542,341

MOVIE AND TV DATA PROVIDED BY IMDb (HTTPS://WWW.IMDB.COM).

TOP 10

TV SHOWS **WITH THE MOST EMMY WINS**

The Emmys have been the most prestigious television awards ceremony for 70 years, and these TV shows have received the most Emmy plaudits...

	SHOW	YEARS ON AIR	EMMY NOMINATIONS	TOTAL WINS
1	SATURDAY NIGHT LIVE	1975–PRESENT	231	50
2	GAME OF THRONES	2011–19	110	38
3	FRASIER	1993–2004	108	37
4	THE SIMPSONS	1989–PRESENT	87	32
5	THE MARY TYLER MOORE SHOW	1970–77	67	29
6	CHEERS	1982–93	117	28
7	HILL STREET BLUES	1981–87	98	26
8	THE WEST WING	1999–2006	95	26
9	ER	1994–2009	124	23
10	MODERN FAMILY	2009–PRESENT	80	22
	BREAKING BAD	2008–13	58	16

MOVIE AND TV DATA PROVIDED BY IMDb (HTTPS://WWW.IMDB.COM).

1 SATURDAY NIGHT LIVE

This multi-award-winning TV series debuted on October 11, 1975. The 850th episode (part of its 43rd season) aired May 19, 2018, hosted by former *SNL* cast member and two-time Golden Globe Award winner Tina Fey. In this picture, the SNL team are shown picking up their Emmy for Outstanding Variety Sketch Series in 2017.

COMIC BOOK WORLDS

SUPERGIRL

Just missing out on this Top 10 is the TV series *Supergirl* (2015–present), with more than 65 episodes to date. Prior to landing the title role, American actress Melissa Benoist had appeared in drumming drama *Whiplash* (2014), and episodes of *Homeland* and *The Good Wife*.

TOP 10

LONGEST-RUNNING COMIC BOOK TV SHOWS (LIVE ACTION)

You may think that the comic book / superhero phenomenon in the film and TV worlds is a recent development, but think again…

	SHOW	YEARS ON AIR	TOTAL EPISODES
1	SMALLVILLE	2001–2011	218
2	SABRINA THE TEENAGE WITCH	1996–2003	163
3	ARROW	2012–PRESENT	139+
4	BATMAN	1966–68	120
5	THE WALKING DEAD	2010–PRESENT	115+
6	ADVENTURES OF SUPERMAN	1952–58	104
7	SUPERBOY	1988–92	100
8	TALES FROM THE CRYPT	1986–96	93
9	LOIS & CLARK: THE NEW ADVENTURES OF SUPERMAN	1993–97	88
10	THE INCREDIBLE HULK	1978–82	86
	SUPERGIRL	2015–PRESENT	65+

MOVIE AND TV DATA PROVIDED BY IMDb (HTTPS://WWW.IMDB.COM).

THE WALKING DEAD COMIC BOOK #1 RELEASED OCT 8, 2003

TOTAL ISSUES TO DATE = 175+

TOP 10

LONGEST-RUNNING **COMIC BOOK TV SHOWS (ANIMATED)**

Although there is a wide range of comic book adaptations in the world of animation, Ninja Turtles appear three times on this chart...

	SHOW	YEARS ON AIR	TOTAL EPISODES
1	TEEN TITANS GO!	2013–PRESENT	204+
2	TEENAGE MUTANT NINJA TURTLES	1986–96	193
3	TMNT	2003–10	158
4	DUCKTALES	1987–90; 2017–PRESENT	146
5	HERGÉ'S ADVENTURES OF TINTIN	1957–64; 1991–92	141
6	TEENAGE MUTANT NINJA TURTLES	2012–PRESENT	124
7	DENNIS THE MENACE AND GNASHER	1996–98; 2009–10; 2013	120
8	CAPTAIN PUGWASH	1957–66; 1974–75	107
9	BATMAN: THE ANIMATED SERIES	1992–95	85
10	X-MEN	1992–97	76

MOVIE AND TV DATA PROVIDED BY IMDb (HTTPS://WWW.IMDB.COM).

4 | **DUCK TALES**

Twenty-seven years after the original run of the cartoon series had finished, *DuckTales* returned on August 12, 2017. The new show's voice cast includes David Tennant as Scrooge McDuck, and Huey, Dewey, and Louie voiced by Danny Pudi, Ben Schwartz, and Bobby Moynihan, respectively.

BIGGEST
INDEPENDENT CREATOR-OWNED COMICS MOVIES

The most famous superhero movies feature the stars of Marvel and DC comic books, but there are a ton of other hit films based on characters from the world of independent comic books...

	MOVIE	PUBLISHER(S)	YEAR OF RELEASE	BOX OFFICE ($ WORLDWIDE)
1	TEENAGE MUTANT NINJA TURTLES	MIRAGE STUDIOS / IDW	2014	493,333,584
2	THE MASK	DARK HORSE	1994	351,583,407
3	WANTED	TOP COW	2008	341,433,252
4	TEENAGE MUTANT NINJA TURTLES: OUT OF THE SHADOWS	MIRAGE STUDIOS / IDW	2016	245,623,848
5	THE GREEN HORNET	DYNAMITE	2011	227,817,248
6	TEENAGE MUTANT NINJA TURTLES	MIRAGE STUDIOS / IDW	1990	201,965,915
7	HELLBOY II: THE GOLDEN ARMY	DARK HORSE	2008	160,388,063
8	JUDGE DREDD	FLEETWAY / REBELLION	1995	113,493,481
9	HELLBOY	DARK HORSE	2004	99,318,987
10	TMNT	MIRAGE STUDIOS / IDW	2007	95,608,995

MOVIE AND TV DATA PROVIDED BY IMDb (HTTPS://WWW.IMDB.COM).

2 THE MASK

Jim Carrey played the title character of this movie. It was based on the comic book written by John Arcudi and illustrated by Doug Mahnke, which was a new spin on Mike Richardson's original idea for the character. The film was Cameron Diaz's movie acting debut.

10 ▶ SPIDER-MAN: HOMECOMING

This Spidey adventure, directed by Jon Watts, is the 16th film in the Marvel Cinematic Universe series of Marvel Studios productions. It was released into theaters three months after *Guardians of the Galaxy Vol. 2.*

TOP 10

BIGGEST **SUPERHERO MOVIES**

The past few years have seen more and more superhero movies smash past the billion-dollar mark from their worldwide box office takings...

	MOVIE	YEAR OF RELEASE	BOX OFFICE ($ WORLDWIDE)
1	AVENGERS: INFINITY WAR	2018	1,914,538,462
2	THE AVENGERS	2012	1,518,812,988
3	AVENGERS: AGE OF ULTRON	2015	1,405,403,694
4	BLACK PANTHER	2018	1,343,859,226
5	IRON MAN 3	2013	1,214,811,252
6	CAPTAIN AMERICA: CIVIL WAR	2016	1,153,304,495
7	THE DARK KNIGHT RISES	2012	1,084,439,099
8	THE DARK KNIGHT	2008	1,004,558,444
9	SPIDER-MAN 3	2007	890,871,626
10	SPIDER-MAN: HOMECOMING	2017	880,166,924

TOP 10

BIGGEST **MARVEL STUDIOS MOVIES**

Marvel Studios' interconnected cinematic universe began on May 2, 2008, when *Iron Man* landed in US theaters. Before the release of *Ant-Man and the Wasp*, *Captain Marvel*, and *Avengers 4*, here's how this chart looks...

	MOVIE	YEAR OF RELEASE	BOX OFFICE ($ WORLDWIDE)
1	AVENGERS: INFINITY WAR	2018	1,914,538,462
2	THE AVENGERS	2012	1,518,812,988
3	AVENGERS: AGE OF ULTRON	2015	1,405,403,694
4	BLACK PANTHER	2018	1,343,859,226
5	IRON MAN 3	2013	1,214,811,252
6	CAPTAIN AMERICA: CIVIL WAR	2016	1,153,304,495
7	SPIDER-MAN: HOMECOMING	2017	880,166,924
8	GUARDIANS OF THE GALAXY VOL. 2	2017	863,756,051
9	THOR: RAGNAROK	2017	853,977,126
10	GUARDIANS OF THE GALAXY	2014	773,328,62

MOVIE AND TV DATA PROVIDED BY IMDb (HTTPS://WWW.IMDB.COM).

9 THOR: RAGNAROK

The third *Thor* movie is directed by Academy Award–nominated director Taika Waititi, who also plays Korg in the film. Waititi also directed the Marvel Studios short films *Team Thor* (2016), *Team Thor: Part 2* (2017), and *Team Darryl* (2018). His other films include *Hunt for the Wilderpeople* (2016), *What We Do in the Shadows* (2014), and *Eagle vs Shark* (2006).

4 ▶ WONDER WOMAN

Actress Gal Gadot (Diana Prince / Wonder Woman) is also a martial artist. The previous work of the film's director Patty Jenkins includes the Academy Award–winning *Monster* (2003). The *Wonder Woman* sequel is set for a November 2019 release, with Jenkins as cowriter and director.

TOP 10

BIGGEST DC MOVIES

Over the past 30 years, film adaptations of DC comic characters and worlds have included Christopher Nolan's epic *Dark Knight* trilogy and Patty Jenkins's record-breaking *Wonder Woman*...

	MOVIE	YEAR OF RELEASE	BOX OFFICE ($ WORLDWIDE)
1	THE DARK KNIGHT RISES	2012	1,084,439,099
2	THE DARK KNIGHT	2008	1,004,558,444
3	BATMAN V SUPERMAN: DAWN OF JUSTICE	2016	873,634,919
4	WONDER WOMAN	2017	821,847,012
5	SUICIDE SQUAD	2016	746,846,894
6	MAN OF STEEL	2013	668,045,518
7	JUSTICE LEAGUE	2017	657,924,295
8	BATMAN	1989	411,348,924
9	SUPERMAN RETURNS	2006	391,081,192
10	BATMAN BEGINS	2005	374,218,673

MOVIE AND TV DATA PROVIDED BY IMDb (HTTPS://WWW.IMDB.COM).

7 SHERLOCK HOLMES

Robert Downey Jr. stars as Holmes, with Jude Law (who also has two Oscar nominations) as Dr. John Watson. *Sherlock Holmes*'s score and art direction were nominated at the 2010 Academy Awards. Sequel *Sherlock Holmes: A Game of Shadows* was released in 2011. A third adventure is in the pipeline.

TOP 10

MOST RECENT (NON-MARVEL) ROBERT DOWNEY JR. MOVIES

The two-time Academy Award–nominated actor behind the Marvel Cinematic Universe's Tony Stark / Iron Man has more than 90 acting credits...

	MOVIE	ROLE	YEAR OF RELEASE
1	THE VOYAGE OF DOCTOR DOLITTLE	DR. JOHN DOLITTLE	2019
2	ALL-STAR WEEKEND	TBD	2018
3	THE JUDGE	HANK PALMER	2014
4	CHEF	MARVIN	2014
5	SHERLOCK HOLMES: A GAME OF SHADOWS	SHERLOCK HOLMES	2011
6	DUE DATE	PETE HIGHMAN	2010
7	SHERLOCK HOLMES	SHERLOCK HOLMES	2009
8	THE SOLOIST	STEVE LOPEZ	2009
9	TROPIC THUNDER	KIRK LAZARUS	2008
10	CHARLIE BARTLETT	NATHAN GARDNER	2007

MOVIE AND TV DATA PROVIDED BY IMDb (HTTPS://WWW.IMDB.COM).

ROBERT DOWNEY JR. WAS NOMINATED FOR BEST ACTOR OSCAR **FOR HIS PORTRAYAL OF CHARLIE CHAPLIN IN *CHAPLIN* (1992)**

6 ▶ SNOWPIERCER

Chris Evans (Steve Rogers / Captain America in the Marvel Cinematic Universe) stars in this adaptation of the French graphic novel. Korean filmmaker Bong Joon Ho is the cowriter and director, also known for *Okja* (2017), *Mother* (2009), and *The Host* (2006).

TOP 10

MOST RECENT (NON-MARVEL) CHRIS EVANS MOVIES

The romantic drama *Before We Go* saw the Steve Rogers / Captain America actor star alongside British actress Alice Eve, but it was also Evans's directorial debut...

	MOVIE	ROLE	YEAR OF RELEASE
1	JEKYLL	TOM JACKMAN	2019
2	THE RED SEA DIVING RESORT	ARI LEVINSON	2018
3	GIFTED	FRANK ADLER	2017
4	PLAYING IT COOL	ME	2014
5	BEFORE WE GO	NICK	2014
6 ▶	SNOWPIERCER	CURTIS	2014
7	THE ICEMAN	MR. FREEZY	2012
8	WHAT'S YOUR NUMBER?	COLIN SHEA	2011
9	PUNCTURE	MIKE WEISS	2011
10	SCOTT PILGRIM VS. THE WORLD	LUCAS LEE	2010

MOVIE AND TV DATA PROVIDED BY IMDb (HTTPS://WWW.IMDB.COM).

TOP 10

FIRST
SCARLETT JOHANSSON MOVIES

The actress behind Natasha Romanoff / Black Widow from the Marvel Studios movies is also an accomplished music artist, and has collaborated with Pete Yorn...

	MOVIE	ROLE	YEAR OF RELEASE
1	NORTH	LAURA NELSON	1994
2	JUST CAUSE	KATIE ARMSTRONG	1995
3	MANNY & LO	AMANDA	1996
4	IF LUCY FELL	EMILY	1996
5	FALL	LITTLE GIRL	1997
6	HOME ALONE 3	MOLLY PRUITT	1997
7	THE HORSE WHISPERER	GRACE MACLEAN	1998
8	MY BROTHER THE PIG	KATHY CALDWELL	1999
9	THE MAN WHO WASN'T THERE	BIRDY ABUNDAS	2001
10	GHOST WORLD	REBECCA	2001

MOVIE AND TV DATA PROVIDED BY IMDb (HTTPS://WWW.IMDB.COM).

10 GHOST WORLD

Scarlett Johansson costars with Thora Birch in this Academy Award–nominated movie version of Daniel Clowes's 1997 graphic novel of the same name. Johansson has more than 60 acting credits. She also wrote and directed the short film *These Vagabond Shoes* (2009), starring Kevin Bacon.

SCARLETT JOHANSSON AND HER BLACK WIDOW STUNT DOUBLE HEIDI MONEYMAKER BOTH WON **THE DYNAMIC DUO ACTION AWARD AT THE 2012 ACTION ICON AWARDS FOR THEIR STUNT / ACTION WORK IN THE MARVEL MOVIES**

1 **NICK FURY**

Samuel L. Jackson made his first appearance as Nick Fury in the tag scene at the end of *Iron Man* (2008). His other numerous appearances in Marvel Studios movies include: *Iron Man 2* (2010), *The Avengers* (2012), *Captain America: The Winter Soldier* (2014), *Avengers: Age of Ultron* (2015), and the tag scene of *Avengers: Infinity War* (2018).

MOST REPRISED
SAMUEL L. JACKSON ROLES

The Academy Award–nominated man behind the Marvel movies' Nick Fury has more than 180 film and TV credits from five decades...

	ROLE	PRODUCTION	TOTAL MOVIES / TV EPISODES / VIDEO GAMES
1	NICK FURY	VARIOUS MARVEL MOVIES & TV SHOWS	13
2	AFRO SAMURAI	AFRO SAMURAI	7
3	MACE WINDU	STAR WARS MOVIES, TV SERIES & VIDEO GAMES	5
=	GIN RUMMY	THE BOONDOCKS	5
5	LUCIUS BEST / FROZONE	THE INCREDIBLES 1 & 2	4
6	AUGUSTUS GIBBONS	XXX MOVIES	3
=	GHOSTWRITER	REGGIE JENKINS	3
8	ELIJAH PRICE / MR. GLASS	UNBREAKABLE (2000), GLASS (2019)	2
=	JOHN SHAFT	SHAFT, SON OF SHAFT	2
=	OFFICER TENPENNY	GRAND THEFT AUTO: SAN ANDREAS	2

MOVIE AND TV DATA PROVIDED BY IMDb (HTTPS://WWW.IMDB.COM).

3 ⟩ GHOSTBUSTERS

Chris Hemsworth stars as Kevin, the receptionist, in the 2016 version of *Ghostbusters*. The 21st-century take on the original 1984 film of the same name features Kristen Wiig, Melissa McCarthy, Kate McKinnon, and Leslie Jones as the paranormal investigators and eliminators.

TOP 10

MOST RECENT (NON-MARVEL) CHRIS HEMSWORTH MOVIE ROLES

Thor actor Chris Hemsworth's two brothers, Liam and Luke, are also actors, and the latter cameos in *Thor: Ragnarok*, playing a stage actor cast as Thor in a play...

	MOVIE	ROLE	YEAR OF RELEASE
1	BAD TIMES AT THE EL ROYALE	TBD	2018
2	12 STRONG	CAPTAIN MITCH NELSON	2018
3	GHOSTBUSTERS	KEVIN	2016
4	THE HUNTSMAN: WINTER'S WAR	ERIC	2016
5	IN THE HEART OF THE SEA	OWEN CHASE	2015
6	VACATION	STONE CRANDALL	2015
7	BLACKHAT	NICK HATHAWAY	2015
8	RUSH	JAMES HUNT	2015
9	STAR TREK: INTO DARKNESS	GEORGE KIRK	2013
10	RED DAWN	JED ECKERT	2012

MOVIE AND TV DATA PROVIDED BY IMDb (HTTPS://WWW.IMDB.COM).

2012'S THE CABIN IN THE WOODS (STARRING CHRIS HEMSWORTH) WAS COWRITTEN AND DIRECTED BY JOSS WHEDON, WHO DIRECTED THE FIRST TWO *AVENGERS* MOVIES FROM 2012 AND 2015

TOP 10

MOST RECENT (NON-MARVEL) MARK RUFFALO MOVIE & TV ROLES

Bruce Banner / Hulk actor Mark Ruffalo has received three Academy Award nominations for Best Actor in a Supporting Role, for *Spotlight* (2015), *Foxcatcher* (2014), and *The Kids Are All Right* (2010)...

	PRODUCTION	ROLE	TYPE	YEAR OF RELEASE
1	I KNOW THIS MUCH IS TRUE	TBD	TV SERIES	2018
2	NOW YOU SEE ME 2	DYLAN RHODES	MOVIE	2016
3	SPOTLIGHT	MIKE REZENDES	MOVIE	2015
4	THE NORMAL HEART	NED WEEKS	TV MOVIE	2014
5	FOXCATCHER	DAVID SCHULTZ	MOVIE	2014
6	INFINITELY POLAR BEAR	CAM STUART	MOVIE	2014
7	BEGIN AGAIN	DAN	MOVIE	2013
8	NOW YOU SEE ME	DYLAN RHODES	MOVIE	2013
9	THANKS FOR SHARING	ADAM	MOVIE	2012
10	MARGARET	MARETTI	MOVIE	2011

MOVIE AND TV DATA PROVIDED BY IMDb (HTTPS://WWW.IMDB.COM).

3 ▸ SPOTLIGHT

In *Spotlight*, Mark Ruffalo stars alongside fellow Marvel Studios movies actors Michael Keaton (who plays Adrian Toomes / Vulture in *Spider-Man: Homecoming*), Rachel McAdams (Christine Palmer in *Doctor Strange*), John Slattery (who plays Howard Stark in *Iron Man 2*, *Ant-Man*, and *Captain America: Civil War*), and Stanley Tucci (Dr. Abraham Erskine in *Captain America: The First Avenger*).

MOST RECENT (NON-MARVEL) CHADWICK BOSEMAN MOVIE & TV ROLES

The record-breaking 2018 Marvel movies *Black Panther* and *Avengers: Infinity War* marked the second and third times Chadwick Boseman starred as T'Challa / Black Panther...

	PRODUCTION	ROLE	TYPE	YEAR OF RELEASE
1	MARSHALL	THURGOOD MARSHALL	MOVIE	2017
2	MESSAGE FROM THE KING	JACOB KING	MOVIE	2016
3	THOTH	GODS OF EGYPT	MOVIE	2016
4	9 KISSES	MUSICIAN	SHORT	2014
5	GET ON UP	JAMES BROWN	MOVIE	2014
6	DRAFT DAY	VONTAE MACK	MOVIE	2014
7	42	JACKIE ROBINSON	MOVIE	2013
8	THE KILL HOLE	LT. SAMUEL DRAKE	MOVIE	2012
9	FRINGE	CAMERON JAMES	TV SERIES	2011 (EPISODE)
10	JUSTIFIED	RALPH "FLEX" BEEMAN	TV SERIES	2011 (EPISODE)

MOVIE AND TV DATA PROVIDED BY IMDb (HTTPS://WWW.IMDB.COM).

5 GET ON UP

Chadwick Boseman portrays music legend James Brown in this biopic of Brown's life, *Get On Up*. Brown's parents, Susie and Joe, are played by Academy Award winner Viola Davis and BAFTA nominee Lenny James.

TOP 10

MOST REPRISED
PAUL RUDD MOVIE & TV ROLES

The Scott Lang / Ant-Man actor has more than 100 acting credits, and he also cowrote *Role Models* (2008), *Ant-Man* (2015), and *Ant-Man and the Wasp* (2018)...

	ROLE	PRODUCTION	TOTAL MOVIES / TV EPISODES
1	KIRBY PHILBY	SISTERS (1992–95)	20
2	MIKE HANNIGAN	FRIENDS (2002–04)	18
3	ANDY	WET HOT AMERICAN SUMMER (MOVIE & SERIES)	15
4	BRIAN GANT	WILD OATS (1994)	6
5	BOBBY NEWPORT	PARKS & RECREATION (2012–15)	5
=	GUY GERRICAULT	RENO 911! (2006–07)	5
7	SCOTT LANG / ANT-MAN	MARVEL STUDIOS' MOVIES	4
8	BRIAN FANTANA	ANCHORMAN MOVIES	3
9	NATE	BURNING LOVE (2013)	3
10	TAMPA ST. PETE	HUDSON VALLEY BALLERS (2013)	2

MOVIE AND TV DATA PROVIDED BY IMDb (HTTPS://WWW.IMDB.COM).

3   WET HOT AMERICAN SUMMER

This comedy debuted as a feature film in 2001. It returned as an eight-episode prequel miniseries in 2015 entitled *Wet Hot American Summer: First Day of Summer*. An eight-episode miniseries, which served as a sequel to the original movie, aired in 2017, *Wet Hot American Summer: Ten Years Later*. Along with most of the original cast, Paul Rudd starred in all three productions.

2 THE HOBBIT: THE BATTLE OF THE FIVE ARMIES

Evangeline Lilly's woodland elf character of Tauriel does not appear in J.R.R. Tolkien's *The Hobbit* or *The Lord of the Rings* books. She was created by the filmmaking team behind the Tolkien adaptations, director / cowriter Peter Jackson, cowriter / producer Fran Walsh, and cowriter / coproducer Philippa Boyens. Lilly's Tauriel first appears in the second *Hobbit* movie, *The Desolation of Smaug*.

TOP 10

MOST RECENT (NON-MARVEL) EVANGELINE LILLY MOVIE & TV ROLES

Hope van Dyne / Wasp actress Evangeline Lilly is also an author, and her debut children's book, *The Squickerwonkers*, was released in 2013...

	PRODUCTION	ROLE	TYPE	YEAR OF RELEASE
1	LITTLE EVIL	SAMANTHA	MOVIE	2017
2	THE HOBBIT: THE BATTLE OF THE FIVE ARMIES	TAURIEL	MOVIE	2014
3	THE HOBBIT: THE DESOLATION OF SMAUG	TAURIEL	MOVIE	2013
4	REAL STEEL	BAILEY TALLET	MOVIE	2011
5	LOST	KATE AUSTEN	TV SERIES	2004–10
6	AFTERWARDS	CLAIRE	MOVIE	2008
7	THE HURT LOCKER	CONNIE JAMES	MOVIE	2008
8	THE LONG WEEKEND	SIMONE	MOVIE	2005
9	WHITE CHICKS	PARTY GUEST	MOVIE	2004
10	KINGDOM HOSPITAL	BENTON'S GIRLFRIEND	TV MINISERIES	2004

MOVIE AND TV DATA PROVIDED BY IMDb (HTTPS://WWW.IMDB.COM).

TOTAL NUMBER OF LOST EPISODES:
121 (2004–2010)

BEYOND THE AVENGERS

8 ▸ TRIPLE 9

John Hillcoat, the director of *The Road* (2009) and *Lawless* (2012), helmed this crime drama. It stars Anthony Mackie alongside Chiwetel Ejiofor, Kate Winslet, Gal Gadot, Aaron Paul, Casey Affleck, Norman Reedus, and Woody Harrelson.

TOP 10

MOST RECENT (NON-MARVEL) ANTHONY MACKIE MOVIE & TV ROLES

Anthony Mackie's Sam Wilson / Falcon debut was in 2014's *Captain America: The Winter Soldier*, and he has more than 50 other acting credits...

	PRODUCTION	ROLE	TYPE	YEAR OF RELEASE
1	THE BLUE MAURITIUS	PETER UNDERWOOD	MOVIE	2019
2	SIGNAL HILL	JOHNNIE COCHRAN	MOVIE	2019
3	IO	MICAH	MOVIE	2018
4	THE HATE U GIVE	KING	MOVIE	2018
5	WETLANDS	(UNNAMED)	MOVIE	2017
6	DETROIT	GREENE	MOVIE	2017
7	ALL THE WAY	DR. MARTIN LUTHER KING JR.	TV MOVIE	2016
8	TRIPLE 9	MARCUS BELMONT	MOVIE	2016
9	THE NIGHT BEFORE	CHRIS	MOVIE	2015
10	LOVE THE COOPERS	OFFICER WILLIAMS	MOVIE	2015

MOVIE AND TV DATA PROVIDED BY IMDb (HTTPS://WWW.IMDB.COM).

ANTHONY MACKIE ALSO STARRED IN THE HURT LOCKER (2008) WITH FUTURE FELLOW *AVENGERS* ACTOR JEREMY RENNER (HAWKEYE)

TOP 10

FIRST (NON-MARVEL) TOM HOLLAND MOVIE & TV ROLES

British actor Tom Holland made his first appearance as Peter Parker / Spider-Man in the Marvel Cinematic Universe in 2016's *Captain America: Civil War*...

	PRODUCTION	ROLE	TYPE	YEAR OF RELEASE
1	THE SECRET WORLD OF ARRIETTY	SHÔ	MOVIE	2010
2	THE IMPOSSIBLE	LUCAS	MOVIE	2012
3	MOMENTS	BOY	SHORT	2013
4	LOCKE	EDDIE	MOVIE	2013
5	HOW I LIVE NOW	ISAAC	MOVIE	2013
6	BILLY ELLIOT: THE MUSICAL LIVE	FORMER BILLY	MOVIE	2014
7	WOLF HALL	GREGORY CROMWELL	TV MINISERIES	2015
8	TWEET	TOM	SHORT	2015
9	IN THE HEART OF THE SEA	THOMAS NICKERSON	MOVIE	2015
10	EDGE OF WINTER	BRADLEY BAKER	MOVIE	2016

MOVIE AND TV DATA PROVIDED BY IMDb (HTTPS://WWW.IMDB.COM).

THE LOST CITY OF Z

In this adaptation of the bestselling nonfiction book by David Grann, Tom Holland plays Jack Fawcett, the son of British explorer Percy Fawcett, portrayed by Charlie Hunnam. Sienna Miller plays Percy's wife, Nina Fawcett. Director James Gray directed the film and adapted the screenplay from Grann's book.

TOP 10

MOST RECENT (NON-MARVEL) JAMES D'ARCY MOVIE & TV ROLES

In Marvel's *Agent Carter* TV series (2015–16), British actor James D'Arcy played Edwin Jarvis, the ever-faithful friend of Hayley Atwell's Peggy Carter...

	PRODUCTION	ROLE	TYPE	YEAR OF RELEASE
1	001LITHIUMX	ADAM BIRD	MOVIE	2018
2	LOVE THY KEEPERS	JULIAN	MOVIE	2018
3	DAS BOOT	TBD	TV MINISERIES	2018
4	INSTRUMENTS OF DARKNESS	BANQUO	MOVIE	2018
5	THE SNOWMAN	FILIP BECKER	MOVIE	2017
6	DUNKIRK	COLONEL WINNANT	MOVIE	2017
7	GUERNICA	HENRY	MOVIE	2016
8	SURVIVOR	PAUL ANDERSON	MOVIE	2015
9	BROADCHURCH	LEE ASHWORTH	TV SERIES	2015
10	JUPITER ASCENDING	MAXIMILIAN JONES	MOVIE	2015

MOVIE AND TV DATA PROVIDED BY IMDb (HTTPS://WWW.IMDB.COM).

6 ▸ DUNKIRK

James D'Arcy's role in Christopher Nolan's three-time Oscar-winning World War II epic *Dunkirk* is another example of the actor's versatility. D'Arcy has also played a scary mobster in *Let's Be Cops* (2017), Anthony Perkins in biopic *Hitchcock* (2012), and Father Francis in *Exorcist: The Beginning* (2004).

2 ► HOWARDS END

Golden Globe Award nominee Hayley Atwell stars in acclaimed British drama *Howards End* (2017–18) alongside Philippa Coulthard, Alex Lawther, Matthew Macfadyen, and Golden Globe winner Tracey Ullman. BAFTA-winning Hettie Macdonald directed this adaptation of E. M. Forster's novel.

TOP 10

MOST RECENT (NON-MARVEL) HAYLEY ATWELL MOVIE & TV ROLES

The Golden Globe Award–nominated actress who plays Agent Peggy Carter in the Marvel films has more than 40 movie and TV credits...

	PRODUCTION	ROLE	TYPE	YEAR OF RELEASE
1	CHRISTOPHER ROBIN	EVELYN	MOVIE	2018
2	HOWARDS END	MARGARET SCHLEGEL	TV MINISERIES	2017
3	CONVICTION	HAYES MORRISON	TV SERIES	2016–17
4	CHICKEN / EGG	LAUREN	SHORT	2016
5	THE COMPLETE WALK: CYMBELINE	INNOGEN	SHORT	2016
6	CINDERELLA	ELLA'S MOTHER	MOVIE	2015
7	TESTAMENT OF YOUTH	HOPE	MOVIE	2014
8	JIMI: ALL IS BY MY SIDE	KATHY	MOVIE	2013
9	LIFE OF CRIME	DENISE WOODS	TV MINISERIES	2013
10	BLACK MIRROR	MARTHA	TV SERIES	2013

MOVIE AND TV DATA PROVIDED BY IMDb (HTTPS://WWW.IMDB.COM).

ANIMATED WORLDS

TOP 10

BIGGEST ANIMATED ANIMAL KINGDOM MOVIES

Of all the animated feature films that include characters based on real-life animals, these are the 10 that succeeded the most at the global box office...

	MOVIE	YEAR OF RELEASE	BOX OFFICE ($ WORLDWIDE)
1	FINDING DORY	2016	1,028,570,889
2	THE LION KING	1994	968,483,777
3	FINDING NEMO	2003	940,335,536
4	THE SECRET LIFE OF PETS	2016	875,457,937
5	MADAGASCAR 3: EUROPE'S MOST WANTED	2012	746,921,274
6	RATATOUILLE	2007	620,702,951
7	MADAGASCAR: ESCAPE 2 AFRICA	2008	603,900,354
8	MADAGASCAR	2005	532,680,671
9	HAPPY FEET	2006	384,335,608
10	SHARK TALE	2004	367,275,019

MOVIE AND TV DATA PROVIDED BY IMDb (HTTPS://WWW.IMDB.COM).

2 THE LION KING

In 1995, *The Lion King*'s music won two Academy Awards, for Best Original Song ("Can You Feel the Love Tonight") and Best Original Score for composer Hans Zimmer. The stage musical version debuted at the Orpheum Theatre in Minneapolis, Minnesota, on July 8, 1997. The live-action film version, directed by Jon Favreau, releases in 2019.

6 **HOW TO TRAIN YOUR DRAGON 2**

Dean DeBlois, the Canadian codirector and cowriter of the first *How to Train Your Dragon* (2010) movie—and also *Lilo & Stitch* (2002)—returned as the sole writer-director for this sequel. DeBlois kept his hand on the reins for the third film in the franchise, released March 2019.

TOP 10

BIGGEST **ANIMATED FANTASY ADVENTURE MOVIES**

Fairy tales, magical lands, and highly imaginative creatures and quests make up the most successful fantasy-based animated movies of all time...

	MOVIE	YEAR OF RELEASE	BOX OFFICE ($ WORLDWIDE)
1	FROZEN	2013	1,276,480,335
2	SHREK 2	2004	919,838,758
3	SHREK THE THIRD	2007	798,958,162
4	SHREK FOREVER AFTER	2010	752,600,867
5	MOANA	2016	643,331,111
6	HOW TO TRAIN YOUR DRAGON 2	2014	621,537,519
7	TANGLED	2010	591,794,936
8	MONSTERS, INC.	2001	577,425,734
9	BRAVE	2012	540,437,063
10	ALADDIN	1992	504,050,219

MOVIE AND TV DATA PROVIDED BY IMDb (HTTPS://WWW.IMDB.COM).

ANIMATED WORLDS

1 ▶ YOUR NAME.

Japanese creative polymath Makoto Shinkai wrote the screenplay and directed this animated version of his novel. The film has won 14 international awards, including Japan's Mainichi Film Award for Best Animated Feature Film. Shinkai also crafted the manga adaptation.

TOP 10

BIGGEST ANIME MOVIES

The term "anime" refers to Japanese animation, and the anime industry has produced countless film and TV successes for decades...

	MOVIE	YEAR OF RELEASE	BOX OFFICE ($ WORLDWIDE)
1	YOUR NAME.	2016	355,298,270
2	SPIRITED AWAY	2002	274,925,095
3	STAND BY ME, DORAEMON	2014	266,542,714
4	HOWL'S MOVING CASTLE	2005	235,184,110
5	PONYO	2009	201,750,937
6	POKÉMON: THE FIRST MOVIE	1999	163,644,662
7	PRINCESS MONONOKE	1999	159,375,308
8	THE SECRET WORLD OF ARRIETTY	2010	145,570,827
9	POKÉMON: THE MOVIE 2000	2000	133,949,270
10	THE WIND RISES	2014	117,932,401

MOVIE AND TV DATA PROVIDED BY IMDb (HTTPS://WWW.IMDB.COM).

THE IRON GIANT, 1999 =
$23,159,305

TRANSFORMERS:
THE MOVIE, 1986 =
$5,849,647

**ROBOT FILM VS.
ROBOT FILM**

TOP 10

BIGGEST ANIMATED ROBOTS & MACHINES MOVIES

If it's an animated feature film with any kind of machine, vehicle, or robot as part of its main cast of characters, then it qualifies for this chart...

	MOVIE	YEAR OF RELEASE	BOX OFFICE ($ WORLDWIDE)
1	BIG HERO 6	2014	657,818,612
2	CARS 2	2016	562,110,557
3	WALL•E	2008	533,281,433
4	CARS	2006	462,216,280
5	CARS 3	2017	383,818,176
6	ROBOTS	2005	260,718,330
7	PLANES	2013	239,258,712
8	PLANES: FIRE & RESCUE	2014	151,386,640
9	JIMMY NEUTRON: BOY GENIUS	2001	102,992,536
10	9	2009	48,428,063

MOVIE AND TV DATA PROVIDED BY IMDb (HTTPS://WWW.IMDB.COM).

3 WALL•E

Director Andrew Stanton won the 2009 Best Animated Film Oscar for *WALL•E*. Stanton's other films include *Finding Nemo* (2003), *Finding Dory* (2016), and *John Carter* (2012). He also directed two episodes of the second season of the TV series *Stranger Things*.

ANIMATED WORLDS

BIGGEST ANIMATED MOVIES

Whether it's with hand-painted cel animation, or computer-generated imagery, these are the most successful animated films...

	MOVIE	YEAR OF RELEASE	BOX OFFICE ($ WORLDWIDE)
1	FROZEN	2013	1,276,480,335
2	MINIONS	2015	1,159,398,397
3	TOY STORY 3	2010	1,066,969,703
4	DESPICABLE ME 3	2017	1,034,799,409
5	FINDING DORY	2016	1,028,570,889
6	ZOOTOPIA	2016	1,023,784,195
7	DESPICABLE ME 2	2013	970,761,885
8	THE LION KING	1994	968,483,777
9	FINDING NEMO	2003	940,335,536
10	SHREK 2	2004	919,838,758
	COCO	2017	804,183,415

MOVIE AND TV DATA PROVIDED BY IMDb (HTTPS://WWW.IMDB.COM).

10 SHREK 2

The first sequel in the *Shrek* franchise was nominated for two Academy Awards in 2005, for Best Original Song and Best Animated Feature Film. Further films include *Shrek the Third* (2007) and *Shrek Forever After* (2010). *Shrek: The Musical* debuted in 2008.

1 SAZAE-SAN

This 50-year-long series is based on the manga publication created by Japanese writer and artist Machiko Hasegawa (January 30, 1920–May 27, 1992). Although the animated TV series became a fully computer-generated animation from 2015, up until then it had featured hand-painted cel animation.

TOP 10

LONGEST-RUNNING **ANIME TV SERIES**

When you think of cartoons that have been on air for years, investigate when they premiered on television and then compare that data to this chart...

	SERIES	YEARS ON AIR	TOTAL EPISODES
1	SAZAE-SAN	1969–PRESENT	7,550+
2	DORAEMON	1973; 1978; 1979–2005; 2005–PRESENT	2,680+
3	NINTAMA RANTARO	1993–PRESENT	2,010+
4	OYAKO CLUB	1994–2013	1,818
5	OJARUMARU	1998–PRESENT	1,665+
6	KIRIN NO MONOSHIRI YAKATA	1975–79	1,565
7	KIRIN ASHITA NO CALENDAR	1980–84	1,498
8	MANGA NIPPON MUKASHI BANASHI	1975–85	1,488
9	HOKA HOKA KAZOKU	1976–82	1,428
10	SOREIKE! ANPANMAN	1988–PRESENT	1,380+

MOVIE AND TV DATA PROVIDED BY IMDb (HTTPS://WWW.IMDB.COM).

TOP 10

MOST RECENT
AGATHA CHRISTIE ADAPTATIONS

Born in Devon, UK, writer Agatha Christie is the creator of the Belgian detective character Hercule Poirot and the longest-running play in the world, *The Mousetrap*...

	PRODUCTION	TYPE	YEAR OF RELEASE
1	DEATH ON THE NILE	MOVIE	2019
2	WITNESS FOR THE PROSECUTION	MOVIE	2019
3	ORDEAL BY INNOCENCE	TV MINISERIES	2018
4	MURDER ON THE ORIENT EXPRESS	MOVIE	2017
5	CROOKED HOUSE	MOVIE	2017
6	LES PETITS MEURTRES D'AGATHA CHRISTIE	TV SERIES	2009–PRESENT
7	SOSHITE DAREMO INAKUNATTA	TV MINISERIES	2017
8	THE WITNESS FOR THE PROSECUTION	TV MINISERIES	2016
9	CHORABALI	MOVIE	2016
10	AND THEN THERE WERE NONE	TV MINISERIES	2015

MOVIE AND TV DATA PROVIDED BY IMDb (HTTPS://WWW.IMDB.COM).

4 MURDER ON THE ORIENT EXPRESS

Penelope Cruz (pictured left) is among the huge cast, led by the film's director, Kenneth Branagh, who also plays Hercule Poirot. This is the second time an adaptation of Agatha Christie's train-based mystery has been adapted for the big screen. Director Sidney Lumet's 1974 film version starred Albert Finney as Poirot.

2 ▷ **THE GREEN MILE**

This supernatural-tinged prison drama received four Academy Award nominations, for Michael Clarke Duncan (Best Supporting Actor), Best Screenplay, Best Sound, and Best Picture. The Stephen King novel the film is based on was released in 1996.

TOP 10

BIGGEST **STEPHEN KING ADAPTATIONS**

American author Stephen King has received multiple awards for his writing, including from the New York Public Library and the National Endowment of the Arts...

	MOVIE	YEAR OF RELEASE	BOX OFFICE ($ WORLDWIDE)
1	IT	2017	700,381,748
2	THE GREEN MILE	1999	286,801,374
3	1408	2007	131,998,242
4	THE DARK TOWER	2017	113,231,078
5	SECRET WINDOW	2004	92,913,171
6	CARRIE	2013	84,790,678
7	DREAMCATCHER	2003	75,715,436
8	MISERY	1990	61,276,872
9	PET SEMATARY	1989	57,469,467
10	THE MIST	2007	57,293,715

ADAPTATIONS

4 ▶ THE NIGHT MANAGER

Danish director Susanne Bier won an Emmy for Outstanding Directing for a Limited Series for *The Night Manager*. The miniseries also won three Golden Globes in 2017: Tom Hiddleston for Best Actor, Olivia Colman for Best Actress, and Hugh Laurie for Best Supporting Actor.

TOP 10

MOST RECENT
JOHN LE CARRÉ ADAPTATIONS

Born in Dorset, UK, on October 19, 1931, David Cornwell (writing under his pen name of John le Carré) has been a novelist for more than 50 years...

	PRODUCTION	TYPE	YEAR OF RELEASE
1	THE LITTLE DRUMMER GIRL	TV MINISERIES	2019
2	THE SPY WHO CAME IN FROM THE COLD	TV MINISERIES	2018
3	OUR KIND OF TRAITOR	MOVIE	2016
4	THE NIGHT MANAGER	TV MINISERIES	2016
5	A MOST WANTED MAN	MOVIE	2014
6	TINKER TAILOR SOLDIER SPY	MOVIE	2011
7	THE CONSTANT GARDENER	MOVIE	2005
8	THE TAILOR OF PANAMA	MOVIE	2001
9	A MURDER OF QUALITY	MOVIE	1991
10	THE RUSSIA HOUSE	MOVIE	1990

MOVIE AND TV DATA PROVIDED BY IMDb (HTTPS://WWW.IMDB.COM).

BIGGEST JAMES BOND MOVIES

Fictional spy James Bond was created by British writer Ian Fleming, and there have been movie adaptations based on Bond's adventures since 1962's *Dr. No*...

	MOVIE	YEAR OF RELEASE	BOX OFFICE ($ WORLDWIDE)
1	SKYFALL	2012	1,108,561,013
2	SPECTRE	2015	880,674,609
3	CASINO ROYALE	2006	599,045,960
4	QUANTUM OF SOLACE	2008	586,090,727
5	DIE ANOTHER DAY	2002	431,971,116
6	THE WORLD IS NOT ENOUGH	1999	361,832,400
7	GOLDENEYE	1995	352,194,034
8	TOMORROW NEVER DIES	1997	333,011,068
9	MOONRAKER	1979	210,308,099
10	LICENCE TO KILL	1989	156,167,015

MOVIE AND TV DATA PROVIDED BY IMDb (HTTPS://WWW.IMDB.COM).

10 ▶ LICENCE TO KILL

This was the second time Timothy Dalton played James Bond, the first being *The Living Daylights* (1987). Both Dalton outings were directed by John Glen, who also helmed three other Bond films and edited an additional three. *Licence to Kill* presented a grittier 007 to the world, 17 years before the Daniel Craig movies embraced a more serious tone.

4 MISSION: IMPOSSIBLE –GHOST PROTOCOL

This fourth film in the Tom Cruise-starring *Mission: Impossible* movie franchise was directed by Brad Bird, the man who also helmed *The Iron Giant* (1999), *The Incredibles* (2004), and Incredibles 2 (2018). Josh Holloway—from TV series *Lost* and *Colony*—appeared in *Mission: Impossible – Ghost Protocol* as Agent Hanaway.

TOP 10

MOST SUCCESSFUL SPY MOVIES

James Bond may be the world's most famous fictional spy, but there are plenty of other undercover agents in the film world who have had huge cinematic success…

	MOVIE	YEAR OF RELEASE	BOX OFFICE ($ WORLDWIDE)
1	SKYFALL	2012	1,108,561,013
2	DESPICABLE ME 2	2013	970,761,885
3	SPECTRE	2015	880,674,609
4	MISSION: IMPOSSIBLE – GHOST PROTOCOL	2011	694,713,380
5	MISSION: IMPOSSIBLE – ROGUE NATION	2015	682,714,267
6	CASINO ROYALE	2006	599,045,960
7	QUANTUM OF SOLACE	2008	586,090,727
8	CARS 2	2011	562,110,557
9	MISSION: IMPOSSIBLE II	2000	546,388,105
10	MISSION: IMPOSSIBLE	1996	457,696,359

MOVIE AND TV DATA PROVIDED BY IMDb (HTTPS://WWW.IMDB.COM).

1 › THE SECRET LIFE OF PETS

The all-star voice cast of this pet-filled adventure includes Kevin Hart as Snowball the rabbit, Jenny Slate as Gidget the Pomeranian, Bobby Moynihan as Mel the pug, and Lake Bell as Chloe the cat. The film's codirector Chris Renaud returns to helm the sequel, *The Secret Life of Pets 2* (2019).

TOP 10

BIGGEST PET MOVIES

If it's live action or animated, as long as pets feature strongly in the movie, it had a chance to compete for a place in this Top 10…

	MOVIE	YEAR OF RELEASE	BOX OFFICE ($ WORLDWIDE)
1	THE SECRET LIFE OF PETS	2016	875,457,937
2	101 DALMATIANS	1996	320,689,294
3	BOLT	2008	309,979,994
4	G-FORCE	2009	292,817,841
5	SCOOBY-DOO	2002	275,650,703
6	BABE	1995	254,134,910
7	MARLEY & ME	2008	242,717,113
8	GARFIELD	2004	200,804,534
9	CATS & DOGS	2001	200,687,492
10	A DOG'S PURPOSE	2017	196,386,854

MOVIE AND TV DATA PROVIDED BY IMDb (HTTPS://WWW.IMDB.COM).

BOURNE COMPARISON

THE BOURNE ULTIMATUM, 2007 = $442,824,138

JASON BOURNE, 2016 = $415,484,914

THE BOURNE SUPREMACY, 2004 = $288,500,217

THE BOURNE LEGACY, 2012 = $276,144,750

THE BOURNE IDENTITY, 2002 = $214,034,224

TOP 10

BIGGEST CREATURE FEATURES

Prior to *Jurassic World: Fallen Kingdom*'s monster box office takings after it opened in the USA on June 22, 2018, these were the Top 10 giant critter movies...

	MOVIE	YEAR OF RELEASE	BOX OFFICE ($ WORLDWIDE)
1	JURASSIC WORLD	2015	1,671,713,208
2	JURASSIC PARK	1993	1,029,153,882
3	THE LOST WORLD: JURASSIC PARK	1997	618,638,999
4	KONG: SKULL ISLAND	2017	566,652,812
5	KING KONG	2005	550,517,357
6	GODZILLA	2014	529,076,069
7	PACIFIC RIM	2013	411,002,906
8	GODZILLA	1998	379,014,294
9	JURASSIC PARK III	2001	368,780,809
10	SUPER 8	2011	260,095,986

MOVIE AND TV DATA PROVIDED BY IMDb (HTTPS://WWW.IMDB.COM).

4 KONG: SKULL ISLAND

This is a prequel to *Godzilla* (2014), and is part of a shared filmic universe that Warner Bros. Pictures and Legendary Pictures call the MonsterVerse. *Godzilla: King of the Monsters* (2019) is the next installment, directed by *Trick 'r Treat* (2007) and *Krampus* (2015) filmmaker Michael Dougherty.

2 E.T.: THE EXTRA-TERRESTRIAL

This film's writer, Melissa Mathison, received an Academy Award nomination for Best Screenplay. Five years before the release of *E.T.: The Extra-Terrestrial*, director Steven Spielberg had made a previous movie about alien–human contact, *Close Encounters of the Third Kind* (1977).

TOP 10

BIGGEST EXTRA-TERRESTRIAL MOVIES

In the film world, aliens have been visiting Earth in their droves for over 80 years, and these 10 productions took box offices around the world by storm...

	MOVIE	YEAR OF RELEASE	BOX OFFICE ($ WORLDWIDE)
1	INDEPENDENCE DAY	1996	817,400,891
2	E.T.: THE EXTRA-TERRESTRIAL	1982	792,910,554
3	MIB III	2012	624,026,776
4	WAR OF THE WORLDS	2005	591,745,540
5	MEN IN BLACK	1997	589,390,539
6	MEN IN BLACK II	2002	441,818,803
7	PACIFIC RIM	2013	411,002,906
8	SIGNS	2002	408,247,917
9	INDEPENDENCE DAY: RESURGENCE	2016	389,681,935
10	HOME	2015	386,041,607

MOVIE AND TV DATA PROVIDED BY IMDb (HTTPS://WWW.IMDB.COM).

BIGGEST **VAMPIRE MOVIES**

For more than 100 years, vampires have been depicted on film, and these bloodsucking tales have captivated audiences around the world the most...

	MOVIE	YEAR OF RELEASE	BOX OFFICE ($ WORLDWIDE)
1	THE TWILIGHT SAGA: BREAKING DAWN PART 2	2012	829,746,820
2	THE TWILIGHT SAGA: BREAKING DAWN PART 1	2011	712,205,856
3	THE TWILIGHT SAGA: NEW MOON	2009	709,711,008
4	THE TWILIGHT SAGA: ECLIPSE	2010	698,491,347
5	HOTEL TRANSYLVANIA 2	2015	473,226,958
6	TWILIGHT	2008	393,616,788
7	HOTEL TRANSYLVANIA	2012	358,375,603
8	VAN HELSING	2004	300,257,475
9	DARK SHADOWS	2012	245,527,149
10	INTERVIEW WITH THE VAMPIRE	1994	223,664,608

DRACULA UNTOLD	2014	217,124,280
BRAM STOKER'S DRACULA	1992	215,862,69S
BLADE II	2002	155,010,032
BLADE	1998	131,183,530
BLADE TRINITY	2004	128,905,366

MOVIE AND TV DATA PROVIDED BY IMDb (HTTPS://WWW.IMDB.COM).

8 ▶ VAN HELSING

Australian Richard Roxburgh portrayed Count Dracula (pictured below) in this tale of vampire hunter Van Helsing, played by fellow Australian actor Hugh Jackman. Their costar Kate Beckinsale starred as a vampire in the *Underworld* movie series.

6 THE WOLFMAN

Joe Johnston—who also helmed *The Rocketeer* (1991), *Jumanji* (1995), and *Captain America: The First Avenger* (2011)—directed this werewolf film. It is based on *The Wolf Man* (1941), one of Universal Pictures' classic monster movies. Johnston's film stars Academy Award–winning actor Benicio del Toro in the title role.

TOP 10

BIGGEST **WEREWOLF MOVIES**

With a similar cinematic tradition to the vampire, the story of a human transforming into a wolflike beast has also been part of film history for more than a century...

	MOVIE	YEAR OF RELEASE	BOX OFFICE ($ WORLDWIDE)
1	THE TWILIGHT SAGA: BREAKING DAWN PART 2	2012	829,746,820
2	THE TWILIGHT SAGA: BREAKING DAWN PART 1	2011	712,205,856
3	THE TWILIGHT SAGA: NEW MOON	2009	709,711,008
4	THE TWILIGHT SAGA: ECLIPSE	2010	698,491,347
5	UNDERWORLD: AWAKENING	2012	160,112,671
6	THE WOLFMAN	2010	139,789,765
7	WOLF	1994	131,002,597
8	UNDERWORLD: EVOLUTION	2006	111,340,801
9	UNDERWORLD	2003	95,708,457
10	UNDERWORLD: RISE OF THE LYCANS	2009	91,353,501

MOVIE AND TV DATA PROVIDED BY IMDb (HTTPS://WWW.IMDB.COM).

TWILIGHT TOTAL (INCL. FIRST 2008 FILM) =
$3,343,771,819

UNDERWORLD TOTAL =
$539,608,743

TWILIGHT VS. UNDERWORLD

INDEX

PICTURE CREDITS

ACKNOWLEDGEMENTS

Paul Terry would like to thank: all of the contributing sources, especially Anna Loynes and BuzzAngle Music / Border City Media; Harry Lin and everyone at IMDb.com; Brett Walton and everyone at VGChartz; paleobiologists Luke Hauser and David Martill; my brilliant Publishing Director Trevor Davies and Assistant Editor Ellie Corbett for the ongoing support and superb Animal Kingdom contributions; Nigel Wright and XAB Design; all the picture researchers, sub-editors, proofreaders, and marketeers for all their hard work; all at Octopus Books and Readerlink; and as always, a massive thank you to my partner in all things, Tara Bennett, who is forever my number one.

DATA SOURCES:

Pages: 10, 11, 12, 13, 24, 29, 33 – data sourced from Luke Hauser and David Martill, paleobiologists **Pages:** 192–223 – data sourced from VGChartz.com **Pages:** 124, 125, 127, 128, 129, 130, 131, 132, 133 – data sourced from the Council on Tall Buildings and Urban Habitat **Pages:** 226–247 – data kindly provided by BuzzAngle Music (BuzzAngleMusic.com) and Border City Media Copyright (C) Border City Media. **Pages:** 178–187 – data sourced from NASA (https://solarsystem.nasa.gov) **Pages:** 256–299 – data sourced from IMDB.com. Box office information courtesy of The Internet Movie Database (http://www.imdb.com). Used with permission.

The Top 10 team collects data on a rolling basis. All data in this book is the most recent data available at the time of going to press.